Other Books by Mel London:

*Getting Into Film*
(Ballantine Books, 1977)

*Bread Winners*
(Rodale Press, 1979)

*Easy Going*
(Rodale Press, 1981)

*Second Spring*
(Rodale Press, 1982)

With Sheryl London:

*The Fish-Lovers' Cookbook*
(Rodale Press, 1980)

*Sheryl and Mel London's Creative Cooking
with Grains and Pasta*
(Rodale Press, 1982)

# Mel London
# Bread Winners Too
## The Second Rising

Rodale Press, Emmaus, Pa.

For Murray
who baked his first bread
here at Fire Island on his
sixty-seventh birthday.

Printed in the United States of America on recycled
paper containing a high percentage of de-inked fiber.

**Library of Congress Cataloging in Publication Data**

London, Mel.
    Bread winners too.

    Includes index.
    1. Bread. I. Title.
TX769.L66 1984          641.8′15          83-24601
ISBN   0-87857-492-1   hardcover

2  4  6  8  10  9  7  5  3  1   hardcover

# Contents

# Acknowledgments

Although the acknowledgments appear at the beginning of most books, it is generally a brief section that is written at the very end of the long journey from empty page to printed volume. The author, his or her name on the jacket and title page, reaps the accolades or brickbats, and too often the names of the people who helped so much along the way are relegated to obscurity. I have learned well in the course of many books that authors cannot do it alone. This is especially true in the writing and the testing of a cookbook. We are terribly dependent upon those who work behind the scenes.

I give particular thanks to Camille Bucci of Rodale Press, to whom I am indebted. Indeed, I am amazed at her dedication, her persistent intelligence, and her remarkable stamina in putting this book into some kind of logical order. Words—even for an author—cannot adequately express my admiration for her and for her patience through the past two years.

My editor, Charles Gerras, is an old hand by this time, and has been through enough books with me to know just when to call to encourage me, when to give me the "good news" before the "bad news," and when to laugh at my funny notes. I have always loved working with him and this book is no exception.

My thanks, too, go to every one of the bread bakers who appear in these pages, for it is really their stories, their lives, and their recipes that make up the volume. Our telephone calls, our exchanges of letters, our mutual working out of baking problems, have developed into many new friendships. I would also like to thank Walter Johnson of the Rosenbach Museum and Library for helping me find the *Via Recta ad Vitam Longam* by Tobias Venner, and Ann Pascarelli and the New York Academy of Medicine Library for giving permission to reproduce from the original edition of that book. Credit, too, goes to my old friend Ann Eisner for suggesting the delightful subtitle for this new book: *The Second Rising*.

My thanks, also, go to the magazine and newspaper editors around the country, who have always been cooperative in putting me in touch with the best of the bread bakers in their areas. I especially appreciate the help and encouragement given by Barbara Gibbs Ostmann of the *St. Louis Post-Dispatch*.

As with all Rodale cookbooks, this one has been tested three times—once by each contributor, once by me, and the final and most important time by the people of the Rodale Test Kitchen, headed by Tom Ney. Breads that did not merit the test kitchen's seal of approval, either as "excellent" or "very good," were eventually dropped from the book, as were loaves that did not test properly. For over a year, the kitchen staff kept the Rodale editorial department from starving by passing around slices of the newly tested, still-hot loaves. And so, for laboring over a hot oven for so many months, I thank Anita Hirsch, who supervised the testing, and JoAnn Coponi and Rhonda Diehl, who so ably assisted her.

Barbara Field, along with Karen Schell, created the striking jacket design, and Barbara adapted the interior design of *Bread Winners* to convey the warmth and fun I aimed for in this book. She also chose Pat Steiner whose cartoons brighten so many pages.

It fell to Mitch Mandel to ride herd on the photographs for this book. Ed Landrock evaluated printing qualities of submitted pictures, and Mitch set up needed retakes and arranged for photographing cooking procedures. Christie C. Tito actually planned and shot the easy-to-follow how-to sequences. Carl Doney gave up a late summer weekend to take last-minute pictures at Fire Island. Ed Landrock and Bob Gerheart printed all of the pictures with masterful skill, enabling us to use some borderline photographs that could not have been reshot. To all these Rodale people I give my deep respect and gratitude.

May their cupboards always be filled with freshly baked bread!

Mel London
Fire Island, N.Y.

# Introduction

It began in the autumn of 1979, almost as soon as *Bread Winners* was published. The evening was cool, I remember, the onset of winter on Fire Island just a few weeks away. It is the season that I enjoy the most, for there is a brisk and bracing chill in the air, the island is at its quietest, and there are still some bluefish roaming the offshore ocean currents before leaving the island and heading south.

Given a moderately successful catch of the feisty fish, accompanied by some just-baked homemade bread, I sometimes have the boyishly impractical and romantic vision that I am a pioneer who is providing sustenance for his family and friends, my wife patiently pacing on the widow's walk as I return home from the sea with the evening's dinner. Always, however, something shatters my dream and twentieth-century reality takes over. That evening it was the telephone.

"Mel London?" the woman questioned. I agreed that she had found the right party. Barely waiting for the acknowledgment, she continued on. *"My bagels don't hold together!"* she wailed. She had tried everything, but the bagels kept separating. Frustration had led her to try binding them with sewing thread, but even that hadn't worked.

The conversation was a delight for me, and putting on my best diagnostic manner, I tried to work it all out with my caller, Martha Hardy, on the phone from Park Ridge, Illinois. We spoke for about half an hour, and I eventually solved the bagel problem by suggesting that she dampen her fingers just before completing the circle and pressing the dough together.

Finally, she offered a useful tip for bread bakers with small children. Martha's daughter, Elizabeth, was then seven months old, and every time that Martha kneaded her bread, she put the child in a backpack on her shoulders. The rhythmic motion of the kneading put Elizabeth right to sleep!

That telephone call was, to say the least, the beginning. Over these past several years, the telephone has continued to ring, and letters have come in from California, Oregon, Illinois, Virginia, Missouri—even from England and New Zealand. Through it all, I have discovered that this bread baking fraternity is even larger and more diverse than I had ever imagined. On my own island, at least 20 more bakers have surfaced. We compare notes, exchange recipes, and share samples. Many say they baked their first loaves as a result of the encouragement given in *Bread Winners,* so it is a joy to see the pride reflected on their faces as they come to the door carrying their newly baked jewels.

Some of the most charming letters and calls about the book came from old, old friends of mine, dating back to my teenage years. One friend, Howard Rosenberg, now lives in Beaumont, Texas, where he works as the senior executive of a large retail chain. He called me after seeing the book in his local store. It was our first contact since we were seventeen years old. He, too, is a bread baker and his prize *challahs* are the joy of Beaumont.

Another letter, this time from a campmate of my teenage years, was accompanied by photographs of me as a skinny counselor. I have shared them with you in the section devoted to the breads of Seena Cowan (nee Cheslow) later on in this volume.

And so, this is, so to speak, "The Second Rising," and all the bakers who appear in this book are the direct result of the response to *Bread Winners.* Some bakers approached me at book fairs; others introduced themselves at the annual American Library Association convention. Still others were recommended to me by bread baking friends of mine, who exclaimed, "If you think *I* can bake bread, you should meet. . . ." I duly followed up the leads to find still new wells of baking creativity. Some of the new bakers became friends during my book tour for *Bread Winners*—Barbara Gibbs Ostmann of the *St. Louis Post-Dispatch* and Anne Byrn Phillips, the food editor of the *Atlanta Journal.*

Nevertheless, there were some doubts about beginning another book about bread. Even in this age of *Rocky III* (and *IV* and *V*?) and *Star Trek II* (and *III* and *IV*?), did the world really need a *Bread Winners Too (The Second Rising)?*

First of all, I have found that there is no such thing as a "complete" bread book. I am amazed at the variety of breads that I discover continually, though all of them are composed of a basic flour, liquid, and leavener (with an occasional omission of the latter ingredient). On a film trip to Ecuador about a year ago, I visited a small market near the village of Quero. There, before my unbelieving eyes, I saw an Ecuadorian Indian circular bread that looks exactly like a *bagel*. It is the same size as a bagel, the same shape as a bagel, but it is not called a bagel, nor does it taste like a bagel. The Japanese also have a traditional bread that looks like an overblown bagel, but it, too, is not a bagel by any means.

In starting yet another book, there is a second point I'd like to make. It is, in some ways, even more important to me than the first one. I am a "missionary" about baking bread. I want to share the mystique that captured me many years ago.

As a result, this new book is less a tribute to the creativity of the author than it is to the amazing variety and potential of bread itself, and to the vast and diverse army of bakers dedicated to their hobby of baking fresh loaves for themselves, their families, and their friends. A loaf of fresh-baked bread brought to your hosts at a dinner party still provokes more enthusiastic and spontaneous appreciation than the best bottle of vintage champagne. The attraction of home-baked bread does not diminish.

As in the first book, our bakers cover a remarkable range of professions—none of them professional baking.

One contributor is president of the largest teachers' union in America. Another is an optometrist in New Jersey. One works in the Chrysler auto plant in Delaware, another is a minister, another a chemist. My favorite is a 2½-year-old baker from Houston, Texas! Our new bakers include lawyers, a sound technician from one of my own film crews, an accountant, a public relations executive, an artist, and a neurologist.

There is one other point that I want to make about this new book. Though I have included a small section (entitled "Postscripts") about the bakers who were featured in the first volume, it is not at all necessary to have read *Bread Winners* in order to become one with both the bakers and the recipes in this sequel. Each book is separate and complete. I have made this volume totally self-contained, including thorough baking instructions, plus full information about ingredients, utensils, and mail-order sources.

One thing remains the same for *both* books, however—the hope that you experience the contagious joy and sensual pleasure that comes from trying the recipes contributed by the people who share these pages. If you have never tried to bake bread before, we urge you to try this most basic and rewarding of experiences. On the other hand, if you are a veteran of the ovens, or if you already own *Bread Winners,* you are sure to make new friends while picking up some new tips, as I do constantly. For the experienced baker, the serendipity of the craft becomes its own reward. Above all, experienced or not, we share in creating a product recognized by virtually every culture as a symbol of hope, nourishment, and loving care.

In the middle European cultures, a loaf of freshly made bread is still given to a family that moves into a new home—along with salt and candles—to symbolize the good wishes for prosperity and plenty, variety and eternal light. Ancient peoples scattered bread crumbs over the heads of the newly married, probably for the same reasons.

Nowadays, the close identification of home-baked bread with the steady qualities of the good life is constantly being exploited for commercial purposes. Our local newspaper carried an article containing tips on selling your home to a prospective buyer. Among others, the writer suggested *baking bread* when the visitors are due to arrive. That way, the entire house will have a "homey fragrance."

My own house here on the island carries a constant essence of loaves just out of the oven, and a visitor's first reaction is to raise the nose and to comment about the aroma. And *my* house is not even up for sale!

# THE CHRISTMAS LOAVES

As most of my readers know, I have carried on a tradition of almost ten years by baking fresh breads for my Fire Island neighbors at Christmas time, delivering the still-warm loaves on my bicycle early Christmas morning to the accompaniment of joyful acceptance and an occasional hug of appreciation. At the time that I was writing *Bread Winners,* Sheryl planned to take photographs of the event, and I thought that they might well appear in the book, since they were so much a part of my baking delight.

And so, on the bright, cold morning of Christmas, 1978, I wrapped the loaves of newly baked Spoon Handle Rye Breads, wore my most colorful scarf for the photographs, and set out on the rounds of the village delivering the breads. To assure that the photographs were well developed and that they would be handled with concern, I did not use the usually reliable Eastman Kodak, but sent them instead to a private company, secure in the knowledge that they would provide the vigilance and attention that these irreplaceable photographs deserved. *They promptly lost the original slides!*

Consequently, *Bread Winners* never contained the photographs—always a source of dismay to me, since the Christmas ritual is so much a part of my Fire Island life, and the breads are so warmly welcomed by the winter people. Last year, I baked 15 Italian round loaves, wrapped them, and set off with my bike and wagon, again accompanied by Sheryl to take photographs of the event. This time, however, I *did* send them to Eastman Kodak and they are included here, some years late perhaps, but here nonetheless.

# Part I THE SATISFACTION OF MAKING YOUR OWN BREAD

# 1 Discovering Real Bread!

We are a society that has been brainwashed (most successfully, I might add) and led to believe that the foods we eat should be processed and preserved with chemical additives. The breads we buy must be light in texture, whiter than white—commercial bakers use bleached flour to make them that way—and the colorfully wrapped loaves must have the feathery touch of facial tissue. I grew up on bread like that. When I was a kid, the after-school snack consisted of two pieces of white bread smeared with gooey drippings of cheap commercial strawberry jam, wrapped in newspaper, and thrown from our third-floor apartment window in the Bronx down to waiting hands below, to be devoured on the run.

It was a marvelously versatile bread they baked then (the commercial bakers told us that they baked it while we slept)—and they still bake what is basically the same bread. When not serving as a base for jam or peanut butter, it could—and still can—be rolled between the fingers to make little puttylike balls to be shot across the room using a rubber band sling. That kind of bread still decorates the supermarket shelves, lying there in all its inflated glory, perfect for mopping up gravy, or anything else that a paper towel can absorb. The loaves are a perfect blend of air, bleached white flour, and the chemical preservatives the industry has such a genius for developing. Did I like that bread as a kid? *I loved it!* I couldn't get enough of it. I built *triple-decker* sandwiches in order to devour more of it. It was, the advertising said, building my body 12 ways—but mostly around the middle!

To this day, I wince when I see supermarket baskets filled to overflowing with brightly wrapped long loaves of processed breads. Well-meaning mothers bring them home to their children who love it as I loved it. They will grow up, as I grew up, thinking that white is best and that chemicals with unpronounceable names are essential to the baking process.

In *Bread Winners,* I introduced the chapter about ingredients with a brief statement about whole grains—that I believed in them, that I used natural ingredients wherever possible, and that there was a new world of discovery awaiting the home baker of bread, a universe apart from the commercial loaves turned out on the assembly line. Since that time, I have spent two years working with Sheryl on a new book about whole grains, *Sheryl and Mel London's Creative Cooking with Grains and Pasta.* During that time, I became even more appreciative of the remarkable qualities of whole grains—wheat, corn, millet, amaranth, rice—not only for the nutrition that they offer, but also for their taste and their impressive versatility in cooking and baking.

Not only did we experiment with new grains, but also with new forms of those grains. The breads that we baked for that book opened new worlds of taste treats for us and for our guests.

We are not the only ones to make that discovery. There is a ground swell of interest in the use of more nutritious ingredients in cooking. Where once it was almost impossible to find whole grains in smaller communities, natural foods outlets that stock them have sprung up all across the country. Many of the more popular supermarkets have added sections where whole grains and truly natural foods can be purchased. Along with their awareness about the nutrition of whole grains, Americans have taken to *reading labels.* They ask questions about the complicated and obstruse ingredients listings on the packages. In short, buyers demand information on what they are really buying. The commercial bakers respond by inundating the marketplace with loaves plastered with the words "natural" and "no preservatives added"; new trade names shout "harvest" and "golden" and "honey," and other catch-words devised by Madison Avenue's marketing geniuses to tell us that they're listening to us.

If you have read any of my previous books, you know that I am not only a curmudgeon, but a devout and outspoken cynic. The more they shout the word "natural" at me, the closer I read the labels and the more disturbed I become at the new world of chemicals I see listed there.

# Chemistry Class

A few weeks ago, one of my baker friends on the West Coast sent me a bread wrapper for a new triticale loaf that had been introduced in her supermarket just that week. My first reaction was one of pleasure, for the commercial bakery had covered the wrapper with words like "bran" and "honey."

I did what I always do. I turned the package over and read the label. Aside from the fact that the major ingredient in the bread was bleached, enriched white flour (more on that later), and that every two-slice serving would give me 375 milligrams of salt, large amounts of brown sugar, and 180 unwanted, useless calories, the balance of the list read like a page from my high school chemistry book!

The label told me that I was also eating ferrous sulphate, thiamine mononitrate, calcium stearoyl-2-lactate, monocalcium phosphate, calcium sulphate, caramel color (more sugar), ammonium sulphate, and potassium bromate.

# The Return to Home-Baked Bread

There are, to be sure, more positive reasons for baking your own bread. No commercial baker in the world could offer the full range of possibilities in flavor and texture open to us at home.

As a home baker I have discovered the remarkable qualities of new grains—of amaranth and millet and sorghum (milo) and triticale—in all their natural forms and with all their remarkable flavors left intact. And my friend, Ed Feiner, has opened new paths for me in the creation and development of sourdough starters. Also, I have begun to use yogurt in more and more of my breads, and I have developed a "feel" for dough that has led me to ignore most of the measuring cups and measuring spoons in my kitchen.

Along the way there have been some hilarious disasters. Just last summer you could have discovered me in my kitchen staring in disbelief at a sourdough starter that I had nurtured for almost two weeks. It had turned so rancid that a visitor inquired politely whether a mouse had expired in the walls of the house! I, a writer of books on baking bread, a failure? But then, if everything went well all the time, what stories would I have to recount in my books?

I can report, however, that the next starter worked, my self-esteem was restored, and I continued with *Bread Winners Too!*

# Time to 2 Discard the Rules

The baking of bread is not a science, by any means. Certainly, it might rise to an art in the hands of some of our more adept bakers. Still, I am always surprised that this most basic, simple, and natural of cooking crafts carries a forbidding aura that prevents so many of my friends from even trying their hands at it for the first time.

I meet a friend one day as I stroll on the narrow wooden walks here at Fire Island. She is a superb cook, and a dinner invitation to her house by the sea is considered by me to be the high point of any week. We come to talk about bread and her plaint is loud and long. "Oh, I've never tried *bread!*" she wails. "What if it should fall!" A few nights later, we are honored by an invitation to her home for dinner. The seven courses include Lobster en Bellevue Parisienne, Potage a la Caravelle, Leg of Lamb *en Croute,* and a dessert of unsurpassed beauty—her triumphant Floating Island (*Oeufs a La Neige*).

*Yet she is in awe of me because I bake bread.*

Possibly it is we writers of bread books who create this mystique. After all, if it's so easy, how can we write whole books about it? The basic ingredients for bread are the same today as they were when our Egyptian forefathers discovered leavening by accident. The breads that I found in Ecuador have exactly the same components as the breads we bake on Fire Island. And special equipment, although useful in baking bread, is not really necessary. Mixing bowls, baking containers, and even ovens can be of almost any kind, and of virtually any serviceable quality. I have an oven here in my home that works on LP gas, sent over from the mainland in large tanks. As a result, the temperature at the top right is 350°, while the bottom left is 275°, and I have not measured the center because my thermometer has not worked in two years. But I bake bread!

In all these seasons of making home-baked loaves, I have discovered one immutable fact—there are no rules to the baking of bread. The recipes that tell you to knead the dough for 8 minutes and 22 seconds, allow the dough to rise for 47 minutes and 10 seconds, tiptoe around the house so that the dough won't fall, and then bake the bread in the center of the oven for exactly 50 minutes and 44 seconds, do a terrible disservice to the joy and the freedom that should accompany the baking of bread.

Certainly, there are things to learn, but in what activity is this not so? Certain ingredients behave differently under varying conditions. For example, here at the island it is usually very damp, and thus the flour will absorb much more water than in an area like Denver, where high altitude creates other conditions. But the solutions are simple. If the dough seems damp, I just add more flour until the texture is right. If the altitude creates a super-fast rise, I just cut the amount of yeast in half. But, above all, don't panic. If *I* can bake bread, anyone can. For I am known as an inveterate bungler in almost everything I attempt— from tying a new fishing line to a hook to making model boats (the glue invariably sticks to my fingers rather than to the rigging).

And if I fail? So what? After all, I failed French three times in high school. My bread baking failures are tossed outside into the garden to feed the birds. But, in spite of the sourdough disaster I mentioned earlier, I have very few failures these days. Once a baker learns the basics about ingredients, how flours and leaveners and liquids handle in making the dough, there is really very little that can go wrong.

I began my bread baking with a sense of freedom that was a reflection of the attitude of my teacher, George Meluso. Always joyful and free in his afternoon of baking, and always accompanied by his glass of red wine, he passed on to me the only rule for bread baking: *There are no rules.* Therefore, I have never owned a thermometer with which to test the temperature of the water before adding yeast. George taught me to run my wrist under the tap water, very much like testing milk for an infant. In recent years, I have thrown away my measuring cups, for I bake by texture now, as you will when you learn the "feel" of bread.

I think the timidity novice bread bakers feel is brought on by the writers of bread books who make it all seem so difficult. But it is fair warning to say that the reader who proceeds to the recipes immediately without checking on the instructions first is likely to have some discouraging failures. I ask, then, that you read these next pages with care, especially if you have never baked a bread before, or if you consider yourself a novice. And then, as a beginning, you might try one of the many "quick" breads included in the book, just to prove to yourself that it can be done. When that first loaf comes hot from the oven, you will be forgiven if you merely stare at it for ten or fifteen minutes as it cools on the rack. At that moment, you will have joined our vast and growing fraternity.

# 3 The Ingredients of Bread

The ingredients I use in my breads are as close to their natural state as I can get them—no bleached white flours, no white sugar, no chemicalized anything. To my taste the flavor and texture of loaves made with whole grains are superior. Flour that has a definite flavor appeals to me, and I like a bread you can chew. I might seem old-fashioned, but I still think of bread as the staff of life; so my breads are rich in nutrition, really good for you!

## Flour

A single kernel of grain—whether we are speaking of wheat, corn, rye, or barley, is a remarkable reservoir of nutrition, *when* it is in its natural state. The wheat berry, for example, contains an outer layer of bran, an oily germ, and a starchy core that we call the endosperm. The outer layers contain most of the minerals, the vitamins, and the other nutrients of the berry, but they are also the most vulnerable to spoilage. For that reason, whole wheat flour needs to be refrigerated if it is to be kept for any length of time. Most commercial flours are processed to eliminate the quick-spoiling elements. We trade nutritional, flavorful ingredients for longer shelf life. It is, over all, a bad bargain.

When the processors mill whole wheat grains into white flour, the values of all but two nutritional ingredients are reduced. The two ingredients that increase are protein (2 percent) and starch (20 percent). The endosperm—the starchy center portion—is what remains after milling. This is one reason that bread has gotten a reputation as a food that "makes you fat."

In addition to being high in starch, the endosperm also carries a protein substance called *gluten.* Naturally, the more endosperm the more gluten, and it is this latter substance that provides the flexible rise of the loaves. Gluten has great properties of elasticity, and when the leavener (yeast) gives off carbon dioxide bubbles, the gluten traps them as it expands and holds the bread together as it rises. As a result, the baker who uses all white flour will find that the loaves rise more easily, that the breads seem to contain more air (they do), and that they begin to resemble the commercial loaves on the supermarket shelves. On the other hand, those of us who bake with whole grains will find that the breads are somewhat more dense, that they have a deeper flavor, and that they are nutritionally richer. A new world of taste and pleasure opens up, while the standard of "white is better" disappears forever.

Of course, we do want our breads to rise, even if we no longer demand skyscraper proportions. Some grains—rye, corn, triticale—have very little gluten or no gluten at all. In order to make the breads rise, they must be mixed with a higher gluten flour, either some white or a finely milled whole wheat. Therefore, this volume, like its sister book, *Bread Winners,* uses white flour in a few situations:

- Where there is need for gluten in order to make the bread rise properly.

- Where the breads are traditional, or have been passed down to the baker from generation to generation. The classic examples are the Mexican breads, *Pan de Nixtamalina* and *Bizchochuelos* and the traditional Jewish loaf, *Challah.* Both types could be made with whole grain flour, but the conversion would take the breads out of the realm of custom. Who am I to tamper with tradition?

- Where a bread has won a baking contest, and white flour was one of the ingredients, I have in some instances left the recipe untouched.

One final word about white flour. If you must use it—and that is your choice, certainly—I strongly recommend that you buy the *unbleached* flour rather than the bleached, enriched, all-purpose flour. The commercial millers generally use yet another chemical to bleach the flour.

# Whole Wheat Flour

Over the past few years, George Meluso and I have been experimenting to determine just how far we can go with whole wheat flour and still have a bread that rises well. We have found, with no great surprise to ourselves, that we can eliminate white flour altogether and get exactly the same results from the use of all whole wheat.

The beauty of whole wheat flour, as I've mentioned, is that it contains *all* the nutrition of the wheat berry, since it is made from the entire kernel—bran, germ, and endosperm. However, some whole wheat flour is made from soft wheat, and some from hard wheat, the latter being a spring wheat that is grown both in the Midwest and in Texas. It is higher in gluten and it absorbs more water than the soft wheat does.

Some whole wheat flour is stone-ground, although much of the commercial variety is ground in high-speed mills with metal blades. For a bread that is of coarse texture, with the feel of the loaf "like grandma used to bake," most of us use the stone-ground flour. The commercial milling also tends to leave the germ in small lumps, and this encourages rancidity. However it is ground, whole wheat flour should be kept in the refrigerator or used within a few weeks after you purchase it.

If you buy whole wheat flour packaged, look carefully at the label to make certain that it is not just white flour that is "enriched" with bran.

For the superb "rise" that I promised you, here are two tips for you to try:

• Use the commercial whole wheat flour, since the millers have now put some excellent flour on the market. Since it is more finely ground, you will probably find that it handles just as well as white flour. You might use George Meluso's recipes (see Index) to test out the theory. Better still, try "Irish Brown Bread" on page 41.

• When using stone-ground flour, either add more leavener, or let the dough rise for a longer period of time than the recipe calls for.

*There is no need to sift whole wheat flour.* What you'd be doing is removing the bran, just as they do in making white flour. Use whole wheat flour just as it comes to you in the package. However, there are times when the flour is packed down tightly and you might want to lighten it. In that case, if you sift, make certain you return the bran that remains in the strainer.

## Whole Wheat Pastry Flour

Basically, this is a finely milled whole wheat flour that is generally used in pies, cakes, cookies, waffles, and pancakes. It can also be used in bread baking to give a lighter texture to the loaf, but when used this way it should be mixed with a larger amount of the regular whole wheat flour.

## Graham Flour

This is the famous flour originally developed by Sylvester Graham. It is simply whole wheat flour in which the endosperm is finely ground and the bran layers are left coarse and flaky and then returned to the flour. Graham flour is superb for rolls and bread.

## Gluten Flour

This flour is an excellent addition to the mixture when baking breads with grains that have a low gluten content— rye, corn, oats, barley, soy, triticale, or milo. Gluten flour is basically a wheat flour with the starch removed. It is sometimes recommended for people on a diabetic diet, which aims to reduce starch intake.

## Oat Flour

People on a wheat-free diet can use this excellent substitute for wheat. Oat flour is finely ground from whole oat groats, and much of the bran remains, making it almost as nutritious as the groats themselves. Oat flour can, of course, be blended with other flours in baking breads, but always remember that its lack of gluten will keep it from rising when it is used by itself.

I've mentioned that the lecithin in soy flour acts as a preservative, and the addition of a small amount of oat flour to bread dough will do the same thing. The grain contains a strong, natural antioxidant that acts to keep baked goods fresh for a longer period of time, and I was fascinated to learn that oats and other derivatives of the grain were used for just that purpose long before the discovery of chemical preservatives.

## Barley Flour

Made up of finely ground, hulled barley, this flour is used for blending with other flours, usually with a high-gluten wheat flour to lighten breads, biscuits, or muffins. This is another grain that is occasionally recommended for people on wheat-restricted diets.

## Rye Flour

Of all bread ingredients, this is one of the tastiest. Those of us who were brought up in city neighborhoods where the local bakery specialized in sour rye loaves still remember the shiny crusts and the semisticky texture of those breads. My brother and I used to quarrel over who would get the heel of the bread, the part that had the paper union label pasted to it. Some commercial bakers have tried to capitalize on these childhood memories by advertising their rye breads as exact copies, but we are not fooled.

Rye flour is very low in gluten and must be used with other higher gluten wheat flours. It also makes a fairly sticky batter, which has a tendency to stick to your fingers, unlike the standard wheat flours. However, the finished loaves have a most unusual and distinctive moist texture.

Rye flour comes in four varieties: white, medium, dark, and pumpernickel. You'll probably find that you achieve your best results by mixing about 30 percent rye flour with 70 percent of the higher gluten whole wheat.

## Soy Flour

Soy flour is ground from the soybean, and since it is a legume, it has no gluten. But it does contain a high amount of protein and it has lecithin, which acts as a natural preservative in breads. As a matter of fact, bakers report that breads baked with soy flour will stay fresh about twice as long as loaves using only whole wheat. Soy flour is also low in fat, but it does have a strong, distinctive flavor and an almost bitter taste if used in great amounts. Recipes vary, but I suggest that soy flour be used by the tablespoon rather than by the cup. As you experiment, you might want to use about one-fifth soy flour in the recipe, deducting the same amount of wheat flour when you add it.

## Corn Flour

Made from finely milled kernels of corn, this flour comes in yellow or white. You'll notice that recipes for southern breads, pancakes, or fritters generally call for corn*meal* rather than corn flour (cornmeal is discussed later in this chapter). However, if you want to add the slight taste of corn to your breads, you can substitute a small amount (up to one cup) of corn flour for the wheat flour.

## Brown Rice Flour

This is an ingredient that is generally recommended for people who are allergic to gluten. However, if it is not mixed with a high-gluten wheat flour when used in breads, muffins, pancakes, and biscuits, it will result in a rather moist and extremely dense-textured product.

## Triticale Flour

After the publication of *Bread Winners,* Frank Ford of Arrowhead Mills and Ron Kershen, who grows the grain down in Canyon, Texas, told me that they were running four months behind in delivering triticale due to the large demand. As the author of the book, I would love to claim credit, but I rather think that the word about this tasty and most unusual grain was already getting around at that time. I have now seen it almost everywhere around the country.

Triticale is a hybrid grain—a cross between rye and wheat, with a higher protein content than either of its original parents. It has a distinctive flavor, sometimes described as "strong rye," but it is low in gluten and thus should be mixed with a wheat flour to get a good rise, at most about half and half.

## Potato Flour

To make this flour potatoes are cooked, dried, and then milled finely. It can then be used in combination with wheat flours, just as you do with soy flour, barley flour, or brown rice flour.

## Sorghum Flour (Milo)

Sorghum is one of those remarkable grains, known around the world as an amazing, drought-resistant crop, and as a staple food source in Africa, China, East Asia, and India. *Yet, it is virtually unknown as human food in America!* We did a lot of experimenting with sorghum when we were writing *Creative Cooking with Grains and Pasta,* and our response was generally, "Where has this been all of our cooking lives?" Well, sorghum was there, but obviously we were not aware of it. Grain sorghum (milo) flour is available from my friend Paul Keene at Walnut Acres (see Mail-Order Sources for the address).

## Amaranth Flour

If we want to consider a really ancient grain, amaranth is clearly the best candidate, since it's been around for well over eight thousand years! Yet amaranth may well be the supercrop of the future, for it grows under the most adverse of conditions, espcially in drought areas. It offers a high-quality protein and an unusual, appealing, nutty flavor. When we mix it with whole wheat flour, the resultant protein balance is close to that recommended for optimum nutrition. Amaranth is available by mail order from Walnut Acres (see Mail-Order Sources for the address).

# Grinding Your Own Grains Can Yield Other Textures

In the section on mail-order sources, I've given some listings for home mills, both hand and electric types. I've also included some tips on what to look for and how to choose a mill, if you think that you'd like to grind your own flour. The most important point to consider, aside from wanting to do it just for fun, is the economics of owning your own mill. When you take into account the cost of a modern, electric mill, you realize that you have to grind an awful lot of grain to make it pay for itself. Most of us are after-work or weekend bakers, and with the vast array of ready-ground flours available through natural foods stores, on our supermarket shelves, and through mail order, you might, as we have, decide against the investment. Nevertheless, friends of mine report that there's nothing like the taste of a bread made with flour just milled in your own kitchen.

When the whole grain is milled coarsely, it's called "meal." It can be made quite easily at home in a spice grinder or a coffee mill. Other potential ingredients are made from just portions of the grain, such as wheat germ or bran. My friend, Andy Esberg (see Index), for example, never makes a bread without adding at least one cup of bran, giving his Fire Island loaves a most distinctive flavor, as well as an excellent dose of fiber. Here are just a few of the ingredients you might be using.

## Cornmeal

So many favorites of southern baking tradition, such as hush puppies, corn bread, and spoon bread, feature this classic ingredient. It is coarsely ground and it comes in either yellow or white forms. Cornmeal also serves another purpose for the baker of bread. Coating the bottom of the baking pan with a light dusting of cornmeal will keep the dough from sticking.

## Whole Wheat Meal

The kernels of wheat are ground coarsely, and rough bits of the bran remain. It adds more "body" to the breads, a rougher texture.

## Millet Meal

Just like sorghum (milo) and amaranth, millet is another of America's underutilized grains, even though it dates back to the Romans and is used today in the Middle East, in Europe, and throughout Africa. In this country we know it as the food we feed to our parakeets! If you'd like to try millet to add crunch to your breads (as well as valuable nutrition), grind some millet seed in your blender, coffee grinder, or spice grinder, adding about one-half cup of millet to five or six cups of flour.

These are the ordinary cereal oats, first steamed and then flattened. When you buy them, be sure to choose the "old-fashioned" kind that cook in five to ten minutes. The commercial "instant" or "quick" versions are preprocessed with heat for faster cooking, and thus have less nutritive value. If you want smaller flakes for your breads, crumble them in the palms of your hands or whirl them in a blender or food processor.

I first became aware of the question when a columnist in one of our major newspapers asserted, "Bulgur is simply cracked wheat," and mentioned that the two were interchangeable. In *Bread Winners,* bulgur was listed as cracked wheat and described as coarsely milled whole grains of wheat, generally used in Greek or Middle Eastern cooking, which add a crunchy texture and nutty flavor to breads.

We were both wrong! Bulgur and cracked wheat are not identical. Both are, indeed, made from whole wheat, but there is one substantial difference:

- *Cracked wheat* is made from whole wheat berries that have been cracked into four to six pieces. It is *uncooked*.

- *Bulgur* is whole wheat that has been cracked, parched, and *steamed*. It is then dried, left whole, or cracked into various grinds. The processing, however, is minimal, so that bulgur retains nearly all the nutrients that we find in whole wheat.

# Extras You Can Add to Flours and Meals

There is no need to stop at the flours and meals that make up the bulk of breads. You can add even more nutrition and texture with the following items.

## Grain Berries

For the past few years, I have been using the whole berry from wheat, rye, and triticale to add texture and nutrition to my breads. The berries are available in most natural foods stores. You'll love the "look" of your loaves when you slice them and see the tiny berries scattered through the slices. They add a bit of crunch too.

However, the berries must be "home-processed" before you use them, since they are quite hard when purchased. For two loaves put about half a cup of the berries into a bowl, cover them with about a cup of warm water, and let them stand overnight to soften a bit. (This will cut down the cooking time.) Next morning, simmer them over low heat for 20 to 40 minutes, or until you taste one and find it tender without being too crunchy. *Do not throw away the water—use it for the loaves!* If, during the simmering process, the water seems to be absorbed, just add a little more to barely cover the cooking berries. Let them cool and add them to your dough before kneading.

I am most enthusiastic about this addition to breads and I think you will be, too. With such extras, they become very personal breads.

## Wheat Germ

In the milling of white flour, the germ is removed from the grain because it is the part that has a tendency to turn rancid and thus reduce shelf life. Germ is the vitamin- and mineral-rich kernel of the wheat grain and it makes a marvelous, natural additive, both for flavor and nutrition. However, because it does contain fat, it should be kept refrigerated. Use a tablespoon or two in your bread dough without changing any other part of the recipe.

## Bran Flakes

This is the outer layer of the hard wheat kernel or berry. You can use it to add extra fiber to your breads.

## Sprouted Grains

"Ain't nature wonderful!" we exclaimed as kids growing up in The Bronx. There, in the midst of large apartment buildings, in barren back lots filled with rocks and rubble, the towering Ailanthus trees forced their way into the air. It always amazed us, for they pushed their way out of every crack and crevice.

I suppose that I feel almost the same emotions when I look at a tiny speck of grain, so versatile, so hardy, and so remarkable. For, if I take that miniscule, dormant seed and I sprout it, it magically multiplies its size and nutritional content in only three to five days! Best of all, sprouting is easy. You can sprout wheat, rye, barley, and even lentils and mung beans, not only for use in breads, but also for a superb addition to salads. If you've never tried it before, I guarantee that you'll look at the results and say with me, "Ain't nature wonderful!"

Along with flour or meal, liquid is the only other essential ingredient in bread. The range of liquids is as vast as the grain forms you can use. Basically, as I've said, bread is nothing more than a combination of these two and, usually, leavener. If you leave out the leavener, you get "unleavened bread"—matzohs being a prime example. I would not, however, plan to leave out the liquid, since I have yet to discover a substitute ingredient to moisten the dough and to develop the gluten in yeast breads. In any case, no matter which liquid your recipe calls for, make certain it is at room temperature, a rule you might well follow with all your ingredients.

# Liquids

## Water

As the most common liquid ingredient in bread, water is sometimes the subject of debate. I have heard arguments that the "taste" of bread is directly related to the water of the city in which it was baked. It is the reason, some tell me, that sourdough bread in San Francisco tastes so different from the bread I bake here on the East Coast. It is what makes the French bread of Paris a very special treat that cannot be duplicated in America. I suppose that there may well be some truth in the concept, but I am sometimes convinced that it is the *being* there in San Francisco or Paris that makes the bread taste so special, rather than the mineral content of the water. My own travel experiences have proven to me that *nothing* from Paris, Rome, San Francisco, or Hong Kong ever tastes the same once you get it home.

In addition to using water as an ingredient in your breads, you can also use it to spray the tops of the loaves while they're baking to produce a crisp and solid crust.

You can use milk as the only liquid in the bread, or you can mix milk with water in varying amounts. It will give your breads a softer, thinner texture, plus milk's extras, calcium, phosphorus, protein, and vitamin A. Grandmother always scalded the milk before using it in bread, mostly because it was not pasteurized. Although there are still recipes that call for scalded milk (brought down to room temperature), for the most part, scalding is no longer done.

## Milk, Skim Milk, and Nonfat Dry Milk

Some people insist that breads made with milk tend to keep longer. However, my own feeling is that it is the fat content of milk that does the job, and that the use of butter or vegetable oil will accomplish the same purpose.

## Potato Water

This is a favorite of mine. It is simply the water left over after boiling potatoes. It acts as an additional leavening agent, and if you leave it at room temperature for a few days, it takes on a superb sour smell and taste. Potato water also gives a smooth crumb to the bread.

## Buttermilk and Sour Milk

Buttermilk is probably the most convenient liquid for baking bread; a container of buttermilk in the refrigerator makes it possible to bake a quick bread within the hour. Since both buttermilk and sour milk have a high acid content, they generally are used with baking soda and baking powder as leavening agents rather than with yeast.

I remember spending summers in the country at a small family farm, and when bread was baked with sour milk, it was the naturally soured milk that had come from the family cows just a few days before. Most modern bakers must find a different source of sour milk. If you decide to use sour milk instead of buttermilk in a recipe, here is a shortcut you might try: Mix one tablespoon of vinegar in one cup of sweet milk and let it stand for a few minutes.

## Vegetable Liquids

Some breads do not require the standard liquids in order to make the dough, especially when watery vegetables such as zucchini are used. In cases such as these, the liquid from the vegetable is all you need for moistening the flour. At other times, you might try the broth that remains from preparing vegetables for lunch or dinner.

## Beer

It stands to reason that if the most common leavening, yeast, is produced commercially from the dregs of beer, then beer itself might well be used in breads. The best way to use beer is to let it stand in a bowl at room temperature for a few days. It adds a pungent flavor to your breads, and any alcohol in the beer cooks off in the heat of the oven.

You may add an egg to your bread dough for extra nutrition. However, in some traditional recipes such as Sally Lunn, *Challah,* or *Brioche,* eggs are considered a standard ingredient in the loaves, and they add a certain richness to the bread. An egg yolk mixed with a tablespoon of water and then brushed on top of the loaf before baking results in a lovely golden glaze.

# Eggs

Except for the rare occasions when I am baking a rich, flaky bread like croissants, I use butter in my recipes mostly for greasing the pans or baking sheets. Butter is probably the best ingredient for that purpose since it does not burn easily during the baking process. If recipes call for fats or oils, you may use butter or any vegetable oil, preferably a polyunsaturated one such as peanut oil or corn oil. Oil acts as a lubricant, letting the loaf expand more easily during rising and baking. Make certain, however, that the oil you use is not rancid; if it is, it will ruin the taste of the bread.

# Fats and Oils

You have shaped the long sourdough loaves, and made them ready for the oven. They have risen into puffy, pale breads that will soon resemble the best that you have ever eaten (even in San Francisco!), for you have made them yourself. Carefully you slice four lines diagonally across the breads, using a straight-edge razor, so that their final rise in the oven will open these thin slits into the rough, distended grooves that make long breads look so professional. But there is one thing yet to do.

# Atop the Bread

After spraying water on top of the loaves, you carefully sprinkle sesame seeds across the entire length of each one. And, thus adorned, the breads somehow look more finished. They will come from the oven as a tribute to your art. It will be time to call someone to, "quick, take a look at what I've done."

The garnishing of bread is another area of imagination. Not only can seeds and whole grains be used inside the loaves, but they constitute a wide range of decorations that make any bread look "finished." I have already mentioned sesame seeds as an adornment for breads, and there is another member of that family that I have used on my French loaves and my sourdough breads—*irigoma,* a Japanese toasted sesame seed that gives the bread an even stronger flavor.

Caraway seeds have been used for centuries. In the Northeast, we were lucky enough to experience black caraway seeds. We called them *chernishkas* (or *charnushkas*). They are very strongly flavored and I would suggest that you use only a few of them on top of the bread until you decide just how much *charnushka* taste you want. I have included a mail-order source for *charnushkas* in the back of the book. A quarter pound will last for a long time.

You can also use poppy seeds or chopped nuts to decorate your breads. Or, put some finely minced onion on top of a rye bread; it will give the loaf both an unusual look as the pieces brown in the heat, and a taste that will linger long after the meal. Keep in mind, though, that some garnishes can turn rather hard and almost inedible when they bake for about an hour—raisins, for example, have a tendency to char and become crisp. If you're in doubt about a garnish, use it—try it—the worst that can happen is that you'll have to scrape off the topping; the bread will remain perfect nonetheless!

# And on the Inside . . .

Fresh herbs from our garden—dill and parsley grow outside our door—end up in many of our breads. And so do blueberries and bananas . . . and sour cream and yogurt . . . and potatoes, onions, garlic, tomatoes, zucchini, apples, apricots, figs, coconut, currants, grapes, walnuts, pecans, peanuts, cloves, nutmeg, sunflower seeds . . . and cheddar cheese, ricotta cheese, and cream cheese. *If you wish to add interest to your breads by incorporating foods like these, keep in mind that fairly dense ingredients, such as nuts and raisins, should be rolled in flour first so that they won't sink to the bottom of the bread as they bake.*

# Sweeteners

I don't remember just when I gave up refined white sugar, but there is a monument to the days of sugar consumption in my kitchen—a never-used container that is half-filled with one of the most important ingredients in America's manufactured and processed foods.

Other food writers, as well as I, have commented adversely upon the large amounts of sugar used in so many of our foods, certainly in commercial breads, and even in the breads we bake at home. I admit to being a victim of America's "sugar fix" just like everyone else. I was brought up on sweets, indulging in an overdose of candy after each meal, including breakfast, and even between meals, as a quick lift for my adolescent energy levels.

Sweeteners are an integral part of bread baking, but the amounts are subject to personal taste. In magazines I find recipes that use up to *three cups* of sweetener. I, in turn, tend to keep the amounts at a minimum. The most common sweetener used by bakers of natural loaves is honey, and we have a wide choice of these, from the light and delicate honeys to the strongly flavored ones. The honey not only adds flavor to the breads, but it also awakens the action of the yeast. Some bakers use molasses and some use natural maple syrup. Molasses and malt syrup are also used to sweeten breads such as pumpernickel as well as to darken them.

It is important to note that if you decide to use honey or a syrup instead of sugar in a recipe that you've found in a magazine or newspaper, *you will be substituting a liquid for a solid.* That means you will probably have to adjust the amount of flour upward somewhat. Don't let it throw you. As I explain later on, it's a matter of knowing the "feel" of the dough rather than being a slave to the amounts called for. Just add more flour.

# Salt

I am convinced, and have been for a long time, that salt is among the leading causes of high blood pressure and fluid retention, and that it is probably a factor in the high incidence of heart attacks in this country.

You can imagine my delight, then, when I came across a book written in 1620 which anticipated today's concern about salt in the diet. The author was an Englishman named Tobias Venner, and the book was called *Via Recta ad Vitam Longam—The Way to Happiness and Long Life.* Venner, along with my dear mother, also warned that eating hot bread "breedeth flatulent and obstructive humors." But salt was Venner's main target. He claimed that, when used in bread, it had many adverse effects on the body. I have no idea how long Venner lived, nor from what dread disease he might have died, but the sage man has been seconded by a great many contemporary experts concerning the bad effect salt has on health and nutrition.

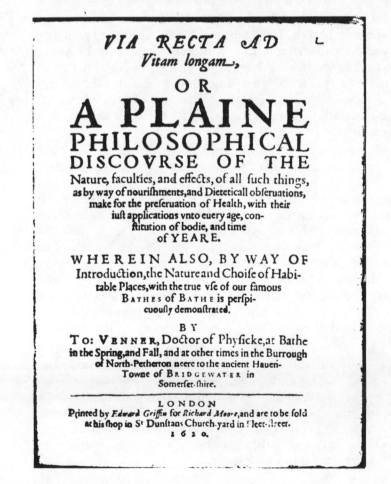

Nevertheless, the food industry continues to use plenty of salt in processed foods (just look at the labels!). Some single products contain *two to three times* the Recommended Daily Amount (RDA) of salt for adult humans in a single serving! On the other hand, some farsighted companies are now using less salt in their processed products.

My wife, Sheryl, and I have written for Rodale Press for several years now. We agree with our publisher that cutting down on salt can only be good for just about any American. We try not to preach, for we still believe, with Bob Rodale, that "the salt shaker is in your hands." However, if you own some of our previous books, you know that we have succeeded in eliminating salt in almost everything we cook by using citrus, spices, or herbs, in place of salt for added flavor and zest.

But when we come to the baking of bread, the problem gets a bit trickier, for it is not just a matter of substituting one ingredient for another. Nor is it just a matter of taste. Salt, in the case of baking bread, is an important chemical ingredient that, among other things, controls the rate of growth of the yeast and thus is responsible in part for the eventual texture and "look" of the bread.

The use of salt will generally make a yeast bread dough rise more slowly, usually double the time it takes without the use of salt. Since the rising rate is slower, more liquid will be absorbed by the dough and the bread will be drier. Over all, by using some salt you get a steadier growth rate during the rise, and thus fewer air holes and a better textured bread, as well as a generally more familiar taste.

Of course, there are other factors that enter into this discussion, since there are no rules in bread baking (remember?). The type of flour you use, the altitude at which you bake, the dampness or dryness of the area in which you live, and the type of yeast you choose, will all affect the time of the rise, the texture of the bread, and the quality of the finished loaf. But we do know that the addition of salt *will* keep the dough from rising too fast, and thus the no-salt bread baker is in a dilemma of sorts. The question is, perhaps, just *how much* salt you are willing to use—and what are the amounts that will control the yeast while still giving satisfactory baking results.

There is one other point worth remembering—while you can add salt to a finished stew if you crave it, and you can sprinkle salt on a cooked egg, you can't add salt to a baked bread. Those who expect the taste that salt imparts to bread find salt-free bread a little flat. That is why we give salt as an optional ingredient.

We arrived at the amount after several experiments in the Rodale Test Kitchen:

- We baked the bread using the contributor's suggested amount of salt.

- We baked the same bread with one-half teaspoon salt per loaf.

- We baked the bread using no salt at all.

Generally, all three textures were acceptable. We chose to go with the minimal amount of salt per loaf (about one-half teaspoon) that satisfied the chemical requirements, yet eliminated the flat or too sweet taste that some of our readers might find objectionable.

Of course, you can go still further by eliminating the salt altogether if you like, or if you must. Just pay attention to the simple rules provided in the box below. I'll say it again: *The salt shaker is in your hands.*

---

## How to Bake Salt-Free Bread

1. Remember, the rising time will be cut, sometimes by as much as half. Just let the dough rise until nearly doubled in bulk, paying no attention to the approximate rising time given in the recipe.
2. If the dough seems too damp after the first rise, since lack of salt will limit absorption of liquids, compensate by adding more flour and kneading it into the dough thoroughly.
3. Quick breads that use baking powder and/or baking soda are not affected by the elimination of salt, except for the taste.

# Yeast

For years now I have been getting my yeast from a little Italian bakery around the corner from where I live, and my friend Angie Tyna, who works there, has become as important to my bread baking as my five-loaf black French baking pan. The bakery owners still get their yeast in one-pound cakes from the local brewery, where it is processed from the remains in their large vats. I, in turn, am very partial to that particular kind of yeast. However, there are several forms of yeast available to the home baker.

Actually, yeast is a living organism that floats in the air around us and exists in the soil as well. It was first produced commercially in Europe early in the nineteenth century, as a by-product of the breweries. It is said that this yeast was so bitter that several days of home processing and washing were needed to make it palatable for bread baking. Today, it is no longer necessary to go to the brewery as grandmother did, or even to have a marvelous Italian bakery around the corner, as I do. Yeast is available in two basic forms, and you can find it just about anywhere.

## Compressed Cake Yeast

I still prefer this form of yeast, which usually comes in a two-ounce package, and obviously I am not alone. I see it often today in my supermarket on the cooled shelves with the cheeses and other dairy products. I prefer cake yeast for handling, and I am convinced that the *taste* of the bread is better when I use it. Others, of course, will disagree, asserting that active dry yeast is just as effective, tastes the same, and gives as perfect a rise. Nevertheless, I love the way cake yeast crumbles when I use it, the smell of it, the feeling that I am baking my breads in the most basic and natural way possible.

Because compressed cake yeast is active and fresh, it will not keep much longer than ten days to two weeks under refrigeration. If you buy a pound of it, as I do, you'll want to use some and keep the rest for use in baking breads at a future time. I suggest that you cut the yeast into one- or two-ounce squares, and freeze them for up to six months.

Some bakers merely wrap the excess yeast in aluminum foil and pop it into the freezer. I prefer the method taught to me by George Meluso, and I find that the results are excellent. I wrap each small piece of yeast in aluminum foil and then bury them all in a large plastic container filled with flour. The wrapped yeast freezes more slowly that way (frozen quickly, the yeast will die) and, when the pieces eventually thaw, they seem to be more fit for their job. When you do take the yeast cakes out of the freezer, though, make sure you don't use them until they're thoroughly thawed at room temperature. And—don't use hot water to speed up the process.

## Active Dry Yeast

This is the most common form of yeast, and I always keep a few packets in my refrigerator as an emergency supply. Produced by a process that removes the moisture from the yeast, it is less subject to spoilage. Nevertheless, it is dated—or should be dated. Some dry yeast is available in natural foods stores, but generally the jars do not carry dates on them. The date is important, but it is not a foolproof way of telling you whether the yeast is still alive or whether it will work when you put it in the batter. To make sure that your yeast is going to work properly, you should *proof* it first.

## Proofing the Yeast

Probably the most common mistake that I've come across in discussing bread failures with friends or with people who've called for advice, is that the yeast had not been proofed before use. The first question I generally ask when someone comes to me with a flat-bread story is, "Did you proof the yeast?" and from the look on his or her face I might just as well have asked the question in Lithuanian.

When yeast becomes active, it gives off carbon dioxide bubbles which, in turn, create the gas that expands the gluten and makes the bread rise. It becomes active at somewhere near 80°F and it remains active until about 140°F. Thus, your "proofing" of the yeast merely tells you whether or not it's going to begin the process—whether it is going to work at all. It is a little easier to tell whether compressed cake yeast is going to work, even without proofing it, for the crumbly texture and the freshness of smell give you more of an indication of its vitality. With active dry yeast, however, the date is not really a useful indicator, for the yeast may have been stored in a hot shed without refrigeration on its way to the supermarket shelves. I proof both kinds of yeast, and it's really so simple that I wonder why anyone would skip this first, most important part of bread baking.

• Crumble the cake yeast or pour the dry yeast into a glass or cup.

• Add about one-fourth to one-half cup warm water. Though there are "rules" that tell you that compressed yeast should be proofed at between 80° to 95°F and dry yeast at a slightly higher temperature, 100° to 115°F, just run warm tap water over your wrist, much as you would for a baby's bottle. It works, it really does, and though water that is too hot will kill yeast and water that is too cold will not activate it, I assure you that water at approximately body temperature *will work*.

• Add a half teaspoon or less of honey to begin the process. Stir and set aside.

In about five minutes or so you will begin to see bubbles appear on top of the yeast mixture. In a few more minutes, the bubbles will rise still further. The yeast is then "proofed." You can use it in your dough.

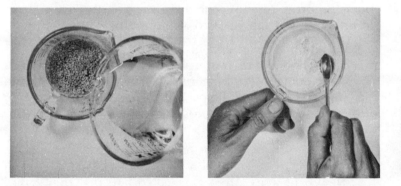 

Of course, you can also use warm potato water, milk, or reconstituted nonfat dry milk both as a proofing agent and in your bread as liquid. The important thing, and the one principle that I follow in proofing yeast, is that *I do not use a thermometer* to test the temperature of the proofing liquid. I can remember my teacher, George Meluso, walking nonchalantly to the tap on the sink to draw water for the proofing. I gasped, "You don't use a thermometer?" The look of anguish on his face as he sipped from his glass of wine was answer enough for me. I have never bought one. And, proofing without a thermometer has remained my one "rule" in this craft with "no rules!"

## How Much to Use

The recipes here and in other books will, of course, specify the amount of yeast to use in breads. With a few exceptions, dry yeast is used in this book, since it is available everywhere. However, you may at times want to convert from dry to compressed yeast or the other way around. Or, you may be buying your yeast in jars and, thus, have to measure the amounts with a tablespoon. There are simple conversions:

- *In a jar:* One tablespoon equals one packet of dry yeast.

- *Dry yeast to compressed:* The packet of dry yeast is about one-fourth ounce or one tablespoon. One packet equals about two-thirds ounce of compressed yeast.

In all measurements, as in everything in the baking of bread, there is no harm done if you are approximate in your conversions. If you use a bit too much compressed yeast, the dough will rise more quickly. If you use too little, the dough will rise more slowly. Most experienced bakers prefer to be on the "short" side of yeast measurements, in order to allow the dough to rise slowly, and to keep the taste of the yeast to a minimum.

People in Denver and in Mexico City (both about a mile high), find that their dough rises quickly in the rarified air. My mountain-climbing friends who bake also report the same phenomenon. I have simply recommended to all of them that they cut the amount of yeast in half, in order to slow the rise.

# Other Leaveners

New bakers are often amazed to find that they have a choice of leaveners. Yeast isn't everything! Here are several alternatives to yeast that can do the job of raising breads very well.

## Baking Powder

This is a leavener that is generally used in "quick breads" or batter breads, among the easiest and most satisfying in the bread baker's repertoire. You'll find that most recipes also call for baking powder in conjunction with buttermilk and baking soda. The dough requires no rising time, and the bread can be popped into the oven just as soon as it's mixed in the bowl and then shaped. The label "double acting" on baking powder means that the action begins when the dough is mixed and the second rise takes place in the oven.

Most brands of baking powder contain aluminum sulfate, but several commercial brands are manufactured without this chemical additive. Just read the label carefully when you buy the product. If you cannot find baking powder without the aluminum sulfate, you can make your own with a recipe developed in the Rodale Test Kitchen:

*Mix one-half teaspoon cream of tartar, one-fourth teaspoon sodium bicarbonate, and one-fourth teaspoon cornstarch or arrowroot. This will be the equivalent of one teaspoon of single-acting baking powder.*

## Baking Soda

Whenever a quick bread recipe calls for an acidic ingredient—buttermilk, sour milk, sour cream, yogurt, fruit juices, or molasses—you'll find that it also calls for baking soda. A tiny amount—generally no more than half a teaspoon—will create carbon dioxide in order to expand the dough and make it rise.

## Sourdough Starters

We bakers of bread, much like collectors of stamps, coins, and rare baseball cards, generally boast of our sourdough starters, and we also trade them from time to time. Shirley Sparr met me on a Fire Island walk one day and within ten seconds I knew that she had been nurturing a 102-year-old starter! Ed Feiner, one of the best and most original bakers that I know, once sent a pungent, sour, remarkably active sourdough starter to me by mail. It arrived at my office and was carried in at arm's length by one of my assistants. With the other hand she held her nose. I have no idea what the Postal Service thought of that piquant package as it made its way to me through sleet and hail and slush and snow. It is now the base for one of my best starters.

There is a very real and practical reason for the development of sourdough starters, aside from the exquisite and unusual taste that they give to breads. It was the only way that the Sourdoughs who traveled to Alaska during the gold rush could bake a leavened bread, since yeast could not survive the long overland trip. They kept their starter alive by keeping it in contact with their bodies at all times—taking it to bed with them, keeping it securely wrapped inside their shirts during the day—and then using it each day for their baking, and replenishing it by "feeding it."

Therein lies the secret—tender concern. The theory behind sourdough is the theory behind all leaveners. Yeast is a live organism which is found in the air, in the soil, and is even carried on the pelts of animals, and it must be fed to keep it growing and healthy. If we mix yeast with flour, water, and sweetener to make it start, it will stay alive so long as we use it and then feed it again after we take from it. Put simply, that is all there is to it—that, and the fact that it will turn sour after a few days and thus add a distinctive taste to the loaves. Sourdough starter is easy to make, though sometimes tricky to keep.

If sourdough starter is not used and fed, and if it is not kept in the refrigerator when unused for long periods of time, it will probably die. But maintaining the vitality of the starter is really fairly simple. For each cup used, replenish the starter with one-half cup flour and one-half cup water and it will remain active and bubbly. If you don't plan to bake bread within a few days, put the starter in a crock or glass jar and store it in the refrigerator, lightly covered, taking it out about a day before you plan to bake again.

If you have any doubt about the effectiveness of the starter, then you simply "sweeten the pot"—a term that has been picked up by poker players around the world. Pour out half the starter, add the same amount as you discarded, made up of one-half flour and one-half water and just a touch of honey, and let the crock stand at room temperature for 24 to 48 hours. Remember, always store your starter in a glass container or a crock—*never in metal!*

Some years ago, I reported making a loaf of sourdough bread for my friend, Len Silver, here at Fire Island. It had ten heels, since he loves the ends of breads. The interesting thing is that he has now become a baker of bread, and a very good one at that. He is also too modest, for he has refused my attempts to get him to join the bakers in this book. Nonetheless, he leaves sliced samples of his bread on my kitchen counter from time to time; and they are excellent.

One lovely summer beach-day in August, Len decided to try some sourdough bread for the first time. He followed the instructions for making the starter, with one exception. The recipe called for a one-quart jar for the starter, to allow it to bubble up and foam. Len hunted but could find nothing larger than a one-pint jar, and he made his starter in it. Then, the day being idyllic, the cool air coming in off the ocean, the temptation of the surf being too much for him, he went off to the beach, leaving his new starter to its own devices.

Late in the afternoon, he returned to the house to find that the starter had had a mind of its own. The day was warm, the jar too small, and the result was a growing, thriving liquid foaming over the top of the jar, down the sides of the counter, and onto the floor! As a result, Len resolved, "Well, that's the last time I begin a sourdough starter on a sunny summer's day!"

A lovely variation for sourdough starter utilizes plain yogurt or skim or low-fat milk along with flour. I began using yogurt starters about four years ago, after a trip to California, where the first recipe was given to me by a friend. They develop the same way as the regular starters, but they add their own distinctive, pungent flavor to the breads. (See Index.)

I have already mentioned the use of potato water, since it was one of the original leavening agents used in Europe. A combination of potatoes and hops was known as "farmer's yeast," and it was dried, crumbled into small bits, then reconstituted with water when the baker wanted to use it, just as we do with today's active dry yeast. Instead of tap water, you might try using potato water for your starter. I find that after a few days at room temperature, or even after a few days in the refrigerator, it takes on an incomparable sour aroma.

# Potato Starters

# 4 Utensils

Whether you live in a cramped urban apartment with a small alcove that passes for a kitchen, or in a large and airy country home with custom-designed counters and cabinets and commercial ovens, you already have the space, and probably all the equipment, you'll need to bake bread. Here is a checklist of basics to reassure you: a large mixing bowl, a wooden spoon, some type of bread pan, baking sheet, or flat metal tray (even a flowerpot, a baking dish, or an empty coffee can will do), some measuring cups and spoons for beginners, and wire racks.

Essentially, that is it. You really can turn out your first loaves with nothing more than what I've listed, plus—of course—the flour, liquid, and leavener. Let's look more carefully at some of the basic equipment, as well as other utensils that you might want to add to your collection as you progress in your baking prowess:

*Mixing Bowl.* It should be either ceramic or glass and rather large at the top—between 13 and 15 inches across. My first mixing bowl was the smaller size and I used to keep it atop the refrigerator. One day, I began to clean the bottom of the refrigerator, failing to remove the bowl before I moved the box. It was a Memorial Day to remember, for the bowl fell on my head and shattered. My scalp required three stitches. The bowl was not so easily repaired. I have now replaced it with an even larger bowl—15 inches across the top. If *it* should fall, it would no doubt kill me this time. However, the larger size is better for mixing several breads at one time. I do like to bake four or more breads simultaneously, since it saves on energy and I can store the extra ones in the freezer or give them as welcome gifts.

*Baking Pans.* There are two basic sizes of metal or glass baking pans:

- Standard (Large): 9 × 5 × 2 inches
- Medium: 8½ × 4½ × 2½ inches

There are also miniature baking pans for tiny, individual breads, as well as special pans for *brioches;* there are cast-iron pans (for crustier loaves), two- and five-section French loaf pans, and muffin tins. If you don't have the required pan around the house, one can sometimes be improvised— you can, for example, fashion long, thin holders out of folded heavy-duty aluminum foil and bake your *baguettes* that way. For free-form breads, just use ordinary baking sheets.

One bit of advice: If you are using glass pans instead of metal, lower the temperature of the oven about 25°, since glass retains more heat.

*Measuring Cups and Spoons.* For a short period of time, you will probably measure everything with the skill and care of a Nobel Prize-winning chemist. It is a good way to begin, and I have no quarrel with it. But I guarantee that, bit by bit, you will eliminate the use of spoons, cups, and other measuring devices as you throw yourself, with wild abandon, into baking your breads. Once you get the "feel" of the dough, the exact and time-consuming method of measuring each and every ingredient is sure to be replaced by imprecise and unmeasured amounts.

I have found, in developing two books about bread baking, that the most difficult task I face is to get my bread baker friends to *measure* the ingredients before they send the recipes on to me. Over and over again, I come across a recipe that reads, "Add *some* honey" or "Season to taste." In *Bread Winners,* I even included a "Table of Non-Measurements," explaining that "a pinch" or "a handful" or "a bit" were the measurements that grandmother used to use, and her recipes were passed down to us carrying just those words.

Just keep in mind that bread baking is flexible, and though your "handful" is not exactly the same as your neighbor's handful or that of your spouse, it will probably work just as well. The recipes in this book, of course, do give exact amounts for the benefit of the beginning baker, but I must tell you that they were wrung out of my friends on pain of taking away their chef's hats.

*Wire Racks.* Small wire racks or even the racks from your oven can be used to cool your loaves after they're baked. If the loaf is left in the pan or is put directly onto a counter, it continues to bake and will probably turn damp. Most breads are turned out onto racks immediately after baking, others after cooling in the pan for a few minutes. The recipes will tell you when to place the loaves on the rack.

# Useful, but Not Necessary

Though there are only a few basic needs for baking bread, listed above, you will no doubt be drawn to the baking department of every specialty shop, hardware store, and mail-order catalog, as your collection of equipment grows and the closets and cabinets and kitchen drawers begin to bulge with the exquisite tools of the baking trade. They are not necessary, but they are nice to collect. My oven will hold but 6 or 8 loaf pans, yet *18* can be found in a cabinet over the counter. I have not one but two of the marvelous black metal five-loaf French bread pans. If you have an insatiable desire for pans or for some of the items that follow, and you cannot find them in your local stores, a list of mail-order sources is provided at the back of the book.

*Cake Tester.* Most breads are tested by tapping the bottom of the loaf; a hollow sound indicates that it is done. However, some quick breads, as well as other breads that are "doubtful," can be tested by inserting a cake tester from the bottom of the loaf toward the top. If the tester comes out completely dry, the bread is done.

*Flat Metal Scraper.* I love this gadget, since it helps me scrape off the scraps of dough that stick to the counter and also makes cleaning up a joy. It is a simple, flat piece of metal with a wooden handle and it is one of the most useful of bread baking tools.

*Curved Plastic Scraper.* This is an excellent tool for scraping out the mixing bowl prior to kneading the dough on the counter. If you can't find this particular item in your specialty shop or hardware store, you can do almost the same thing with a firm rubber spatula.

*Large and Small Firmly Capped Glass Jars.* As your bread baking inventory increases—new types of flour, seeds, meal—you'll probably find that the most attractive and practical way to keep them all is to display them on a top shelf somewhere in your kitchen. Certainly, it is better than keeping them hidden in sundry boxes, bags, and containers all around the house or the pantry. Some whole grain flours should be kept refrigerated, and so should wheat germ, and you'll find that rubber-sealed apothecary jars are easier and neater to store than the original bags or boxes.

*Pastry Brush.* I use this tool to glaze the tops of some of my loaves both before baking and while they're in the oven. If you don't have a pastry brush, a soft paper towel will do.

*Small Plastic Plant Spray Bottle.* This little item is perfect for spraying the tops of your loaves with a thin film of water in order to create a crustier bread. Spray them right before placing the loaves into the oven, and then again about 15 minutes into the baking process to add crispness to the crust.

*A Brick and a Large Cake Pan.* Later on, in discussing the process of making and baking your breads, I will suggest that you use a hot brick in a pan of water to create steam, very much the way the old commercial bakers used to do it. I'll give instructions in a later chapter, but you might hunt around the house for a plain old red brick and put it with your baking tools.

*Electric Mixer with Dough Hook.* I love the sensuality of kneading bread by hand, but some people find the task difficult, or their strength gives out after a few minutes. The major problem with the mixers that are not designed for commercial loaves is that they just do not hold enough dough for more than one or two breads. However, I must admit that the *taste* of home-baked bread made in an electric mixer is just as good as the taste of my loaves, dutifully kneaded by hand.

*Food Processor.* This remarkable machine, the only mechanical invention to which I nod my head in homage, is also designed to knead dough with a special plastic blade. However, here too, you will find that the amount of dough that can be handled at one time is severely limited.

*Quarry Tiles.* Some of my bread baking friends attribute the fine quality of their breads to these unglazed, clay tiles. They're about five and one-half inches square and when they're lined up across your oven rack, they distribute the heat evenly, something to consider in ovens such as mine, where temperature varies from place to place. They also give crustiness to the breads that you bake on them. If the breads are placed directly on the quarry tiles, it's a good idea to dust them with a thin layer of cornmeal to keep the dough from sticking.

*Oven Thermometer.* Mine hangs near the door of the oven, so I only know the temperature at that particular spot. By the time I kneel to read it, and realize that I cannot see the dial without my glasses, the temperature has changed radically. However, it's good enough for an approximate idea as to whether the oven is too hot or too cool.

You will, of course, want asbestos gloves, or some equivalent, to handle the hot pans, trays, and loaves, and you will certainly discover other baking gadgets on your own. But, always keep in mind that the basic craft of baking bread requires very few tools.

# Some Non- 5 Rules to Know before Baking

I believe that reassurance is the most important thing you can give to a new baker. Nothing is really crucial in bread baking. It is helpful to know what *not* to worry about.

• Remember that all recipe amounts are *approximate* and should be used only as a preliminary guide. Flour measurements and liquids will vary depending upon altitude, weather, type of flour, and leavener. If you live in a damp climate, the amount of flour required to make a given recipe will increase by as much as a cup or more over what is written. Learn to get the "feel" of the dough, rather than being a slave to the mathematics of the recipe.

• Some bakers like to put the flour in first and then pour in the liquid bit by bit. Others prefer to put the liquid in the bowl and then add the flour. It makes very little difference, if any. There are times that I take a full container of buttermilk and pour it in, followed by whatever flour it takes to make a batter. At other times, I reverse the procedure. Both batches come out exactly alike.

• Experiment. Don't be afraid. If there's a particular ingredient that you'd like to try—nuts or berries, for example—just add them by the handful, even if the recipe does not call for them. (But be sure to dip them in flour before adding, so they won't sink to the bottom.) Solids will not affect the batter. However, if you decide to add a liquid or a highly liquid item— fruit juice, zucchini, or juicy tomatoes—make certain you reduce the amount of liquid called for in the recipe.

• The same goes for recipe ingredients that you'd like to eliminate. (Some people, I find, do not like caraway seeds.) Merely leave them out of your bread; only the taste will change, and maybe you'll discover a whole new loaf you love.

• Almost any logical utensil in the kitchen cabinet will do for baking bread, so don't think you have to run out to the corner hardware store in search of a particular pan or shape. Certainly, there are some breads, such as *brioche,* that do require a special pan if the bread is to have the traditional shape, but these are rare occurrences. You can bake on baking sheets and make your own free-form or braided breads, you can use flowerpots, or you can even use regular bread pans!

• Ovens are notorious for having temperatures that vary from minute to minute, or place to place within them. Don't let such variations bother you. Twenty-five degrees more or less will make very little difference in the final result. If the temperature is too low, the bread will simply take a bit longer to finish. The most important thing to know is when "done" is done. In most cases, a loaf can be tested by taking it into the palm of your hand while wearing an asbestos glove, turning it over, and tapping it on the bottom. If the bread sounds hollow, it is finished.

In *Bread Winners,* I mentioned what I called the "fear of trying"—that tentative, awesome concern about the chance of failure that beginners still associate with the simple and ancient process of baking bread. It is easy, believe me. Every new loaf that comes out of the oven is a joy and a revelation to those of us who share the craft, no matter whether we are new to it or have baked for many years. We leave slices or whole loaves of a new bread at each other's doorstep. (Recently, I stopped by the house of Gerry Franklin and was presented with a lovely slice of his freshly baked Blueberry/Orange/Nut Bread.) We send bread through the mails. We exchange recipes. Some of us even win prizes at our state and county fairs.

It is time, then, for you to join us.

# Baking a 6
# Quick Bread

Imagine an occasion that calls for a quick, tasty, beautiful home-baked bread that can serve as the table centerpiece, one that looks just like a bread your grandmother was supposed to have baked (but probably didn't)—

- If you are a beginner who has never baked before and you have the "fear of trying" . . .

- If you are a veteran baker but just don't have the time to bake your regular yeast loaves . . .

- If dinner company is coming on short notice (or even long notice) . . .

I strongly suggest that you try a quick bread.

You need very few ingredients to make a quick bread—flour, buttermilk or another sour liquid, baking powder, and baking soda. The bread requires no yeast and no kneading—nor does the loaf have to rise before being placed in the oven. And it's finished in less than an hour!

I generally make a quick bread in a free-form shape, sometimes as a large loaf that resembles the crusty middle-European whole grain breads still sold in some small bakeries in France, Belgium, and Germany. Or, the bread can be baked in a regular pan if you prefer. Either way, with a bold slash across the top to allow it to rise in the heat of the oven, the loaf comes out puffed and fragrant and very professional looking!

Later on in this book, I have written of several occasions where I needed to bake bread quickly, efficiently, and with a show of great dexterity. Once, while publicizing *Bread Winners* for the book trade, I baked bread at the American Booksellers Association convention in Los Angeles (page 205). Then, on the book tour that told the world that another bread book had been written (*another bread book!*), I needed a bread that would always work on live television (page 186). And finally, working in northern New York State on a film project, I baked bread for an entire restaurant, replacing the commercial loaves on every table in the place, and did it within two hours (page 150)! In all three cases, I baked the same bread—a quick bread—for in all three cases I simply could not afford to fail!

On another occasion, a quick bread may have helped me to make another convert to bread baking. I was speaking about the joy and the ease of baking bread at a department store demonstration in Portland, when a woman in the audience, showing her disbelief, interrupted me. She said it was no wonder I could speak that way, I was a professional (bringing a small glow to my ego). To prove that anyone could do it, I asked her eight-year-old daughter to come up to the demonstration counter and had the child make the bread. The outcome was successful—and her mother bought the book!

So, here is a bread that is delicious, beautiful, and reliable. It is as close as you will get to a foolproof recipe. Though its real name is "Irish Brown Bread," I call it "Old Faithful."

# Irish Brown Bread ("Old Faithful")

(2 loaves)

In a large bowl, combine the flour, salt, baking soda, and baking powder. Add the raisins and stir to coat them thoroughly. This will prevent them from sinking to the bottom of the batter. Add the caraway seeds and stir. Add the honey and then gradually pour in the buttermilk, mixing with a wooden spoon as you do so. The dough should be sticky but easy to handle. If it feels too sticky, just add more flour. Once again, the measurements should be used according to "feel." In my damp area, I find I use the larger amount of flour. Don't be afraid to add more. Using floured hands, mix the dough thoroughly in the bowl in order to blend the ingredients more completely. I sometimes like to turn the dough out onto a floured board in order to get a smoother texture. Note that this is *not* kneading. You are merely blending more thoroughly. When the dough has a smooth texture, and it is still damp, it is ready for shaping and baking.

Divide the dough into 2 parts and form any shape that suits you—round, oval, square, or oblong. Place the loaves on a buttered and floured baking sheet. Take a sharp knife and dip it into the flour and then cut a *deep* cross into each loaf. Don't be afraid to cut deeply, for this will allow the bread to expand evenly in the oven instead of bursting at the seams as it rises; and it will also give your loaf that professional-looking texture where it has expanded. Dust each loaf lightly with flour and blow off the excess. Bake in a preheated 425°F over for 40 to 50 minutes, or until loaves test done. The crust will turn a dark, crunchy brown and you will get a hollow sound when the bottoms are tapped with a gloved hand.

7 to 8 cups stone-ground whole wheat flour
1 teaspoon salt (optional, see page 22)
½ teaspoon baking soda
2 tablespoons baking powder
½ cup golden raisins
½ cup caraway seeds
1 tablespoon honey
4 cups buttermilk, room temperature

# 7 Baking a Yeast Bread

There is, of course, a basic difference in the baking of a yeast bread as compared to a "quick" bread that can be whipped up and served in very little time. A yeast loaf is done in stages, and you really can't "whip one up" in an hour from start to finish. But, the very fact that it is *not* done all at one time can be a distinct advantage.

First of all, while the dough is rising, other things can be accomplished around the house. But, more important perhaps, is the fact that making yeast breads gives the baker a continuing series of delightful revelations; no matter how long you've been at it, it will always amaze you that dough that is put aside to rise *does rise*. My friends and I, none of us professional bakers, are continually in awe that what we have created is actually *alive,* expanding, puffing itself up to become a real, honest-to-goodness homemade bread. Not long ago, while testing her new recipes for this book, Sheryl walked past the large bowl in which the dough was rising. About an hour had passed since she had put a shapeless, satiny mass into the bowl, but now the covering towel had formed a large, round, expanding bump. "My God!" she exclaimed, "My towel is pregnant!" It was not too long afterward that the oven gave birth to a set of healthy twin loaves, so her comment had some truth in it.

## Laying Out the Ingredients

In baking bread, every ingredient should be at room temperature (except, of course, the warm water with which you proof your yeast). If the yeast has been in the refrigerator, take it out and let it warm up before you proof it. The same procedure should be followed for your liquids (milk, for example), and everything else that is called for in the recipe. I generally put an apron on first, since flour manages to coat my clothing each time I measure out a cupful.

A tip given to me by Bernice Beenhower, who appeared in my first book, led to one other thing that I do before beginning the baking process. We all know that the one time the telephone is bound to ring is when we are up to our elbows in sticky dough during the first tacky stages of mixing or kneading. I put a plastic bag nearby—and I would suggest that you do the same. When the phone rings (not *if* it rings), just put your hand inside the bag and pick up the phone!

# Mixing

All recipes in this book give you the order in which ingredients are added, so there should be no problems about whether the flour comes before the water or the dry ingredients precede the wet. Simply add them one by one and stir them well with a wooden spoon, blending them as much as you can before kneading.

- Remember to proof the yeast first, so that it is active and ready when you add it to the recipe (see page 26).

- If the batter feels too wet, don't be afraid to add a bit more flour. The humidity in your area, the temperature, and the type of flour will all play a role in determining how much flour above or below the recipe amount should be added.

- Whole grain bread dough, by its nature, is a bit stickier than dough made with white flour. You'll find that rye and triticale, for example, are naturally sticky grains.

- Put aside some flour in a small cup, so that you can add it to the dough while you knead or reflour your hands to keep the dough from sticking.

Remember, that it's the *feel* of the dough that counts rather than the amounts listed in the recipes. At first the texture of the dough will be fairly rough. When all the ingredients are blended it will probably be fairly soft and biscuitlike. As you mix with the wooden spoon, you'll see crumbs of dough or extra flour lying at the bottom of the bowl. Pay no attention, for when you turn out the dough for kneading, you will blend these "leftovers" with the rest of the dough.

- A reminder again. If you are adding raisins or nuts, roll them in flour first so that they won't sink to the bottom of the batter.

- Do not sift whole grain flours. You'll be removing the very ingredients that make them so nutritious, such as the bran.

# Kneading

Flour a surface on which you can apply some leverage, for you will be pushing with your arms and shoulders. Another tip straight out of *Bread Winners* (Corinne Wastun) might be of help to bakers of shorter stature or those who just do not have strength in their shoulder muscles. Sheryl uses it with great success, and it's a perfect solution to the fact that the house builders who make our kitchen counters are generally six feet, seven inches tall and can reach anything unaided. Just put a large, floured bread board down on the kitchen floor and knead the dough on your knees, Indian-fashion.

Kneading is, perhaps, my favorite part of baking bread—with the exception of *tasting* the fresh loaves. I love the feel of the dough, I love the fact that I can change this sticky, lumpy mass into a glistening, vibrating shape. I have called the process "sensual" and I am not alone. Bread baker friends have compared the feeling of the finished dough to the textural quality of *a baby's bottom!* (Others, with less inhibited imaginations, have suggested still more exotic comparisons!)

Kneading is, indeed, the most physical part of baking. In addition to the pleasurable qualities that are inherent in kneading, it has also been recommended as a superb way of getting rid of stress caused by contemporary problems. When everything seems to turn out wrong and the day seems to be going down the drain, when our twentieth-century computerized society has made a mess of our bank accounts, charge accounts, and credit card records, the act of kneading bread can be a remarkably therapeutic way of working off our aggression and our anger. One of my favorite writers about nutrition and health, Jane E. Brody, commented about just this phenomenon in an article for the *New York Times* (February 10, 1982). She wrote that her grandmother (who lived to be 95), when upset by some turn of events, "used to scrub clothes on the washboard" and worked off her bad feelings by "scrubbing floors, thrashing rugs, sawing wood, scything weeds, *kneading bread*. . . ." Her point, well-taken, is that our contemporary society provides few if any physical outlets of that kind, so "we lash out at others or we turn on ourselves."

And so, whether your reasons for kneading are sensual or aggressive, you can begin by dusting the counter or board with a light coating of flour. This will keep the dough from sticking. As you knead, don't be afraid to add more flour to the surface if the dough begins to stick. Most recipes tell you to knead the dough for 8 to 10 minutes, but those of you who are stronger and more rapid in your kneading technique will probably find that you can cut down the time by a couple of minutes.

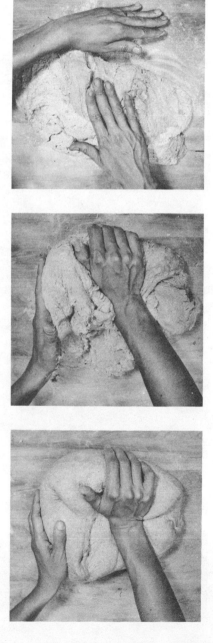

Dip your hands in flour and turn the dough out onto the surface. As you knead the dough, you will be blending the gas bubbles of the yeast into it, and this fermentation will react with the gluten to create the rise later on. First, gather all the crumbs and add them to the dough. The initial few movements will be nothing more than pushing and pulling it all into one large lump. After you have it all together, you can begin to knead, and the more rhythmic you can make the process, the easier it will be.

Using your right hand, take the rear of the dough and pull it toward you, pushing it down into the middle. Push it as hard as you can—you can't hurt the dough. Then, using your left hand, turn the dough about half a turn in a clockwise direction. (Left-handed bakers can merely reverse the process.) Just continue the kneading, developing your own speed and your own rhythm:

- Right hand pulls the dough from the back and presses it down into the middle.

- Left hand turns the dough clockwise.

- In a few minutes, you may find that the dough becomes sticky again, particularly if you are using rye flour. Just add some more flour to your hands and to the dough itself.

The marvelous part about kneading is that as you do it the dough actually changes texture right before your eyes and under your working fingertips. The transformation is miraculous. On one TV show I demonstrated the kneading technique and just as I poured the unkneaded batter onto a counter the host said, "My, doesn't that look ugly!" He later agreed with me that we had created Cinderella from the Ugly Duckling. As you knead, then, the dough will change and take on a smoother appearance. Suddenly, too, it will push back at you, the elasticity beginning to make itself felt, the look of it shinier and more satiny. You will *know* when it's ready. Those of us who are crazy about bread baking will swear that the dough lies there smiling back at us!

## Kneading with a Food Processor or Electric Mixer

This is a perfectly acceptable way of kneading. If you don't have the strength to mix by hand, I suggest that you use an electric mixer with the dough hook attachment or the plastic blade of the food processor. Just remember that you will probably not be able to mix the amount of dough needed for more than one bread at a time, unless your machine is a professional model. On the other hand, the job is done quickly and efficiently. These new machines have been recommended by food editors across the country, but my own feeling is that a great part of the joy and gratification of home baking is lost when they are used; if there is no *physical* reason for using the mixer or processor, I suggest that you knead by hand your first time. After all, if you're kneading for sensual reasons, you'll like the feel of the dough under your hands. If you're doing it to release your aggressions, kneading by hand offers an excellent outlet.*

## The First Rise

While the kneaded dough is resting, wash out your bread bowl and dry it thoroughly, then cover it with a light coating of oil. Put the dough into the bowl and turn it over a few times to coat all sides with the oil. This will keep it from drying out as it rises. Then place the bowl in a warm spot in your kitchen and cover it lightly with a towel.

Bread writers seem to make a federal case out of where to place the bowl of dough for the best rise. I have always used the same corner of my kitchen, winter or summer, although I am not really certain if it is the recommended 85° (doubtful, except in August) or cooler. Some writers recommend that you use a gas oven with only the pilot light working. There are bakers who go so far as to put a small amount of warm water into their bathtubs, placing the bowl on a rack over it. Others swear that you cannot use the outdoor sun, while a friend of mine places her bowl in a field right on the same rock that her grandmother used fifty years ago! If one place is cooler than the next, it will take a bit longer for the dough to rise. Just make certain that the spot is fairly warm and that it is draft-free; then leave the dough alone.

It will generally take 45 to 60 minutes for the dough to rise to about double its bulk (less time if you've omitted salt). However, even here, I suggest that you do not go by the clock. Judge the rising dough by *appearance*—has it almost doubled in size? Stone-ground grains will take longer to rise, or cooler temperature may delay the process. I have had bread dough take almost two and a half hours to double because I have cut down on the amount of yeast while using low-gluten flours for a whole grain bread.

To test the risen dough, just press two fingers into it. If the indentations remain, then you are ready for the next step. If the dough fills out after you have pushed down on it, let it rise a bit longer.

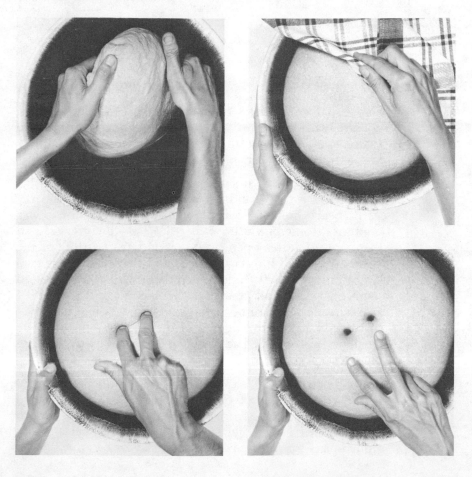

*Baking a Yeast Bread*

# Pounding Down: After the Rise

Turn the dough out onto a lightly floured surface, and let it lie there for a moment while you admire it. Then punch it down a few times with your hand. This is the time that I lift the dough and slam it down on the counter a few times to distribute the gluten even more completely. Don't be afraid to be rough with the dough. And notice, too, that it seems to be much more elastic than it was before it was put aside to rise. Knead the dough three or four times. Slam it down again just for good measure, and proceed to your next step.

# The Shape of Your Bread

If the recipe does not call for one more rise in the bowl before shaping, as some finer-textured breads require, then you are ready to choose the shape of your bread. And here again, a new world of imagination, sculpture, and whimsy awaits the adventurer.

This past year, my friend Tom Ervin celebrated his seventieth birthday, and we were invited to a small party at his beach house. I could not bring flowers, for it was winter. I don't know how to bake a birthday cake, and there are no stores open on our island at that time of the year. So I baked him two breads and shaped them as two large numbers—"70." I decorated them with candles, placed them on a tray, and presented them as my gift to Tom. I also had the pleasure of tasting the bread as it was served that evening, and by the end of the celebration, only one small piece of the "7" had not been devoured by the hungry guests!

The choices of bread shapes are legion, as reflected in the wide variety of pans available to bakers: standard bread pans that range from very small to very large, French loaf pans for long *baguettes* or sourdoughs, specially designed pans for muffins or *brioches,* clay or ceramic bowls, flowerpots, coffee cans, or just plain baking sheets for free-form ideas. Breads can be made in loaves or they can be braided. Bagels (the "roll with a hole") have their own special shape. If you want a huge peasant-type middle-European bread, use the entire batter to make one exquisite, round bread. Or, divide the dough into two or three parts and shape one as a round bread, another as an oval, and a third as a braid and bake them all on the same sheet.

You can make a "jelly-roll" shape by rolling out the dough with a rolling pin or just patting it out flat with your hands and covering the surface with herbs or nuts or any other filling you can think of. Then roll up the dough and put it on a baking sheet to bake. When you cut it, the "jelly-roll" effect will be quite evident and your guests will love it.

Another lovely bread can be made in the same jelly-roll fashion, but instead of placing filling on the dough, just add another layer of a *different* dough. By using a bottom layer of a lightly colored dough and covering it with a layer of pumpernickel, for example, then rolling it up and baking it, you will have made a two-toned bread that shows its spiral colors when you slice it.

If you want to shape long loaves and you don't have a French loaf pan, simply form heavy-duty aluminum foil into the long shape that you want and bake your breads in that, just as you would with the professional pan.

And, of course, there are always shapes like the ones I baked for Tom's birthday party! Whichever shape you've chosen, just flour your hands and divide the dough into the number of loaves that you plan to bake. If you're using the standard loaf pan, the dough should fill about two-thirds of the pan. Keep in mind that the breads will rise again before baking and yet again in the oven when they are exposed to the heat.

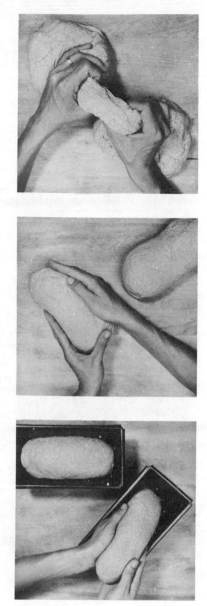

# The Rise before Baking

Put your pans or baking sheets in a warm spot in the kitchen and cover them lightly with a towel. This second rise is one area where beginners sometimes make their first mistake. *Don't let the rise go too far!* At this point, panic may set in among beginning bakers. What does he mean by "too far"? Is it much further than "not enough"?

Keep in mind that the loaves must have sufficient elasticity to rise just a bit further when they're put in the oven. If you've let them go too far in the second rise, there is a chance that the heat of the oven will make them burst at the seams. So, in judging the amount of your second rise, *too little* is better than *too much*. Let them rise to about double their bulk in the pan—and, this time, *don't* punch your fingers into the dough to see if it's gone far enough!

This is the point where the baker can begin to see what the finished bread is going to look like.

# Preheating the Oven

While the bread is rising for the second time, the oven should be turned on and the temperature adjusted. This is also the time that you might want to use the technique of creating steam in your oven to get a crustier bread.

I have an old red brick, taken from a construction site about ten years ago. While I'm preparing the dough for baking, I put the brick atop the stove on one of the burners and keep the flame at medium. This heats it thoroughly. (Remember to use asbestos gloves during this whole procedure.)

I then boil a pot of water on the stove, and when I'm ready to bake, I pour the water into a long pan. Then I place the hot brick in the water and put the pan on the bottom of the oven. The steamy atmosphere that is created is a replica of conditions in a professional baker's oven, and it's quite simple to do.

This particular baker's trick has been the cause of a great deal of frustration for me. I received a letter some time ago—passed on to me by Rodale Press—from a professional baker who signed himself: "Paul Voiland, Elm Street Bakery (one of the last bakeries in New York State that bakes in a real brick oven)." Although generally complimentary about the book, his letter mentioned several instances where he thought that information was misleading and I wanted to acknowledge the letter immediately. However, *there was no return address on the letter* and the envelope had not been forwarded to me! To this day, I do not know *where* in New York State to find the Elm Street Bakery, and I am acknowledging Paul Voiland's efforts by printing a part of his correction here:

> *We professional bakers steam our breads to give them a fabulous hard, shiny crust, not to keep them moist. The steam is only necessary for the first 25 percent of the baking, after which the bread's crust is formed and should be baked dry to yield the firm crustiness that is absent in most commercial breads.*

I now remove my pan and brick about 20 minutes into the baking period. And I do thank Paul Voiland and the Elm Street Bakery (wherever you are!).

When the energy crisis struck, some food writers began to recommend that we start our breads in a *cold* oven, letting the heat work up to the correct temperature gradually. It was supposed to save energy, but the recipes called for *longer* baking time because of the cold starting temperature. Logic tells me that breads that bake longer by starting with a cold oven, will use just as much energy as breads that are put into a preheated one. I still prefer to preheat my oven, though the other method will work for most breads. Some, however, require a preheated oven. Pita breads, for example, must be placed in a very hot oven in order to make them puff up.

# Decorating the Bread

Before you place the breads in the oven, you can proceed to make them even more beautiful than they look at that point. This is the time for the seeds, the glazes, the slashing of the dough. Even if the recipe doesn't call for a particular seed, you might want to add some for your own taste: caraway or poppy or sesame, for example.

One of the questions that bread bakers frequently have is how to keep the seeds from falling off during baking. I lightly spray the tops of the loaves with water (using a regular hand plant sprayer), then I sprinkle the seeds across the tops of the breads, and finally I run my finger lightly over the seeds to set them more completely into the dough. Although loose seeds will always appear after the baking, this method keeps most of them where you want them.

Some recipes call for the slashing of the loaves with a razor blade (such as sourdough loaves) or with a sharp knife (such as most quick breads baked in free-form shapes). Old superstition said that a cross should be slashed in the tops of breads in order to let Satan escape. But the more practical reason for slashing is to encourage the breads to expand where *you* want them to, instead of bursting at the seams where *they* want to. However, beginning bakers (including the author when he first started) are in awe of a recipe that says, "Slash the loaves deeply." Certainly, they will fall! Yet, they do not. The slashing will make your breads look even more perfect (and let Satan escape).

# . . .Into the Oven

This is the time for the unexpected visitor to call, for this is the time that the *aroma* of baking bread fills the house.

- Make certain that the temperature of the oven is at the proper setting. Remember that temperatures will vary, even within the same oven, but don't let it worry you. A small variation will make no difference, and you can always move the breads around in the oven when they begin to firm up. If one loaf looks like it's getting darker than the others, move it to a cooler part of the oven and replace it with a loaf that does not seem to be baking as quickly.

- If you want crusty breads, put the pan of water on the floor of the oven and set the hot brick in it. Use gloves. And, don't put the brick in before the water— it will burn the pan. The steaming will begin.

- Place the loaves in the oven so that there is enough room for the air to circulate freely around them.

- Close the door.

- Relax.

- Enjoy the aroma of baking bread.

# Testing the Loaves

Most breads can be tested by simply picking them up with a gloved hand, turning them over, and tapping the bottoms. Generally, the bottom of a bread will have a hard, firm crust that when tapped will produce a "hollow" sound. If the amount of baking time is approximately correct, the bread *looks done,* and you get the hollow sound when you tap it, it is, indeed, done.

- If the bread is in a pan instead of being free-form, just invert the pan, drop the loaf into your gloved hand, and test as described above.

- If you're still in doubt, use a cake tester, pushing it from the bottom of the bread toward the top. If it comes out dry, the bread is finished.

- If the bread still seems soggy, put it back into the oven and check it in another five to ten minutes.

- If the bread seems done on top, brown and lovely and just as a bread should be, but the bottom is still soggy, cover the top with aluminum foil and put the bread back into the oven for further baking.

When the bread is finished, turn it out of the pan and put it on a wire rack. The rack will keep the bottom from getting too damp and soggy as it cools. Now is the time to pace back and forth awaiting the first taste, or to summon family, neighbors, and friends to take a look at your handiwork.

# The Taste of Warm Bread

Back in the fifteenth century, an anonymous writer (probably related to my mother) wisely counseled: "Hote bread is unholesome for any man for it doth lye in the stomache like a sponge . . . yet the smell of newe breade is comfortable to the heade and herte."

The reason bread should be left to cool slightly is not just that our predecessors recommended it, but also that it firms up and can be cut easily. There is no taste in the world like that of warm, freshly baked bread, and all of us who bake cannot wait for that first slice, covered with butter, eaten with our eyes closed in ecstasy. That is quickly followed by a second slice, followed by still another for a neighbor or a family member, followed by yet another for the baker who created the heavenly loaf. It is no wonder that, where once we had four lovely loaves cooling, barely three and a half remain!

# Freezing Your Breads

I feel that starting the oven for one or two breads is a waste of energy, so I either double recipes or make two breads that need the same temperature for baking. Thus, I have a bounty of loaves when I'm finished. Since we can only eat one loaf at a time, the others must be kept.

Because home-baked breads have no preservatives, freezing is the best way to maintain their flavor, texture, and nutritional value if they won't be eaten in a day or two. Just let any extra loaves cool to room temperature and wrap each one in heavy-duty aluminum foil. Label the loaves and put them in your freezer. If they're properly wrapped, with no air inside the foil, they should keep well for three to four months.

When you want to use a loaf that's been frozen, remove it from the freezer and let it come to room temperature. I strongly suggest that you do not take the frozen bread and pop it into the oven to thaw. The moisture will probably make the loaf soggy and tasteless.

When you are ready to serve the bread, *open the foil wrapper* and put the loaf into an oven that has been preheated to about 250° to 300°F. Let it warm for about ten minutes before you remove it, slice it, and serve it. The beauty of using foil is that it can go right into the oven with the bread and then be used as a wrapper to keep the loaf warm when it comes out ready to slice and serve.

# And So. . .

When *Bread Winners* was published, nothing gave me greater joy than to read that some food editors had called it a "family album" of bread bakers. Since that time, the "family" has expanded somewhat, as you shall see in these next pages.

The rest of the book, with the exception of some other stories that I simply must recount, and the addition of some of my own new recipes, belongs to them. The tips about baking, their approach to this marvelous pastime, and the recipes reflect *their* personalities and *their* experiences.

Though their professions vary, and their locations span the country from coast to coast, their common interest is what brings us together—the same one that brought 45 other people together in the volume that preceded this one: Bread. It is, I hope, the interest that also brings the new reader to this book, and my old acquaintances back to meet these new members of the family.

# Part II MEET THE BAKERS AND ENJOY THEIR BREADS

# Tina Gonzalez

*The Breads:*

**Amaranth Whole
Wheat Bread
Mincemeat Milo Loaves
Double Millet
Skillet Bread**

Though Tina is, first of all, an integral part of our small film production company, Symbiosis, Inc., working as a producer and production manager on our documentaries, she is also a superb cook and baker. During the writing of our book, *Sheryl and Mel London's Creative Cooking with Grains and Pasta,* she provided her own input by devising original amaranth recipes.

When this book was being developed, I asked Tina to work on some breads that would include three underutilized, tasty, nutritious grain forms—amaranth, sorghum (milo), and millet. In a sense, these grains are very much where triticale was when I wrote *Bread Winners,* and yet they are easy to work with, very high in nutrition, and just marvelous in flavor.

Tina brought her packages of grains and flours out to the Fire Island house, where she dug in for a spell of creative bread baking. And each week, when we'd arrive on the ferry, a new bread was waiting for us. I think you'll like them—and I think you'll find them delicious and unusual enough to elicit compliments and inquiries from your guests. If you can't find the ingredients in your local stores, I've included a list of sources in the back of the book; and the grains can be ordered through the mail.

Although the Mexican alegria candies are made from popped amaranth and honey, amaranth is a grain that has been lost to us since the Aztecs used it for their sacrificial ceremonies. In fact, it is a grain that dates back almost eight thousand years to the Tehuacan cave dwellers. It is ironic, therefore, that amaranth has been rediscovered only recently and is now being called "the grain of the future."

Amaranth has a slightly peppery taste. As a flour, it works best in conjunction with other gluten flours, since its own gluten content is very low. Though it can be purchased by mail order (see Mail-Order Sources), many families around the country grow their own amaranth plants, since it does well in almost any type of soil, even where water is a problem.

This bread is rich and very dark, with the unusual spicy flavor of the amaranth. You might also note the very short kneading time, because, Tina explains, "I hate kneading!"

In a small bowl, dissolve yeast in warm water. Add 1 tablespoon honey and blend.

In a small saucepan, heat the remaining honey, milk, molasses, and oil. Remove from heat and add beaten eggs.

In a large bowl, combine the flours. Add the liquid ingredients and yeast mixture. Blend well until mixture forms a smooth dough. Turn out onto a floured surface and knead briefly, 2 to 3 minutes. If dough is too sticky, add more whole wheat flour. Place dough into an oiled bowl and cover. Let rise in a warm spot until doubled in bulk, 1 to 1½ hours.

Punch down, knead again for 2 to 3 minutes, divide dough in half, and place each loaf into a buttered and floured 8½ × 4½-inch loaf pan. Cover and let rise in a warm spot until doubled in bulk, 45 to 60 minutes.

Bake in a preheated 375°F oven for 35 to 40 minutes, or until the loaves test done.

Cool on a wire rack.

# Amaranth Whole Wheat Bread

(2 medium-size loaves)

2 tablespoons dry yeast
½ cup warm water
3 tablespoons honey
1 cup milk
1 tablespoon molasses
⅓ cup safflower oil
2 eggs, beaten
2 cups amaranth flour
2 cups whole wheat flour
1½ cups gluten flour

# Mincemeat Milo Loaves

(2 medium-size or 8 small loaves)

2½ cups buttermilk
2 cups milo flour
1 cup whole wheat flour
1 cup gluten flour
1 teaspoon baking soda
3 teaspoons baking powder
1½ tablespoons grated
orange rind
2 eggs, beaten
1 cup chopped walnuts
1½ cups Vegetarian
Mincemeat (see recipe
below)

Milo is another grain that is well known all over the world, but is very little utilized in the United States and Canada. Over 300 million people in Africa, East Asia, India, Japan, and China use it as a valuable part of their daily diet, yet almost all of our sorghum goes to feed our cattle! It is, without doubt, one of the best-tasting grains that we've discovered, and the flour is available through mail order (see Mail-Order Sources). Try it. It's unusual, it's tasty. This quick bread makes a delicious breakfast dish, served warm.

In a large saucepan, heat 2 cups buttermilk, stirring in milo flour until the mixture is thick and stiff. Spoon mixture into a large bowl. Then add the whole wheat and gluten flours, baking soda, baking powder, and orange rind, and combine. Stir in beaten eggs and the remaining buttermilk. Add walnuts and mincemeat and mix well.

To make 2 medium-size loaves, spoon batter into buttered 8½ × 4½-inch loaf pans and bake in a preheated 375°F oven for 50 minutes. To make 8 small loaves, spoon batter into buttered 4 × 2-inch pans and bake in a preheated 375°F oven for 30 minutes.

Cool on wire racks. Serve warm.

# Vegetarian Mincemeat

(about 2 cups)

¼ cup raisins
¼ cup currants
¼ pound dried apples,
coarsely chopped
½ teaspoon ground
cinnamon
⅛ teaspoon ground cloves
½ teaspoon grated peeled
ginger root
1 tablespoon grated lemon
rind
1½ cups apple cider
½ cup coarsely chopped
walnuts
2 tablespoons butter,
softened (optional)

Mix together all ingredients except nuts and softened butter, if used, in a medium-size nonstick saucepan. Bring to a boil and then simmer, uncovered, stirring occasionally, for 45 to 60 minutes, or until liquid is absorbed and mixture is very thick. Stir in nuts and softened butter, if used, and cool.

Millet is the third of the underutilized grains that we worked with during the testing of our book on grains and pasta. Considering that Americans only feed millet to their birds, we could not understand why this grain goes unloved and unused. It is probably my favorite-tasting grain, and among the most nutritious of the grain family. It's easy to digest, rich in amino acids, phosphorus, and B vitamins, with an iron content that is higher than any grain except amaranth. Yet it remains a "stepchild" in our food chain. This bread, developed by Tina, is very much like corn bread in texture, with the unusual and surprisingly good taste of the millet flour.

To prepare the millet: In a large heavy skillet, heat 1 teaspoon melted butter or oil over medium heat. Add millet and toast, stirring and shaking the pan, until the grains are light and tan and you begin to smell a nutty aroma.

In a medium-size nonstick saucepan, bring water to a boil. Add the remaining butter or oil and the grains; stir, cover pan, and simmer over very low heat for 25 to 30 minutes, or until all the water is absorbed. Slip a double sheet of paper toweling between the pot and the lid. Cover pot again and let stand to absorb moisture for 10 minutes. Remove cover and discard towels. Fluff with fork. There should be 4 cups.

To prepare the bread: Melt butter in a small saucepan. Stir in honey and cool. Then turn into a small bowl and mix in milk and beaten eggs.

In a large bowl, combine flours and baking powder. Add the liquid ingredients to the dry ingredients. Then add cooked millet and blend. Pour batter into a buttered 12-inch cast-iron skillet and bake in a preheated 375°F oven for 20 to 30 minutes, or until a tester comes out clean.

Serve warm, cut into wedges.

Note: Cooked millet can be stored in a covered container in the refrigerator for 7 to 10 days, or in the freezer for 3 to 4 months.

# Double Millet Skillet Bread

(8 servings)

*Millet:*
 2 teaspoons butter, melted, or safflower oil
 1 cup millet
 2 cups water

*Bread:*
¼ cup butter
 1 tablespoon honey
 1 cup milk
 2 eggs, beaten
 1 cup whole wheat flour
 1 cup millet flour
 1 tablespoon baking powder

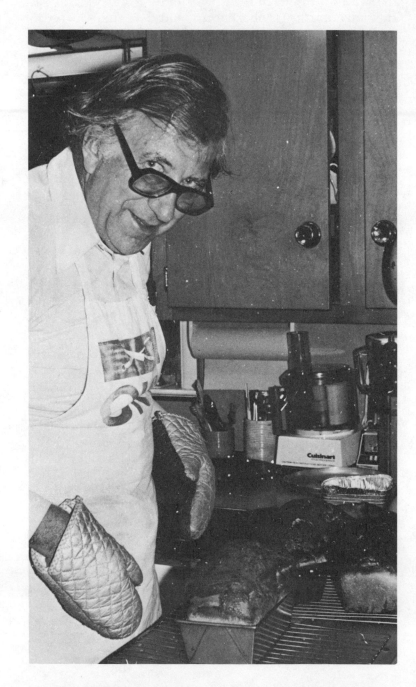

*Bread Winners Too*

# Albert Shanker

*Some years ago, I had to go to an important meeting at the White House, and I went there straight from the plane, carrying loaves of freshly baked bread that I had made for my Washington staff. The White House guards must have thought it was a little strange, but they let me in with the loaves anyway!*

Al Shanker is probably one of the best known labor leaders in the United States—president of the American Federation of Teachers (AFT) and of the United Federation of Teachers (UFT), and a participant in international labor meetings on the Executive Council of the AFL-CIO.

*My jobs are very demanding and they involve a lot of travel both in this country and abroad. Baking is one of my favorite ways of relaxing—although these days I don't get to do it as much as I'd like.*

Al grinds his own grains into flour, and he feels as most of us do, that bread baking provides a lot of gratification, in addition to some very funny stories.

*It happened during New York City's fiscal crisis some years back. The municipal labor leaders had just emerged from a negotiating session with the city officials. We were on our way to lunch and I was walking with Jack Bigel, who serves as a consultant to a number of unions. Some reporters were watching us and they saw Jack and me pounding our fists into our palms and twisting our hands. One of them drew the conclusion that it must have been a very tough session to make us so angry. However, Jack—who's also a bread baker—and I were just comparing notes on kneading techniques!*

*The Bread:*

**Bran Whole Wheat Bread**

# Bran Whole Wheat Bread

(2 large loaves)

4 cups warm water
1 tablespoon dry yeast
¼ cup malt powder
7 tablespoons dark molasses
3 cups bran
10 cups whole wheat flour
2 tablespoons vegetable oil
1 teaspoon salt (optional, see page 22)

*The UFT and AFT staffs in New York and Washington are fans of my bread baking efforts, although dieters usually complain that I'm unfairly tempting them. I often bring a weekend's worth of bread baking into the office, especially if I'm trying a new recipe. This one was taste-tested in my New York office.*

Place warm water in a large bowl. Then add the yeast, malt, and molasses. Add bran and about one-third of the flour, followed by oil and salt. Stir with a wooden spoon. Continue stirring and add the remaining flour, 1 cup at a time, stirring as you do so.

Turn dough out onto a floured surface. It should be soft, but it should not stick to the fingers. If you need more flour than the recipe calls for, add just enough so that the dough no longer sticks to your fingers. (The amount of flour can vary considerably, depending upon humidity or temperature.) Knead dough for 8 to 10 minutes, or until smooth and elastic. Place into a large oiled bowl, turn to coat, and cover. Let rise in a warm spot until doubled in bulk, 1 to 1½ hours.

Punch down, turn dough out onto a floured surface, and divide into 2 loaves. Place into 2 well-buttered 9 × 5-inch loaf pans, cover, and let rise until almost doubled in bulk.

Bake in a preheated 400°F oven for 15 minutes, then reduce the heat to 350°F, and bake for another 30 minutes, or until the loaves test done.

Remove from pans and place on wire racks to cool.

# Nancy Cross Eckert

Nancy is one of the most joyful, delightful, enthusiastic people that I have come to know through the publication of my first bread book. Our friendship began with a letter from Everglades, Florida—addressed to Rodale Press, and forwarded to me. The two typewritten, single-spaced pages began:

> *This morning I noticed a large container of cottage cheese dated October 19th and I realized that since my husband and I along with my daughter, my son-in-law-the-Jewish-automobile-mechanic, and my two grandchildren were leaving for Disney World tomorrow, I had better find something to do with the cottage cheese. So last night I started reading* Bread Winners *and found the solution to my problem in Dill-Onion Bread!*

She continued on about her family (seven children and six grandchildren); her work as her husband's literary agent, answering his fan mail, playing accountant, preparing the tax information for the *real* accountant; cooking, cleaning, doing laundry; designing and working knitted, crocheted, and needlepointed garments; swimming and keeping the pool clean; and currently working on four books—plus baking cookies, cakes, and breads and distributing them in the most unusual place.

> *Once I get started on a baking binge, I can't seem to stop. Obviously, my neighbors help me by taking some of the output. But, we have a road prison about seven miles from here and "the gang" help keep our little city (pop. 350) free of palm fronds. As they passed the other day, I ran out with warm cookies and slices of fresh-baked bread and offered it to them. I suggested to Allan that I might get rid of a lot of my baking by delivering it to the prison and then I might*

*even take it off my income tax. Allan laughed and said that a prison is not a charitable institution. Well, I tried. Short of opening up my own bakery or restaurant, I'm going to have to find someplace to dispose of all my creations!*

And, in closing, Nancy wrote, "Do I always carry on this way with a person I've never met? As a matter of fact, yes!"

Since then, there have been several letters and as many telephone calls from Fire Island to Everglades. One of these included an invitation to Nancy to publish some of her recipes here, along with her delightful notes.

# Megawheat Bread with Raisins and Nuts

(2 large loaves or 4 small loaves)

2 tablespoons dry yeast
1½ cups warm water
¼ cup honey
½ cup nonfat dry milk
¼ cup toasted wheat germ
¼ cup bran
¼ cup soy flour (optional)
5½ to 7 cups whole wheat flour
3 eggs
1 teaspoon salt (optional, see page 22)
⅓ cup vegetable oil
1 cup raisins (seeded muscat raisins are good)
1 cup chopped walnuts (other nuts may be substituted)
1 egg, beaten (optional), for brushing loaves

*If you've never tried baking bread in South Florida, you don't know what you're missing. Allan and I moved here a year and a half ago from Barrington, Illinois, and I spent the better part of the first three months watching bread dough rise. With an afternoon temperature between 85° and 90° and high humidity, this place is a bread person's dream!*

This bread, Nancy tells me, is heavy and substantial; it's delicious when toasted.

In a large bowl, dissolve yeast in warm water and then stir in honey. Then add the nonfat dry milk, wheat germ, and bran, stirring as you do so. Add soy flour, if using, and 3 cups of the whole wheat flour. Add the remaining ingredients and enough whole wheat flour to make a nonsticky dough. (If the dough is too soft, it will not be able to support the fruit and the nuts; and they'll sink to the bottom.)

Turn out onto a lightly floured surface and knead for 8 to 10 minutes, or until the dough is smooth and does not stick to your hands. Add more flour as you knead, if necessary. Place dough into an oiled bowl, turn to coat, cover, and let rise in a warm spot until doubled in bulk, about 1½ hours.

Punch down, turn out onto a lightly floured surface, and knead for 1 to 2 minutes. Then return to oiled bowl, turn to coat, and cover again. Place in a warm spot to rise until almost doubled in bulk, 1 to 1½ hours. If you like, you can eliminate this second rise, but the bread will not have the texture that it should.

*Bread Winners Too*

After the second rise, turn the dough out onto a floured surface and divide into 2 parts. (You can make 4 smaller loaves if you wish.) Place into 2 buttered 9 × 5-inch loaf pans, or 4 buttered 4 × 2-inch loaf pans, cover, and place in a warm spot to rise until almost doubled in bulk. This should take another hour or more.

Bake in a preheated 350°F oven for about 40 minutes, or until breads test done. If you make 4 smaller loaves, bake for 30 minutes. If desired, the loaves may be brushed with beaten egg before baking.

Cool on wire racks.

*When my children were young, one of my delights was to make sure that fresh loaves were coming out of the oven when they were returning home for the evening. I guess I must have been impressed by the* Better Homes and Gardens *ethos early in life!*

# Apricot Oatmeal Bread

(2 large loaves)

    2 tablespoons dry yeast
 ½ cup warm water
 ¼ cup plus 1 teaspoon
       honey
2½ cups buttermilk, room
       temperature
2½ cups rolled oats
    1 teaspoon salt (optional,
       see page 22)
 ½ teaspoon baking soda
 ¼ cup vegetable oil
 ½ cup toasted wheat germ
    5 cups whole wheat flour
    8 ounces dried apricots,
       chopped*

In a small bowl, dissolve yeast in warm water. Stir in 1 teaspoon honey, and set aside.

In a large bowl, combine the buttermilk, oats, and ¼ cup honey. Then add the remaining ingredients and the proofed yeast mixture. Use only enough flour to make a soft dough.

Turn out onto a lightly floured surface and knead until smooth and elastic, 8 to 10 minutes. Place dough into a well-oiled bowl, turn to coat, and cover. Let rise in a warm spot until doubled in bulk, about 1½ hours.

Punch dough down, cover, and place in a warm spot for a second rise, about 1 hour. Punch down, turn out onto a floured surface, and form into 2 loaves. Place into 2 well-buttered 9 × 5-inch loaf pans, cover, and let rise in a warm spot until almost doubled in bulk, about 45 minutes.

Bake in a preheated 350°F oven for about 45 minutes.

Cool on wire racks.

*If you are chopping the apricots in a food processor, add a little flour to prevent the fruit from sticking to the blades.

# Picnic Bread

(2 rolled loaves)

*Bread:*
2 tablespoons dry yeast
2 cups warm water
1 cup nonfat dry milk
5 cups whole wheat flour
3 tablespoons honey
¼ cup toasted wheat germ
1 teaspoon salt (optional, see page 22)
¼ cup vegetable oil

*Filling:*
½ cup butter
1 cup slivered almonds
2 cups thinly sliced onions
1 pound Swiss cheese, shredded (cheddar or other hard cheese can be substituted)
1 to 2 tablespoons coarsely ground black pepper
1 egg, beaten with 1 teaspoon water, for brushing loaves

This is another festive bread from Nancy, rolled up jelly-roll style, so that cutting it will reveal the swirl of the filling. Any bread calling for 5 to 6 cups of flour will do. But here is an easy recipe.

To prepare the bread: In a large bowl, dissolve yeast in warm water. Then add the remaining ingredients in order, using only enough flour to make a smooth dough.

Turn out onto a lightly floured surface and knead for 8 to 10 minutes, or until dough is smooth and does not stick to your hands. Place into an oiled bowl, turn to coat, and cover. Let rise in a warm spot until doubled in bulk, about 1½ hours.

Turn out onto a floured surface and knead for 1 to 2 minutes. Return dough to the oiled bowl, cover, and let rise again in a warm spot for about 1 hour.

Turn out onto to floured surface, divide in half, and roll each half into a circle about 14 inches in diameter. Set them aside and make the filling.

To prepare the filling: In a large skillet, melt butter over high heat, watching it carefully so that it does not burn. Add nuts and onions, stirring as you sauté, until lightly fried, but not burned and not steamed in the onion juices. Set aside to cool.

When filling is cool, spread on both circles of dough. Sprinkle cheese and pepper evenly over filling. Roll up circles jelly-roll style and place, seam-side down, on a well-buttered jelly-roll pan. Brush with mixture of egg and water. Cover and set aside to rise in a warm spot for 30 to 45 minutes.

Bake in a preheated 350°F oven for about 45 minutes. Half way through the baking time, reverse position of loaves in oven for even browning.

Serve warm or cold.

The loaves may be frozen. Before serving, reheat for maximum flavor.

One of the constant complaints that I hear from my friends is that they "have no room to bake bread." Nancy writes:

*You should see this kitchen. I think it measures about 8 by 11 and is arranged in the most unlikely way imaginable. However, I cooked for nine people morning, noon (if one includes school lunches), and night for years and years from a kitchen that was not much better. I was always organized. The only time that this kitchen really bothers me is when we have guests and I have to knead dough on one of the two microscopic counters!*

Here, then, is another superb loaf from her microscopic counters.

In a large bowl, dissolve yeast in warm water. Then stir in honey. Add nonfat dry milk, and 3 cups flour and stir vigorously. Mix in the eggs, salt, butter, and only enough of the remaining flour to make a slightly sticky dough. (Too much flour will make the bread too dense.)

Turn out onto a lightly floured surface and knead for 8 to 10 minutes, adding only enough flour to make dough easy to handle. Place into a well-oiled bowl, turn to coat, cover, and let rise in a warm spot until doubled in bulk, about 1½ hours.

Punch dough down, turn out onto a lightly floured surface, and knead for 1 to 2 minutes. Return dough to the oiled bowl, cover, and let rise in a warm spot until almost doubled in bulk, about 1 hour.

Punch down, turn out onto a lightly floured surface, and divide dough into 2 sections. Divide each section into 3 strands about 12 inches long and 3 inches wide. Roll each of these sections flat and then sprinkle the seeds down the center of the strips. (Save some seeds for the tops.) Roll the strips over the seeds lengthwise and pinch the ends firmly to seal in the seeds. Braid 3 strips and then repeat with the remaining 3 to make 2 loaves. Place braids into 2 well-buttered 9 × 5-inch loaf pans, cover, and let rise in a warm spot until almost doubled in bulk, about 45 minutes.

Brush loaves with egg mixture and sprinkle with reserved seeds. Bake in a preheated 350°F oven for 40 to 45 minutes, or until loaves test done.

Cool on wire racks.

# Seeded Egg Braid

(2 large loaves)

2 tablespoons dry yeast
2 cups warm water
¼ cup honey
½ cup nonfat dry milk
6 to 7 cups whole wheat flour
3 eggs
1 teaspoon salt (optional, see page 22)
¼ cup butter
1 cup seeds (poppy, toasted sesame, or toasted and chopped pumpkin or sunflower)
1 egg, slightly beaten with 1 teaspoon water, for brushing loaves

# Bread for a Celebration Morning

(6 loaves)

2 tablespoons dry yeast
2½ cups warm water
½ cup plus 1 teaspoon honey
1½ cups nonfat dry milk
5 eggs
8½ cups whole wheat flour
¼ cup ground cardamom
1 teaspoon salt (optional, see
page 22)
½ cup butter
1 pound dried, mixed fruits,
chopped into small pieces
½ cup raisins
½ cup golden raisins
grated rind of ½ orange
grated rind of ½ lemon
½ cup chopped almonds
½ cup chopped pecans
1 egg, beaten with 1
teaspoon water, for
brushing loaves
¾ cup sliced almonds

These are glorious little breads, almost like coffee cakes, excellent for breakfast on *any* morning, or served to guests who drop in for tea on a quiet afternoon.

*You'll notice that I never add salt or shortening to a yeast mixture until I incorporate some of the flour. I find that salt and/or fat inhibit yeast growth. Or maybe it's my imagination.*

In a small bowl, dissolve yeast in ½ cup warm water, stir in 1 teaspoon honey, and set aside.

In a very large bowl, combine 2 cups warm water, ½ cup honey, nonfat dry milk, eggs, and 3 cups flour. When yeast mixture is bubbling, stir it into flour mixture. Add the cardamom, salt, butter, and about 5 cups flour, using only enough flour to make a slightly sticky dough. Don't overdo it; you can always add more flour later. Toss ½ cup flour with the dried fruits, orange and lemon rinds, and nuts.

Turn dough out onto a lightly floured surface, add the floured fruits, rinds, and nuts, and knead very well for 10 minutes, making sure that fruits and nuts are incorporated throughout. Place dough into a well-oiled bowl and turn to coat. Cover, place in a warm spot, and let rise until doubled in bulk, about 1½ hours.

Punch dough down, cover, place in a warm spot, and let rise until doubled in bulk, 1 to 1½ hours.

Turn out onto a floured surface, knead for 1 to 2 minutes, and form the dough into 6 braided loaves, about 12 inches in length. Place the breads on 2 lightly buttered jelly-roll pans or baking sheets, cover, and let rise in a warm spot until almost doubled in bulk, 45 to 60 minutes.

Brush with egg mixture and sprinkle top with almonds.

Bake in a preheated 350°F oven for about 45 minutes.

Cool on wire racks.

# Frank Howard

I don't know how many late-night telephone conversations I've had with Frank Howard over the past few years. Soon after *Bread Winners* was published, he found me at Fire Island and we began a long, continuing relationship based upon our love for bread baking. Frank recalls, "I received a copy of *Bread Winners* from my brother and sister-in-law. It sure was a lot better than a tie!"

Frank is a journeyman machine repairer for the Chrysler Auto Plant in Newark, Delaware. He and his wife, Ann, have been married for 32 years. They have five children and seven grandchildren, all of whom like his baking.

*But the grandchildren only like the ends of the bread with lots of butter. I've been baking about six years and I don't follow all the rules. I sometimes mix all my flours in one big bowl. I use a plastic spray bottle to steam the oven when I want a crisp crust. I don't worry about temperatures, and I've found that powdered buttermilk saves me time and money. For my round loaves, I've started using new enamel pans, the likes of which my mother-in-law used for 48 years when she baked her holiday breads.*

*The Breads:*

**Whole Wheat
  Pumpkin Bread
Triticale Herb Bread
Ukranian Easter Bread**
*(Pashka)*

# Whole Wheat Pumpkin Bread

(1 medium-size loaf)

1¼ cups honey
½ cup vegetable oil
2 eggs, beaten
2 cups whole wheat flour
¼ teaspoon baking powder
1 teaspoon baking soda
¼ teaspoon ground
cinnamon
½ teaspoon ground cloves
½ teaspoon ground nutmeg
1 cup cooked strained
pumpkin
½ cup chopped nuts
1 cup raisins

This is a quick bread, a tasty bread, and an excellent one in which to use the leftover Halloween pumpkin.

In a large bowl, mix the honey, oil, and beaten eggs. In a medium-size bowl, combine the dry ingredients and then add them to the liquid mixture. Mix well. Stir in the pumpkin, nuts, and raisins. Turn batter into a buttered 8½ × 4½-inch loaf pan and bake in a preheated 350°F oven for 1 to 1½ hours, or until bread tests done.

Cool on a wire rack.

I *never* wash my loaf pans. The older and darker they get, the prettier the color of the bread will be.

Suzanne Gosar

One of the most delightful developments in recent years is the increased popularity of triticale flour with bread bakers across the country. The flour, flakes, and whole grain are now readily available in the natural foods stores and even in some supermarkets. If you have trouble finding the flour, use the list of mail-order sources at the back of the book.

Here is a tasty bread from Frank Howard. Because of the low gluten content of triticale, he combines it with whole wheat flour.

In a medium-size bowl, blend 1 cup whole wheat flour with triticale flour and set aside. Reserve the remaining whole wheat flour for the kneading, should the dough become too sticky.

Heat the buttermilk, butter, honey, and salt in a small saucepan and then cool to lukewarm.

In a large bowl, sprinkle yeast over warm water and stir until dissolved. Add the lukewarm buttermilk mixture, beaten egg, onions, parsley, and oregano. Stir in 2 cups of the blended flour, beating until smooth. Add enough additional flour to make a stiff dough.

Turn out onto a lightly floured surface and knead until smooth and elastic, about 10 minutes. Place into a well-oiled bowl, turn to coat, cover, and let rise in a warm spot until doubled in bulk, 1 to 1½ hours.

Punch dough down, turn out onto a floured surface, and shape into a large, round loaf. Place into a buttered 9-inch pie plate. Cover lightly and let rise in a warm spot until almost doubled in bulk, about 45 minutes.

Bake in a preheated 400°F oven for 10 minutes, then reduce the heat to 375°F, and bake 20 to 25 minutes longer, or until bread is well browned.

Cool on a wire rack.

# Triticale Herb Bread

(1 round loaf)

1½ cups whole wheat flour
2 cups triticale flour
¾ cup buttermilk
2 tablespoons butter
2 tablespoons honey
½ teaspoon salt (optional, see page 22)
1 tablespoon dry yeast
¼ cup warm water
1 egg, beaten
¼ cup chopped onions
2 tablespoons minced fresh parsley
1 teaspoon dried oregano

# Ukranian Easter Bread
## (Pashka)

(4 medium-size loaves)

2 tablespoons dry yeast
4 cups warm water
½ cup plus 2 teaspoons
honey
1 cup buttermilk
10 to 12 cups whole wheat
flour
3 eggs, beaten
½ cup butter, melted
½ teaspoon salt (optional, see
page 22)
½ teaspoon ground
cinnamon
2 cups raisins
1 egg yolk, beaten
1 tablespoon milk

This version of *Pashka* replaces the traditional white flour with whole wheat. The bread comes out a little darker, but the flavor is heavenly.

In a small bowl, dissolve yeast in ½ cup warm water. Add 2 teaspoons honey, mix, and set aside to proof.

In a large bowl, combine 3½ cups warm water, buttermilk, proofed yeast mixture, and 5 cups of the flour, adding 1 cup at a time, mixing as you do so. Beat until smooth. Cover and let rise in a warm place until doubled in bulk, about 1½ hours.

After the batter has risen, add the beaten eggs, melted butter, salt, remaining honey, cinnamon, and raisins. Work in the remaining flour until you have a dough that can be kneaded.

Turn out onto a lightly floured surface and knead for about 15 minutes. Place into a well-oiled bowl, turn to coat, cover, and let rise in a warm spot until doubled in bulk, about 1½ hours.

Punch dough down, turn out onto a floured surface, divide into 4 portions, and shape into the loaf of your choice. Place into 4 well-oiled 8½ × 4½-inch loaf pans, cover, and let rise in a warm spot until doubled in bulk, 45 to 60 minutes. (Frank uses enamel dish pans for large breads.)

Mix beaten egg yolk with milk, brush this mixture on the loaves, and bake in a preheated 375°F oven for 30 to 35 minutes, or until the loaves test done.

Cool on wire racks.

Keep a plastic bag near your workplace. If the phone rings while you're kneading (and it always does), just put your hand in the bag and answer the call.

Bernice Beenhower

# Connie Hartland

A few years ago, while producing a documentary for the National Council of Farmer Cooperatives and the American Institute of Cooperation, I traveled the country from north to south and from east to west, filming the stages of America's agricultural bonanza as well as many of its problems. As a special treat, I imagined meeting hundreds of farm families, all of whom baked their own bread, filling the kitchen with the redolence of fresh loaves. With the exception of just one or two people who finally appeared in *Bread Winners* (such as Joyce Slinden), I learned that I was terribly naive in my anticipation. Farm wives, for the most part, are *too darned busy* to spend their time baking fresh bread; it is the city folk who seem to squeeze time for the craft into their schedules. As Connie Hartland describes her work on the farm in Fairview, South Dakota:

> *My husband, Rolland, and I raise corn, barley, soybeans, hay, and hogs. We have two children—our older daughter, a freshman at St. Olaf College in Northfield, Minnesota, our youngest, a senior in high school and soon to go to Luther College in Iowa next year. Besides caring for my husband, kids, pets, large house, and lawn, I raise a large garden and, though I seldom do field work on the tractor, my summers are busy with "walking" beans (chopping weeds out of soybean fields) and helping to chase the pigs or cattle—and like all farm wives, I'm sent to the implement dealer to buy parts for machinery repair.*

Connie does all her own baking, she adds with pride. In that sense, Connie is most unusual in these days of convenience foods and "store bought" breads. In addition, her baking is done entirely with natural ingredients:

*The Breads:*

**Basic Honey Graham Bread**
**–Seven-Grain Bread**
**Buckwheat Buttermilk Pancakes**
**No-Knead Caramel Rolls**
**Whole Wheat Hamburger Buns**
**Bread Bowls**

*Several years ago, while on a weight loss diet, I became conscious of good nutrition and totally eliminated white flour and sugar from my breads, substituting whole grains and honey or molasses. I found, too, that using whole grains presented a much more creative opportunity to experiment with my recipes.*

Here are just a few of Connie's breads. Though I don't think that pancakes really fall into the "bread" category, I could not resist including one of her favorites.

# Basic Honey Graham Bread

(4 medium-size loaves)

3 tablespoons dry yeast
1 cup warm water
⅓ cup vegetable oil
⅓ cup honey
5 cups milk
2 teaspoons salt (optional, see page 22)
14 to 16 cups graham flour

This basic recipe makes a dense and satisfying loaf which can be varied according to your mood and the ingredients you have on hand.

*I use this basic recipe on which to vent my creative energies. Sometimes I add one-half cup toasted sesame seeds or millet or raw sunflower seeds—or I substitute one cup of cornmeal or cracked wheat, rolled rye, or rolled oats for one cup of graham flour. I use molasses instead of honey, now and then.*

Sprinkle yeast over warm water in a small bowl and set aside. Do not stir.

In a medium-size saucepan, combine the oil, honey, and milk and heat slowly to lukewarm.

While milk mixture is heating, place salt and 6 cups of the flour into a large electric mixer bowl. Pour warm milk mixture into flour and stir with a rubber spatula until ingredients are well moistened. Then stir in dissolved yeast. Beat with electric mixer at low speed for 5 minutes. Pour mixture into a large bowl and, with a wooden spoon, stir in 4 cups of the flour until well blended. Stir in 4 more cups of the flour, 1 cup at a time. With your hands, mix in enough of the remaining flour to form a soft dough.

Turn out onto a lightly floured surface and knead for 10 minutes. Place dough into an oiled bowl, turning once to coat top. Cover with plastic wrap or a towel and let rise in a warm place until doubled in bulk, about 1 hour.

Turn dough out onto a floured surface and divide into 4 parts. Knead each portion lightly, place dough back into the bowl, cover with plastic wrap or a towel, and let dough rest for about 10 minutes.

Form each ball into a loaf by rolling it into an elongated triangle 8 by 18 inches. Peel the dough off the surface, flip it over, and roll it up, beginning with the point of the triangle. Seal the edge and ends of the loaf by pressing down with the side of your hand. Place loaves into 4 buttered 8½ × 4½-inch loaf pans, turning once to coat tops. Cover each pan with a piece of plastic wrap and place a towel over all. Let rise in a warm spot until loaves increase in size by about one-third, 30 to 45 minutes.

Bake in a 375°F oven for 15 minutes. Then reduce the temperature to 350°F and bake 30 to 40 minutes longer.

Remove from pans and cool on wire racks.

## Seven-Grain Bread Variation

A tasty, nutritious, and unusual variation can be made by using the recipe for the Basic Honey Graham Bread and substituting a mixture of flours for some of the graham flour. Mix ½ cup each rye flour, barley flour, soy flour, oat flour, buckwheat flour, and brown rice flour—or any other combination—to make a total of 3 cups. Then, at the point in the recipe where Connie calls for 4 cups flour to be mixed into the batter, add this mixture along with *1 cup whole wheat flour* to make the 4-cup addition.

## Buckwheat Buttermilk Pancakes

(12 medium-size pancakes)

2 cups buckwheat flour
1½ teaspoons baking powder
1 teaspoon baking soda
½ teaspoon salt (optional, see page 22)
2 eggs, beaten
¼ cup vegetable oil
2½ cups buttermilk

Stir together the buckwheat flour, baking powder, baking soda, and salt in a large bowl.

In a medium-size bowl, combine the beaten eggs, oil, and buttermilk. Pour the buttermilk mixture into the dry ingredients and stir until thoroughly mixed. Cook in a lightly buttered electric frying pan set at 380°F, or on a well-buttered hot griddle on top of the stove. Turn pancakes when bubbles appear on surface and cook until done.

# No-Knead Caramel Rolls

*Although it makes me sound a hundred years old, I remember my mother baking bread in her wood-fired cookstove when I was little. This recipe is one that she used to make quite often, but I have converted it to whole wheat flour and natural sweeteners.*

(12 rolls)

*Rolls:*
½ cup milk
3 tablespoons butter
2 tablespoons plus 1 teaspoon honey
1 teaspoon salt (optional, see page 22)
½ cup warm water
1 tablespoon dry yeast
1 egg
3 cups whole wheat flour

*Filling:*
¼ cup honey
1 teaspoon ground cinnamon

*Caramel:*
⅓ cup honey
1 tablespoon molasses
¼ cup heavy cream

To prepare the rolls: Scald milk in a small saucepan. Stir in the butter, 2 tablespoons honey, and salt. Cool mixture to lukewarm.

Mix 1 teaspoon honey with warm water in a small bowl. Sprinkle yeast over water but do not stir. Set aside.

In a large bowl, beat egg well and then add lukewarm milk mixture and dissolved yeast. Add 2 cups flour and beat with a wooden spoon until smooth. Stir in the remaining flour and stir until ingredients are well mixed. Cover bowl with buttered wax paper and a towel and let rise in a warm place until doubled in bulk, about 1 hour.

To prepare the filling: In a cup, blend together honey and cinnamon.

Turn dough out onto a floured surface, pat into a 12 by 18-inch rectangle, and drizzle the filling over top. Roll up dough, starting with long edge, and cut into 12 slices.

To prepare the caramel: In a small bowl, mix honey and molasses with heavy cream. Pour into a buttered 7 × 11-inch or 9-inch round pan. Place slices of dough into caramel mixture, cut-side down. Cover pan with a piece of buttered wax paper and a towel. Let rise in a warm place until rolls have doubled in bulk, about 45 minutes.

Bake in a preheated 400°F oven for 20 minutes.

The rolls are best when eaten warm. Any leftover rolls can be kept in the pan and reheated when you're ready to serve them again.

*When our kids were younger, I always timed my bread and rolls to come out of the oven around the time that the school bus brought them home. The smell of fresh-baked bread is a signal for our family to gather at the end of the baking time to sample the results while we talk. My children have always loved these hearty buns.*

# Whole Wheat Hamburger Buns

(32 large buns)

2 tablespoons dry yeast
1 cup warm water
¼ cup vegetable oil
¼ cup honey
2½ cups milk
2 teaspoons salt (optional, see page 22)
10 to 11 cups whole wheat flour
2 eggs, beaten

Sprinkle yeast over warm water in a small bowl and set aside. Do not stir.

In a small saucepan, heat the oil, honey, milk, and salt to lukewarm.

Place 5 cups flour into a large bowl. Add warm milk mixture and dissolved yeast. Stir with a wooden spoon until well blended. Add beaten eggs, mixing well. Gradually add the remaining flour to make a soft dough, mixing in the last 1 to 1½ cups of flour with your hands.

Turn out onto a floured surface and knead for 10 minutes. Place into an oiled bowl, turning to coat. Cover with plastic wrap and a towel and let rise in a warm spot until doubled in bulk, about 1 hour.

Turn dough out onto a floured surface, divide into 4 parts, and knead each part lightly. Return to bowl, cover with plastic wrap, and let rest for about 10 minutes. Roll each portion of dough into a 12-inch square. Divide each square into 8 parts and form into 32 bun shapes. Place on buttered baking sheets. Press buns to flatten slightly and round out tops. Cover with plastic wrap and let rise in a warm spot until almost doubled in bulk, about 45 minutes.

Bake in a preheated 375°F oven for 15 minutes, placing baking sheets on lower and middle racks. Then reverse the pans and bake 5 to 10 minutes longer, or until buns are lightly browned.

Cool on wire racks.

# Bread Bowls

(24 small bowls)

Whole Wheat Hamburger
Buns recipe (see page 79)
1 egg
1 tablespoon water

*Since writing to you last, I have been experimenting with these bread bowls. They use the basic Hamburger Bun recipe and they're a marvelous way to serve chili or stews. That way, you can eat everything—bread bowl and all!*

Use the hamburger bun recipe to make the dough. Divide dough into thirds after it has risen. Place the portions back into the oiled bowl, cover with plastic wrap, and allow to rest while buttering the *outside* of 8 10-ounce custard cups. Place the buttered cups *upside down* on 2 baking sheets.

Divide 1 of the dough portions into 8 pieces and form each piece into a ball. Roll each ball into a 6-inch circle. Lay each rolled circle over a custard cup. Mold dough over the entire cup, making sure no air is trapped under dough. Let stand, uncovered, for 20 minutes.

Bake in a preheated 375°F oven for 15 minutes, placing 1 sheet of bread bowls on lower rack and the other on middle rack.

Remove from oven. In a cup, beat egg and water together and brush outside of bread bowls with mixture. Return baking sheets to oven, reversing their positions, and bake 5 minutes longer.

Remove from oven. Turn bread bowls right side up, removing custard cups gently. Brush inside of bread bowls with egg and water mixture and bake again for 10 to 15 minutes, or until lightly browned.

Cool on wire racks.

Repeat the process with the remaining pieces of dough; or, if you wish, refrigerate them and use for Whole Wheat Hamburger Buns.

# Steve and Carrie Price

*The Bread:*

**Soy Whole Wheat Bread**

When I wrote *Bread Winners,* the youngest baker in the book was Amy Seltzer, then 13 years old (and now a senior at Princeton!). I don't know if we qualify for *The Guinness Book of Records* in this volume, but our youngest baker is Carrie Price, *2½ years old* at the time of this writing. She and her father, Steve, an attorney, live in Houston and their bread baking is a family effort.

*Carrie began baking bread with me as soon as she could stand on a chair and help at the work surface. She was about 18 months old at the time. She has her favorites—anything with raisins, for example—and we make muffins frequently because they're fast and she gets the finished product quickly.*

Steve says that it took him quite a while to realize that the amounts of flour would vary, especially in humid Houston, and at that point he began to make his recipes flexible, as we all do. He began to receive more compliments from his dinner guests, and now he enjoys making bread even more than eating it.

*Then, when Carrie came along, baking bread gave my toddler and me something in common and it helped to bring us together. Also, it provided an opportunity to teach her the value of good nutrition and to show her how easy it is to eat good food. Commercial bread is tasteless in comparison to what we bake at home. But, as my wife, Robin, tells me, "You know, you'll have to bake bread for the rest of your life now!"*

Here is a recipe that Steve and Carrie bake together.

# Soy Whole Wheat Bread

(3 long loaves or 4 medium-size *baguettes*)

2 tablespoons dry yeast
½ cup warm water
½ cup plus 1 tablespoon honey
4 cups milk, warmed
½ cup vegetable oil
2 eggs
2 teaspoons salt (optional, see page 22)
½ cup toasted wheat germ
¾ cup brown rice flour
1½ cups soy flour
10½ cups whole wheat flour
cornmeal for dusting pans
water for brushing loaves

*I developed this recipe at a time when Carrie was eating mainly apple juice and bread. It was an easy way to get protein to her in an acceptable form. It has since become my favorite bread.*

Place yeast in a small bowl. Pour in warm water. Add 1 tablespoon honey, stir, and let proof while warming milk.

Warm milk to about 85° to 110°F in a medium-size saucepan and then pour it into a large bowl. Stir in ½ cup honey, oil, eggs, salt, and wheat germ. Add yeast mixture and stir. Add the brown rice flour, soy flour, and about half of the whole wheat flour, stirring after each addition. Then, add the balance of the flour, 1 cup at a time, until dough is no longer sticky, stirring after each addition.

Turn dough out onto a lightly floured surface and knead until smooth and elastic, about 10 minutes, adding additional flour as needed if dough gets too sticky and clings to your hands. Place the dough into an oiled bowl, turn to coat, cover, and let rise in a warm place until doubled in bulk, about 1½ hours.

Punch dough down, turn out onto a floured surface, and knead for 1 to 2 minutes. Then shape into 3 long loaves or 4 medium-size *baguettes*. Sprinkle a baking sheet or French loaf pans with cornmeal. Place the loaves on the sheet or into the pans, cover lightly with a towel, and let rise in a warm spot for about 30 minutes.

Brush the loaves with water, and then bake in a preheated 400°F oven for about 30 minutes. At 5- to 7-minute intervals, brush the loaves again with water. When done, the loaves will be dark and will have a hollow sound when tapped on the bottoms.

Remove from sheet or pans and cool on wire racks.

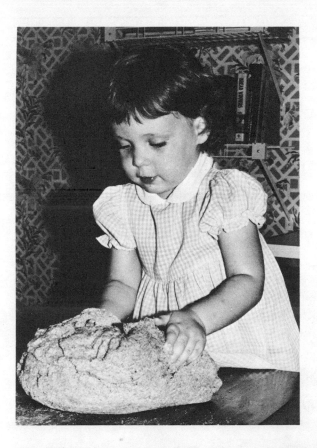

# AN EAST INDIAN HALLOWEEN

*The Breads:*

**Poori**
*Naan*
**Whole Wheat** *Chapati*

This past year, Halloween on our island reminded us that winter was not too far away. The day broke gray and cloud-covered with a chill wind that swept in off the ocean. It was a great day for baking bread. Sheryl and I invited George Meluso over to the house for an East Indian bread baking session, since he is not only an afficionado of Indian cuisine, but also a vegetarian by preference.

George came over on his bicycle early in the morning, equipped with a tiny Indian rolling pin, a *tava* (stove-top griddle), and a *karhai* (a small woklike heavy pan used for deep frying). We, in turn, provided a heavy eight-inch

cast-iron skillet, a ten-inch SilverStone-lined griddle, and a large pastry rolling pin. And so, throughout the day, East met West in our kitchen, accompanied by cold apple cider to keep the spirit of Halloween alive. We baked from early morning until late afternoon, the rain clouds offering a perfect excuse to stay indoors near the warm oven.

We made *66 breads* that day—*chapati, poori,* and *naan*—and then we sat down and, naturally, tasted them one by one. Though these breads are generally made in India on *karhais* or *tavas,* or in *tandoori* ovens (clay ovens), you will find that your ordinary kitchen utensils will do the job very nicely.

All of the breads for which I've given recipes are served hot, and each bread has a different shape and taste, ranging from the simple to the sophisticated. Actually, these three provide only a small sample of the variety to be found in India, but almost all are unleavened. They are used to scoop up the meat and vegetables that are served as a main course. Incidentally, all Indian breads are called *roti,* while Western breads are known as *double roti.*

Try them. It may take a little practice, but the first time the *poori* puffs up in the hot deep fat, we guarantee that you'll laugh aloud as we did with a sense of accomplishment. And you don't have to wait until Halloween to try them!

# *Poori*

(11 or 12 *pooris*, 5 inches in diameter)

2 tablespoons *Ghee* (see page 89)
1 cup fine whole wheat flour
¼ cup tepid water (approximate)
*Ghee* for brushing dough
peanut oil for deep frying

These festive breads puff up like little pillows as steam forms in the center. Keep them warm while they are being made one at a time. *Pooris* are a mixture of whole wheat flour, tepid water, and clarified butter (*ghee*) which is fried in peanut oil. They are easy to prepare but cooking them requires skill.

Sprinkle *ghee* over flour in a large bowl and mix with the tips of your fingers until crumbly. Add a bit of water at a time, mixing until a ball of dough is formed. Knead for 5 to 10 minutes. Brush ball of dough with *ghee* and cover with a dampened tea towel. Let rest 1 to 2 hours in a warm place.

When ready to prepare, heat oil to 350°F in an 8-inch heavy cast-iron skillet, or *karhai,* or wok. Roll dough into a 14-inch rope and cut into about 12 equal pieces. Roll each piece into a ball between palms of hands. Keep dough covered while making each bread. Roll each ball into a thin 5-inch circle and slip into hot oil. The *poori* will bubble and rise to the surface in a few seconds, and then suddenly it will puff up with steam, like a pillow. When this happens, hold it gently under the hot oil with the back of a slotted spoon for a few seconds before turning it over for another few seconds. Lift out and drain on paper towels. Keep warm while preparing the rest. They will keep their puff for about 40 minutes. You must work quickly and deftly. Once you've mastered the technique, you will find *pooris* fun to make and impressive to serve.

*Bread Winners Too*

## Ghee
## (Clarified Butter)

(about 1½ cups)

1 pound butter, cut into
    pieces

In a heavy, 5-quart saucepan, melt the butter slowly over low heat, while stirring. Do not brown. Increase the heat and bring the butter to a boil. When the surface is covered with white foam, reduce heat to the lowest possible setting, using a flame tamer if necessary. Simmer, uncovered, and do not disturb for about 30 minutes, or until the milk solids on the bottom of the pan are golden and the butter on top is transparent. This slow cooking evaporates the water and adds a lovely nutlike flavor to the butter.

You can use a gravy separator to pour off the clear top liquid, discarding the solids that remain on the bottom of the pot. However, if you do not own one, slowly pour the clear liquid through a strainer lined with several layers of dampened cheesecloth. Make certain there are no solids in the *ghee,* since they will turn rancid. It is the clear mixture that keeps so well and tastes so good.

Note: *Ghee* has a distinctive flavor and marvelous keeping power. Though I do store mine in the refrigerator in a tightly covered crock, it can be safely kept without refrigeration for 2 to 3 months. After cooling, the *ghee* will solidify. Before you use it, let it melt slowly over very low heat.

# *Naan*

(24 *naans*, 4 × 3 inches each)

3 cups fine whole wheat
flour*
1 tablespoon baking powder
¾ teaspoon baking soda
1 egg, beaten
¾ cup milk, warmed
4 tablespoons yogurt
2 tablespoons *Ghee* (see page
89)
*Ghee* for rolling *naan*

These teardrop-shaped loaves are among the few leavened
flat-breads of India. They're traditionally made by slapping
them onto the sides of a clay *tandoori* oven. *Naans* usually
accompany meat dishes but leftover *naan* dough is sometimes deep-fried in oil and served with tea for breakfast.
It is then called *bhatura*.

Mix all the dry ingredients together in a large bowl and
form a well in the center.

In small bowl, mix all the liquid ingredients together with
a whisk. Then slowly pour the liquid ingredients into the
well, pulling the flour toward the center until a dough
forms. Add more flour if the dough is sticky.

Turn out onto a floured board and knead for 5 to 10 minutes, or until smooth and elastic. Divide dough into about
24 golf-ball-size pieces. Roll balls in *ghee,* cover with a
dampened tea towel, and let rest at least 2 hours.

Pat, roll, and stretch balls into rough 4 × 3-inch teardrop
shapes, about ¼-inch thick, and place on a preheated baking sheet that has been lined with foil, about 6 at a time.
Bake in a preheated 450°F oven for about 3 to 4 minutes,
or until loaves are slightly puffed and golden. Then slip
under the broiler for a few seconds before removing from
baking sheet with a wide spatula. Keep warm while baking
remaining *naans* and serve hot.

*You must use a finely milled whole wheat flour for this recipe. We
use Hecker's whole wheat flour from our local supermarket, but special
*chapati* flour can be purchased from East Indian stores or by mail order
(see Mail-Order Sources).

*Chapatis* are the simplest of the Indian breads, prepared using only fine whole wheat flour and tepid water and baked in a dry skillet. These flat, crisp breads are eaten throughout India with all kinds of main dishes. The larger and slightly puffed breads, prepared in almost the same way, are sometimes called *phulkas*.

Place flour into a large bowl. Sprinkle ½ cup water over it, mixing with a wooden spoon and adding additional water, if necessary, to form a semifirm dough that is not sticky. Sprinkle with a few drops of water and knead until smooth and springy, 5 to 10 minutes. Cover dough with a dampened tea towel and let rest about 30 minutes. Roll dough into a 20-inch rope with palms of hands on a floured surface. Divide rope into 16 equal pieces and roll into balls between palms of hands. Cover with a damp towel again and let rest.

Heat a nonstick 10-inch skillet. Dip ball of dough into flour and roll out to a ¼-inch thickness. When skillet is hot, place *chapatis* on skillet and then, with a folded paper towel, press down on *chapatis* with your fingers and cook for about 30 seconds. Remove your fingers and the paper towel; *chapatis* should puff up. Continue to cook a few more seconds, turn over, and cook on second side for 1 to 2 minutes. Keep warm on a plate covered with foil.

*Chapatis* can be made in advance. When ready to serve, wrap them in foil and warm in a 350°F oven for about 10 minutes.

*You must use a fincly milled whole wheat flour for this recipe. We use Hecker's whole wheat flour from our local supermarket, but special *chapati* flour can be purchased from East Indian stores or by mail order (see Mail-Order Sources).

# Whole Wheat *Chapati*

(16 *chapatis*, 5 inches in diameter)

1 cup fine whole wheat
  flour*
½ to ¾ cup tepid water

# Bobbie Leigh

Bobbie, an avid bird watcher, tennis player, and sailor, is but the most recent "victim" of the epidemic "Fire Island Bread Baking Fever"—a new convert, though one of my oldest friends out here on the island. As almost everyone knows, George Meluso (see Index), the man who passed the fever on to me some years ago, was my teacher and mentor. Quietly, it turns out, he has made still another disciple on our island:

*George saw me eating a store-bought bran muffin on the ferry boat. He reached into a shopping bag and presented me with a bran muffin that he had made just that morning. It was terrific! I'd already flunked paté brisé and pizza and considered myself a hopeless cook. George, however, volunteered to teach me. In exchange for two slices of each loaf I baked at the beach, George said he would go back and forth between his house and mine until I produced a loaf of bread.*

Bobbie's results have been nothing short of phenomenal—almost every day she is at my door with a delicious sample, all of them worked out in her kitchen on the bay. As a result, the baking of bread has become almost an integral part of her profession, which is writing scripts for film:

*I travel back and forth from the bedroom, where I write, to the kitchen several times a day. At one time, I would go there to overdose on tea. Now I go to test the warmth of the kitchen, knead and push my dough, or just put the pans in the oven.*

She assigns herself a certain number of pages to complete and begins to write. At her break point, she goes to the kitchen to assemble the ingredients for a bread. Then she returns to work. Next she proofs her yeast, which is followed by proofing her pages.

*It works like a charm. The dough doubles in bulk. I double my output. I not only end up with an acceptable pile of pages next to my typewriter, but I also have something wonderful to help improve a simple dinner—a fresh-baked loaf of bread!*

The two breads that follow are simple and quick to make.

# Whole Wheat Orange Bread

(2 medium-size loaves)

4 tablespoons vegetable oil
2 cups water
1 cup honey
2 tablespoons dry yeast
5 cups whole wheat flour
1 egg, beaten
grated rind of 2 oranges
½ cup toasted wheat germ
½ cup bran

Bobbie says that she once added a cup of currants to this recipe, and she liked the results. You might want to try it as a variation.

Heat oil and water in a small saucepan until warm. Add 1 teaspoon of the honey and then yeast to the saucepan, stir, and set aside to proof, about 10 minutes.

Place 3 cups of the flour into a large bowl. Add yeast mixture. Then add the remaining honey, beaten egg, and orange rind and beat with a dough hook (or use a wooden spoon) until thoroughly mixed. Add the remaining flour, wheat germ, and bran. Beat again with dough hook.

Turn dough out onto a lightly floured surface and finish kneading by hand for 5 to 8 minutes.

Warm a bowl with hot water and then dry thoroughly. Oil the bowl, add the dough, and turn to coat. Cover with plastic wrap and let dough rise in a warm spot until doubled in bulk, about 1 hour.

Turn dough out onto a floured surface, knead lightly for 1 to 2 minutes, and then shape into 2 loaves. Place loaves into 2 well-oiled 8½ × 4½-inch loaf pans, cover, and let rise in a warm spot until dough just comes over edge of pans, about 30 minutes.

Preheat oven to 400°F and then reduce heat to 375°F. Place loaves in oven and throw in a handful of ice cubes to create steam. Bake for 35 to 40 minutes, or until loaves test done.

Cool on a wire rack.

Another method of steaming the oven for a crisp crust, aside from using a hot brick in a pan of water, is to throw some ice cubes on the bottom before putting the loaves in.

George Meluso

In a cup, dissolve yeast in warm water. Add honey, stir, and set aside to proof.

Combine the milk, oil, molasses, and yeast mixture in a large bowl. Work in all the flour, 1 cup at a time, the wheat germ, bran, and salt. Use a dough hook to blend.

Turn dough out onto a lightly floured surface and finish kneading by hand for 5 to 7 minutes. Place into a well-oiled bowl, turn to coat, cover, and let rise in a warm spot until doubled in bulk, 1 to 1½ hours.

Turn dough out onto a lightly floured surface and divide in half. Knead each piece for 1 to 2 minutes. Place the loaves into 2 well-buttered 8½ × 4½-inch loaf pans, cover, and let rise in a warm spot until doubled in bulk, about 1 hour.

Brush tops of loaves with water and bake in a preheated 400°F oven for 10 minutes. Then, reduce heat to 375°F and bake about 1¼ hours longer, or until loaves test done.

Cool on a wire rack.

# Molasses Whole Grain Bread

(2 medium-size loaves)

2 tablespoons dry yeast
¼ cup warm water
1 tablespoon honey
2 cups milk, scalded and cooled to room temperature
1 tablespoon vegetable oil
⅓ cup molasses
5½ cups whole wheat flour
½ cup toasted wheat germ
½ cup bran
1 teaspoon salt (optional, see page 22)
water for brushing loaves

If you think the bread is done, but find when you cut it that the loaf is still too damp inside, don't be afraid to return it to the oven, even several hours or a day later, to finish baking.
Valerie Rogers

# Art Hartman

For a collector/author who is writing a book such as this, Art Hartman is a veritable gold mine of bread lore and recipes. We first met at the American Library Association convention at the New York Coliseum, where Rodale Press had a booth. Art's wife, Mary Ann Ferrarese, is Assistant Chief of Photoduplication Service at the Library of Congress, and both of them were in town for the convention.

*We live in a condominium apartment in College Park, Maryland, with our dog Lefty, a Belgian Tervuren. Mary Ann usually brown bags her lunch, which contains home-baked bread (of course). Lefty is my chief taster and resident sourdough maven.*

Before retiring some years ago, Art was a psychologist. Today he is a "houseperson" who is also studying the craft of photography, when he's not experimenting with his breads.

*In our house, I do most of the cooking, and bread baking is a part of that. The gratification I receive is that of nurturing others, as well as self-nurturance. Feeding is, after all, the basic act of love. And when all goes well, and family and friends are appreciative, there is much ego satisfaction as well.*

You'll notice that Art uses the "sponge" method of baking, as do I. It's simply a matter of making a soft mixture either the night before or just an hour or so before preparing the final dough. He feels that it gives him superior and more consistent results than any other method. Some of his other theories are interesting too:

• *A dough with seeds can help a novice baker learn the feel of a properly kneaded dough. When the dough begins to force the seeds out—and they fall out clean—the gluten has developed and the dough needs only a few, say five, minutes more of kneading.*

• *I use a heating pad wrapped in a heavy towel to provide constant warmth for fermenting a sponge and raising dough, no matter what the room temperature.*

• *Heavy mixed-grain breads, especially sourdoughs, can look done and sound done, yet still be gummy inside. I insert a bamboo skewer or cake tester into the bottom of the loaf; if it comes out clean, the bread is really done.*

For this new book, Art has contributed a basic bread that includes the use of anise seeds, as well as several Mexican favorites.

# Anise-Raisin Bread

(2 medium-size loaves)

*Sponge:*
1 tablespoon dry yeast
1 tablespoon honey
⅔ cup nonfat dry milk
3 cups whole wheat flour
2 cups warm water

*Dough:*
1 cup raisins
2 teaspoons anise seeds
8 black peppercorns
1 teaspoon salt (optional, see
page 22)
¼ cup butter, melted
¼ cup honey
3 cups whole wheat flour
(approximate)

*Glaze:*
1 egg white
1 tablespoon water
anise seeds

To prepare the sponge: In a large bowl, dissolve the yeast, honey, nonfat dry milk, and flour in warm water. Blend well. Cover and let ferment in a warm spot for about 1 hour.

To prepare the dough: Steam raisins in the top of a double boiler for about 15 minutes. Crush anise seeds lightly between sheets of wax paper with a rolling pin. Grind peppercorns in a mortar until they are very fine and light.

Then, add the anise, pepper, salt, melted butter, and honey to the sponge. Sprinkle some flour over raisins and rub with your fingers to coat, making sure raisins do not stick together. Stir into sponge. Stir in the remaining flour until a dough forms.

Turn out onto a lightly floured surface and work in more flour until dough is no longer sticky. Knead for about 15 minutes. Then place dough into an oiled bowl, turn to coat, cover, and let rise in a warm spot until doubled in bulk, about 45 minutes.

Punch dough down, turn out onto floured surface, and knead again for several minutes. Cover and let rest for 5 minutes.

Shape dough into 2 loaves and place into 2 buttered 8½ × 4½-inch loaf pans. Cover and let rise in a warm spot for about 30 minutes.

To prepare the glaze: In a cup, beat egg white and water together and brush this mixture over tops of loaves. Sprinkle with anise seeds and bake in a preheated 375° oven for 40 to 45 minutes, or until breads test done.

Cool on a wire rack.

Knead to your favorite music. It gets the yeast creatures moving and gives you something to concentrate on—besides your tired arms.

Bethami Auerbach

These breads are fun to make, though the simplest ones may not be as easy as they look.

*The only outright failures I recall were my early tortillas, which were total disasters. For such a simple bread, tortillas require a great deal of skill to make properly. If you have never made tortillas before, your first ones will probably be rather odd looking and may not even be edible. Not to worry, all that's needed is practice, practice, practice. By the time you have worked your way through a 5-pound bag of nixtamalina, you should be fairly proficient.*

Two of Art's recipes call for *nixtamalina*, which is simply a flour made from parched lime-treated corn kernels (*nixtamal*); from that the Mexicans make their *tortilla* dough (*masa*) and *tamal* dough. Often called "instant *masa*," it's widely available from Quaker under the trade name of *Masa Harina*.

*Traditional whole wheat Mexican breads are rare, but here is one, and a most unusual bread it is. I have never made this bread in anything but fine weather, but if you make it on a rainy day or when humidity is high, I suggest reducing the water by one-third to one-half cup.*

In a large bowl, dissolve yeast in warm water. Stir in honey and then fennel seeds. Let stand for 15 minutes.

Stir in salt and flour to form a dough. Knead in the bowl for 15 minutes. Add oil, a little at a time, to keep dough from sticking. (But don't be too fussy about the stickiness.)

Turn dough out onto wax paper. Divide in half, oil each half, shape into rectangles, and place into 2 oiled 8½ × 4½-inch loaf pans. Cover and let rise in a warm place for 15 minutes.

Bake loaves in a preheated 450°F oven for 15 minutes. Reduce oven temperature to 350°F and bake for 1 hour. Then reduce heat to 250°F and bake 1¼ hours longer.

Let breads cool in pans for 30 minutes before turning out onto a wire rack.

# Some Mexican Breads

# Pan Entero

(2 medium-size loaves)

2 tablespoons dry yeast
3½ cups very warm water
½ cup honey
1 tablespoon fennel seeds
1 teaspoon salt (optional, see page 22)
8 cups stone-ground hard whole wheat flour
¾ cup olive oil (approximate)

# *Tortillas*

(about 12 *tortillas*)

2 cups *nixtamalina* (see page 99)
1¼ cups water

Making *tortillas* successfully is a classic example of having "feel" for a bread. Art gives explicit instructions just in case things don't seem to be going well. I've tried this recipe with a *tortilla* press, and once the *tortillas* begin to turn out just like the Mexican version, there is a great feeling of achievement.

Place *nixtamalina* into a large bowl. Add water and mix thoroughly with your fingers. Pat dough into a ball, cover with a towel, and let stand for 15 to 20 minutes.

Meanwhile, heat a griddle, skillet, or *comal* (the Mexican pan used for *tortillas*) over medium heat. If you're using an electric griddle, set the thermostat for 400°F. The griddle should be perfectly flat and ungreased.

Place a square of polyethylene, such as a sandwich bag, on the base of a tortilla press. Pinch off a piece of *masa* (dough) about 1¼ inches in diameter and roll into a ball between your palms. Flatten slightly and place in the *tortilla* press, a little off-center, toward the hinge. Place another sheet of plastic on top of the *masa* and close the press. If you do not have a *tortilla* press, use a table or counter top as a base and press out *tortillas* between plastic by using a heavy, flat-bottom skillet or saucepan. Open the press and carefully peel off top plastic. If *tortilla* sticks to the plastic, the *masa* is too damp. Scrape if off the plastic and return it to the big ball of *masa*. Mix in another tablespoon of *nixtamalina* and try another *tortilla*.

After peeling off top plastic, lift *tortilla* by bottom plastic and invert it on to your other hand. Peel off plastic. If *tortilla* looks granular at the edges, or if it tears apart, or is crumbly, the *masa* is too dry. Scrape it off and return it to the big ball of *masa*. Mix in 1 teaspoon water and try again. The moisture content of the *masa* can be adjusted this way indefinitely, until you find just the right consistency. Handling does not harm it.

When the *masa* is right and you have an intact *tortilla* in your hand, lay it gently on the griddle. After about 1 minute, the edge of the *tortilla* will curl up slightly. Turn it over with a spatula and cook 1½ to 2 minutes more. Turn again, and in a few moments the *tortilla* should puff up. Remove from the griddle and wrap in a napkin. As you cook more *tortillas,* stack them together and keep them wrapped in a napkin.

You may prepare *tortillas* well in advance of serving them, but they should be served warm. To reheat, spray each *tortilla* very lightly with water from a plant mister, pile them up in foil, and reheat slowly in a 250°F oven for about 10 minutes.

You can also freeze *tortillas* for several weeks. When you're ready to use them, just remove from freezer and reheat in foil in a low oven.

*Tortillas and* pan francés *are at opposite poles, but mix* tortilla *dough into French bread dough and this is the result.*

To prepare the sponge: Pour warm water into a large bowl. Then add yeast and honey. Stir in flour and *nixtamalina* and blend well. Cover with plastic wrap and let ferment in a warm spot for 1½ to 2 hours.

To prepare the dough: Stir the salt, oil, and *nixtamalina* into the sponge. Cover and let rest for about 15 minutes.

Mix in enough flour to make a dough that pulls away from the bowl. Then scrape dough out onto a floured surface and work in more flour until dough is stiff. Knead 20 minutes or longer. Place dough into an oiled bowl, turn to coat, cover with plastic wrap, and let rise in a warm spot until doubled in bulk, about 45 minutes.

Punch dough down, turn out onto a floured surface, and knead briefly. Then divide dough in half, cover, and let rest for 10 minutes.

Shape dough into 2 round loaves, place well apart on an oiled baking sheet, and brush tops and sides lightly with melted butter. Cover and let rise in a warm spot until nearly double in bulk, about 30 minutes. (They will spread more than they will rise.)

Brush loaves lightly with butter again and bake in a preheated 400°F oven until lightly browned and loaves test done, about 35 minutes.

# Pan de Nixtamalina

(2 loaves)

*Sponge:*
2 cups warm water
1 tablespoon dry yeast
1 tablespoon honey
2 cups unbleached white
    flour
1 cup *nixtamalina* (see
    page 99)

*Dough:*
1 teaspoon salt (optional, see
    page 22)
3 tablespoons vegetable oil
1 cup *nixtamalina*
2 cups unbleached white
    flour (approximate)
    melted butter for brushing
    loaves

# Bizchochue-los

*The pan dulce of Mexico range from just the vaguely sweet to the overwhelmingly sweet. This one lies somewhere in between, and it's delightfully flavored.*

(3 loaves)

*Sponge:*
1½ cups milk, scalded
1 tablespoon dry yeast
1 tablespoon honey
3 cups unbleached white
    flour

*Dough:*
1 teaspoon anise seeds
1½ teaspoons salt (optional,
    see page 22)
¼ cup butter, melted
1 cup honey
2 eggs
1 egg yolk
4 cups unbleached white
    flour (approximate)

*Glaze:*
1 egg white
1 tablespoon water
anise seeds
sesame seeds

To prepare the sponge: Let milk cool to warm. Pour into a large bowl. Stir in the yeast, honey, and flour until well blended. Cover with plastic wrap and let ferment in a warm place for 2 hours.

To prepare the dough: Place anise seeds between sheets of wax paper and crush lightly with a rolling pin. Stir into sponge along with the salt, melted butter, and honey. In a small bowl, beat together whole eggs and egg yolk and add to sponge. Mix in enough flour to form a dough that pulls away from the bowl.

Scrape dough out onto a floured surface and work in more flour until dough is no longer sticky. Knead for 10 minutes. Place dough into an oiled bowl, turn to coat, cover with plastic wrap, and let rise in a warm place until doubled in bulk, about 1½ hours.

Punch dough down, turn out onto a floured surface, and knead again briefly. Shape into 3 balls. Place 2 of them well apart on a large oiled baking sheet and the third one on another oiled baking sheet. Cover loosely and let rise in a warm place until doubled in bulk, about 45 minutes.

To prepare the glaze: In a cup, beat egg white with water and brush tops and sides of loaves with this wash. Sprinkle half of each loaf with anise seeds and the other half with sesame seeds. With a sharp knife, slash each loaf ½ inch deep from side to side. Bake in a preheated 425°F oven for 5 minutes. Then reduce the temperature to 350°F and bake until loaves are well browned and test done, about 30 minutes.

# Anne Byrn Phillips

Anne is food editor of the *Atlanta Journal*. She is a charming and delightful young woman. I first met her when I was on the book tour for *Bread Winners,* and her articles about the book did much to publicize it in the Atlanta area. After the "formal" interviews, however, Anne and I spoke about—bread. She told me that if I ever thought of doing another bread book, she'd very much like to contribute some traditional southern recipes, as well as some of her own favorites.

*I started making biscuits when I was 13 or 14 and that progressed into quick breads of all kinds—banana, pumpkin, carrot. My mother soon left the baking to me. But, yeast breads were another story. I began making them only six years ago, and I finally feel that I've caught on. And I finally have a draft-free kitchen in which the dough can flourish.*

At the newspaper, Anne edits food stories for the Wednesday section, does restaurant and travel stories, writes on subjects ranging from gourmet cooking to nutrition, tests the recipes that are published in the food section, and styles food for the color photographs that accompany them.

*I also enjoy picnics, playing soccer, and taking my chocolate brown Labrador, Bailey, on long walks. Though I now live in Atlanta, my husband, Chris, and I hope someday to move outside the city and into a comfortable farmhouse where the country kitchen could easily handle my 60-inch South Bend commercial range—which bakes beautiful bread.*

The Breads:

**Spoon Bread with Corn**
**Georgia Sweet
 Potato Bread**
**Whole Wheat
 Buttermilk Biscuits**
**Whole Wheat
 Cheese Straws**
**Mile-High Biscuits**

And does a professional food editor have her failures just like the rest of us mortals?

*Oh sure. My yeast breads are sometimes too hard because I have a tendency to add too much flour. But I find that by greasing my hands with oil before kneading, I can handle the dough without having to add too much flour. And besides, Chris loves all my breads, even those I consider failures. Occasionally, he also helps me knead.*

# Spoon Bread with Corn

(4 servings)

3 ears white or yellow corn, husked
3 cups milk
½ teaspoon salt (optional, see page 22)
1 cup stone-ground cornmeal (preferably white)
½ cup butter, softened
3 egg yolks
2 teaspoons honey
¼ teaspoon ground nutmeg
⅛ teaspoon cayenne pepper
3 egg whites

Shred corn from ears and place into a large saucepan, along with any liquid that comes from the corn while shredding. Add 2 cups milk and salt and bring to a boil over high heat.

Pour in cornmeal slowly, so that the boiling continues rapidly, and stir with a wooden spoon to keep the mixture smooth. Reduce heat to low and while stirring constantly, simmer, uncovered, until mixture is so thick that a spoon will stand up in the middle of the pan. Remove pan from heat and beat in softened butter. Add the remaining milk and when it is completely incorporated, beat in the egg yolks, 1 at a time, honey, nutmeg, and cayenne pepper.

In a small bowl, beat egg whites until stiff and then fold into corn mixture. Pour mixture into a buttered 2-quart casserole, spreading it evenly with a spatula. Bake, uncovered, in a preheated 350°F oven for 45 to 60 minutes.

Serve at once.

This is a traditional bread from Anne's kitchen. The unbleached white flour can be converted to whole wheat flour if you like. Anne comments:

*This bread should be only slightly sweet. If you like a sweeter bread, just add more honey. It should be moist, and the flavor actually improves if you store it in the refrigerator for a day. It's excellent served with pork.*

In a small saucepan, combine raisins and water and bring to a boil. Set aside to cool.

Combine honey and oil in a medium-size bowl and mix well. Add eggs, 1 at a time, and beat well after each addition.

In a large bowl, mix together all the dry ingredients, except for baking soda.

Add sweet potatoes to honey/oil mixture, blending well.

Stir baking soda into raisin/water mixture and then add it along with sweet potato mixture to the dry ingredients, alternating a small amount of each at a time, until well blended. Stir in nuts. Fold into 2 buttered and floured 8½ × 4½-inch loaf pans and bake in a preheated 350°F oven for about 1 hour, or until loaves test done.

# Georgia Sweet Potato Bread

(2 medium-size loaves)

1 cup raisins
½ cup water
1 cup honey
1 cup safflower or sunflower oil
4 medium or 3 large eggs
1 cup whole wheat flour
2½ cups unbleached white flour
3 tablespoons nonfat dry milk
2 tablespoons toasted wheat germ
1 teaspoon salt (optional, see page 22)
1 teaspoon ground cinnamon
2 cups mashed sweet potatoes (about 3 large potatoes), boiled until tender, peeled, and then mashed
2 teaspoons baking soda
½ cup chopped pecans

# Whole Wheat Buttermilk Biscuits

(12 2½-inch biscuits)

1¾ cups whole wheat flour
¼ teaspoon salt (optional, see page 22)
1 tablespoon baking powder
¼ teaspoon baking soda
¼ cup butter
¾ cup buttermilk
1 teaspoon honey

Sift flour before measuring. Combine dry ingredients in a medium-size bowl. Cut in butter until mixture resembles coarse crumbs. Then add buttermilk to form a soft dough. Stir in honey.

Pat dough out onto a floured surface to a thickness of ½ to ¾ inch. Cut into rounds with a floured glass. Arrange close together (for soft-sided biscuits) or about ½ inch apart (for crusty-sided biscuits) on an ungreased baking sheet and bake in a preheated 450°F oven for 12 to 15 minutes.

I find that buttermilk powder saves me time and money.

Frank Howard

These are delicious with tomato soup or gazpacho. Anne's recipe calls for New York State black rind cheese, but any cheddar can be used, either very mild or very strong, depending upon your taste buds.

Combine all ingredients in a large bowl.

Form into rolls about ½ inch thick and 3 inches in length. Place on an ungreased baking sheet and bake at 350°F for about 15 minutes, or until golden brown.

Serve hot or cold.

# Whole Wheat Cheese Straws

(about 5 dozen straws)

1 pound New York State black rind cheese, shredded
2 cups whole wheat flour
1 teaspoon salt (optional, see page 22)
1 teaspoon cayenne papper
¾ cup butter, softened

These are the traditional biscuits that Anne baked when she was still a teenager. They work very well with whole wheat flour in place of the white she used back in her high school days.

Sift together flour, baking powder, cream of tartar, and salt into a large bowl. Cut in butter until mixture resembles coarse meal.

Combine egg and milk in a small bowl and beat with a fork. Add to the flour mixture, stirring to make a dough. Add honey.

Turn out onto a lightly floured surface and knead a few times. Do not over-knead. Biscuits are much better when they're blended roughly. Roll out to a thickness of 1 inch and cut into rounds with a floured glass. Place on an ungreased baking sheet and bake in a preheated 450°F oven for 10 to 12 minutes, or until golden brown.

# Mile-High Biscuits

(16 large biscuits)

3 cups whole wheat flour, sifted
4½ teaspoons baking powder
¾ teaspoon cream of tartar
½ teaspoon salt (optional, see page 22)
¾ cup butter
1 egg, beaten
¾ cup milk
1 tablespoon honey

# Paul Stitt

*The Breads:*

**Sunny Millet Bread**
**Happiness Bread**

*We've got to change the demands we make of bread . . .
bread should be crumbly, so it can be easily digested. Bread
should be chewy, so it is more satisfying and provides needed
fiber. The flour from which it is made should undergo only
coarse grinding, rather than the nutrition-stealing pulveri-
zation that white flour gets. We should no longer demand
bread that can sit for a week on a shelf, unless we are willing
to accept the chemical poisons that go into bread.*

Paul Stitt
*Fighting the Food Giants*
(San Mateo, Calif.: Natural World Press, 1980)

Paul Stitt is a most remarkable man. I could probably
write a book about him, though he has described his views
and activities very well by himself, both in the book I've
quoted above, and in a second one published in 1982 by
Natural World Press, *Why Calories Don't Count,* pursuing
his premise that people who eat whole grains and raw fruits
and vegetables never have to count calories. Possibly all
this would not be unusual, were Paul still involved in his
original career as a biochemist and researcher in the food
industry.

However, after years of working to produce protein
from waste products in order to feed a hungry world, he
found, much to his chagrin, that the commercial companies for whom he worked were *just not interested.*

*Protein produced from waste could be nothing but bad news
for sales. Not only were protein bars expensive to make,
but they were so satisfying a person couldn't finish more
than one at a meal. A box of breakfast bars might last one
family an entire week!*

The major food manufacturers, according to Stitt, are involved only in trying to produce a profit, and they've committed themselves to expanding their markets by processing, sweetening, and adding salt, as well as color dyes and flavor chemicals. In 1976, Paul changed his life by purchasing a commercial bakery in Manitowoc, calling it Natural Ovens, and setting out to make a 100 percent whole wheat bread.

> *The so-called experts say that you can't make a 100 percent commercial whole wheat bread. What the baking industry really means is that you can't make a 100 percent whole wheat bread in 15 minutes!*

Natural Ovens is now a well-known name in seven midwestern states. It takes four hours to produce a loaf of bread, but they still turn out over five thousand loaves a day, and 16 different types of bread. More unusual, perhaps, is the fact that Paul and his staff are quite willing to give their recipes to their customers, something highly unlikely when dealing with one of the commercial bread baking giants.

> *Our goal behind Natural Ovens was not profit (as any accountant looking over the books those first years would attest), but* nourishment. *I believe that people ought to be more self-reliant when it comes to food. If they want to bake Sunny Millet themselves, or if they're simply curious about what goes into a loaf, they ought to be given the information. Our customers really appreciate the candor— and sales keep climbing!*

Paul Stitt is, indeed, a most unusual man. And though I have said in two books that I have not included a "commercial baker," I still feel that I have held to that credo. Paul Stitt is really one of *us*. Here are two of the favorites he shares with those who admire the breads from Natural Ovens. They appear as Paul prepares them.

# Sunny Millet Bread

(2 medium-size loaves)

¼ cup millet
2 tablespoons vegetable oil
2 tablespoons honey
1 ounce cake yeast
¼ cup sunflower seeds
½ cup cracked wheat
1 cup whole wheat flour
2 cups gluten flour
2 cups rolled oats
1 teaspoon salt (optional, see page 22)
1 teaspoon barley malt
1 tablespoon sesame seeds

Paul's Doberman Pinscher, Lady, is, like Paul, a vegetarian and one of her favorite snacks is this bread. Enhanced by the crunchiness of millet, Sunny Millet is now the best-selling item in about 300 supermarkets in Illinois and Wisconsin.

In a large bowl, mix all ingredients at once.

Turn dough out onto a floured surface and knead for 10 minutes. The dough should be slightly sticky. Place in an oiled bowl, cover, and let rise in a warm place, about 1 hour.

Punch dough down and wait 15 minutes. Then form dough into 2 loaves. Work out all possible air. Place into 2 buttered 8½ × 4½-inch loaf pans and let rise in a warm place until doubled in bulk, but not higher than ½ inch below the top of the pans.

Bake in a preheated 350°F oven for about 30 minutes.

Turn out onto a wire rack to cool. Each loaf will be about 3½ inches high and will weigh about 1½ pounds.

Note: It is very important to use high-gluten flour so that the flour has enough strength to rise with the heavy seeds in it.

*Bread can either be the most nutritious food in the supermarket or barely nutritious at all. If you can squeeze it like bathroom tissue, chances are it's a poor source of nutrition. If it has the ingredients in this bread, and tastes the way this one does, it's among the best. It isn't called Happiness Bread for nothing!*

# Happiness Bread

(2 medium-size loaves)

 3 cups whole wheat flour
 2 cups gluten flour
 1 cup rolled oats
 1 tablespoon potato flour
 1 teaspoon malt
 1 teaspoon ground cinnamon
 ½ teaspoon salt (optional, see page 22)
 3 tablespoons vegetable oil
 ¼ cup honey
 2 ounces cake yeast
2¼ cups warm water
 1 cup raisins
 2 tablespoons pecan pieces

In a large bowl, combine the whole wheat flour, gluten flour, oats, potato flour, malt, cinnamon, and salt. Then add the oil, honey, yeast, and warm water. Mix for 12 minutes. Then evenly distribute raisins and pecans. The dough should be slightly sticky. Cover and let rise in a warm place for 1 hour.

Punch dough down and let rest for 15 minutes. Knead for 10 minutes. Divide dough into 2 loaves and place them into 2 buttered 8½ × 4½-inch loaf pans. Cover and let rise in a warm place until almost doubled in bulk, 20 to 30 minutes.

Bake in a preheated 350°F oven for 30 to 40 minutes, or until the loaves test done.

Turn out onto a wire rack to cool.

The loaves will weigh about 1½ pounds each, and their size will be approximately 4 inches high and 8 inches long.

Instead of just punching down the dough after it rises, pick it up and *throw it down on the counter—hard!* Do it again and again. It distributes the gluten and gets rid of aggression.

Margaret Peabody

# Seena Cowan

*The Breads:*

**Onion Honey
Wheat Bread
Bit O' Honey
Crunch Muffins**

Just a few months after *Bread Winners* was published, I received a letter from Newburgh, New York, which read in part:

*My insatiable curiosity has finally gotten the best of me! It has pervaded my existence for the past eight months. Before it makes a permanent dent in my psyche, I'd like to clarify a question in my mind. Were you, by chance, a counselor at Camp Kanawha in the forties? My gut feeling tells me you were—and my intuition is usually 90 percent accurate . . . . If you are the gentlemen who performed with me in* Iolanthe *at camp 40 years ago, I'd certainly get a kick out of hearing from you to confirm my intuitive feelings.*

*Curiously,*
*Seena Sheslow Cowan*

Forty years ago! If you can recognize the unlined face of the young man in the photograph, as yet unscathed by life and a war that had just begun, you will know the answer. Indeed I was "Uncle Mel," a counselor to a group of undisciplined nine-year-olds, just at the beginning of a college life that was soon to be interrupted for four years. And, indeed, I did remember Seena Cowan.

I answered her letter by telephone, she came down to New York for a long, long remembrance conversation over coffee, and soon after, the photos arrived along with memorabilia from that distant time, "ghosts" recalled vividly, and a friendship renewed after so many years.

During those years, Seena taught English to Spanish-speaking students and instructed disadvantaged children. She is now a gourmet caterer in Newburgh, as well as the mother of three grown children, and a grandmother to three-year-old twin boys. And, as a caterer, she is also a baker of bread.

*Of course, I've done a lot of entertaining, experimenting with anything and everything for my guests—with total success. But, for years, I never tried baking bread with yeast! To tell the truth, I was leery of trying it for fear that I might fail, thus negating my expertise as a cook and a baker.*

She had baked many quick breads, muffins, for example, but never "real" breads, as she calls them. Then, one day, that was all changed by a quirk of winter fate.

*I awoke to discover that the pipes had frozen! Feeling angry, disgusted, and frustrated because I had to stay home to wait for the plumber, I decided that* this was it! *B-Day.* Bread Day! *I cleared the counter, rolled up my sleeves, and got to work.*

And so, she improvised—added a little of this, a bit of that, including some wine and cheese that was left over from a party the night before—and voila! "I did it! I really did it! And it was tempting, tasty, and tangy."

"ME"

"MEL"

The recipes that follow are a few favorites whipped up by an old friend from 40 years back!

# Onion Honey Wheat Bread

(2 medium-size loaves)

1 tablespoon dry yeast
¼ cup lukewarm water
⅓ cup plus ½ teaspoon honey
2 cups milk
2 tablespoons butter
1 teaspoon salt (optional, see page 22)
2 cups sifted rye flour
1 small onion, finely diced
3½ to 4½ cups whole wheat flour

*My experience with this bread was frustrating at first. The dough was extremely sticky and for a while I thought my fingers were permanently fused together! I thought that if I used too much flour, the bread would be too heavy, but I kept flouring my fingers and adding flour to the dough, and surprisingly, when the bread was baked and sliced, it had a lovely, light texture.*

All of us have had the feeling that our rye breads are too sticky, but that is the very nature of the grain. Don't be afraid to add wheat flour to your rye loaves in order to bring the dough to the proper consistency. Remember that it's the "feel" of the dough that is much more important than the *amounts* given in the recipes.

In a large bowl, dissolve yeast in lukewarm water. Add ½ teaspoon honey, stir, and set aside to proof.

Scald milk in a small saucepan and then stir in the butter, ⅓ cup honey, and salt. Cool until lukewarm and then stir into yeast mixture.

Stir rye flour into yeast mixture, beating until smooth. Add onion and enough whole wheat flour to make a stiff dough.

Turn out onto a floured surface and knead for 10 minutes, or until smooth and shiny. Place dough into an oiled bowl, turn to coat, cover, and let rise in a warm place until doubled in bulk, about 1 hour. (I like to cover the dough with a towel wrung out in warm water.)

Punch dough down, turn out onto a floured surface, and let rest for 15 minutes.

Form dough into 2 loaves and place them into 2 well-buttered 8½ × 4½-inch loaf pans. Cover again and let rise in a warm spot for 30 to 45 minutes.

Bake in a preheated 375°F oven for about 35 minutes, or until breads test done. Cool on a wire rack.

These are easy to make. The crunch comes from the sunflower seeds.

In a large bowl, stir the dry ingredients and sunflower seeds together.

Combine the beaten egg, milk, honey, oil, orange rind, and vanilla in a small bowl. Add all at once to dry ingredients. Stir until moistened. Fill a buttered 12-cup muffin tin two-thirds full and bake in a preheated 375°F oven for 20 minutes.

Serve warm.

# Bit O' Honey Crunch Muffins

(12 muffins)

1½ cups whole wheat flour
 2 teaspoons baking powder
½ teaspoon salt (optional, see page 22)
½ cup sunflower seeds
 1 egg, beaten
½ cup milk
½ cup honey
¼ cup vegetable oil
 1 teaspoon grated orange rind
 1 teaspoon vanilla extract

Since temperatures vary so much, a good oven thermometer is a must, even if your oven is new.
Sam Kirk

# Samuel Kirk

Sam and I "met" in a rather strange way. He had been asked by Pat Hanna, the food editor of the *Rocky Mountain News,* to review the first bread book. I later learned that Sam conducted baking classes in Denver with the unusual title of: "Not for Women Only."

*The classes are not exclusively for men, but I guess I named them to focus on my own initial reluctance as a male to (1) be in the kitchen and (2) effectively perform in the kitchen.*

Though his "real" profession is heading his own career counseling firm, Sam is a veritable treasure of bread lore and the traditions of bread. He's researched the religious, historical, and national origins of numerous recipes, especially those of Mexican, Swedish, Scottish, Mennonite, and Navajo background. For neighborhood international dinners, the host family selects the country that will

be featured, while Sam invariably researches and bakes the breads of that nation. As he puts it, he gets great pleasure from "eating my art."

One of the discussions that we've had about baking has to do with achieving success in high-altitude locations such as Denver, a subject which I covered in *Bread Winners*. Because of the quick rise of breads at high altitudes, I suggested that the amount of yeast be cut down. Sam has still another good idea:

> *Contrary to public opinion, baking breads at high altitudes (Denver is one mile above sea level) means little if any change in recipe. Further, because there is less atmospheric pressure at a mile above sea level, the bread may rise faster, so if one wishes, one can punch it down after it's doubled and get in* another *rise within the recipe's stated time. Thus, better texture results—and, some contend, better taste.*

Sam also suggests that you use plastic wrap to cover dough in a dry atmosphere. It holds in the moisture better, while a towel or cloth tends to let the bread dry out. He also has an unusual trick to cover the mistake of putting *too much* flour into a recipe:

> *If you mistakenly knead in too much flour, making the dough dry and unmanageable, put the dough into a bowl of tepid water, with the water just covering the top of the dough. When it floats to the top (in about 15 minutes), take it out and pat it dry with a paper towel, then proceed to knead it again on a floured surface. Usually, it will knead into a smooth and elastic dough.*

Sam says that a fringe benefit from teaching bread baking is that he receives, unsolicited, delightful recipes from class members, friends, and family. The following breads are just a few of their most delectable and unique contributions.

# Molasses Skillet Bread

(1 loaf)

*Bread:*
1 tablespoon dry yeast
¼ cup lukewarm water
⅔ cup milk, scalded, or ⅔
cup hot water mixed with
⅓ cup nonfat dry milk
¼ cup honey
½ teaspoon salt (optional, see
page 22
¼ cup butter, melted
¼ cup molasses
3¾ to 4 cups whole wheat
flour
1 egg, beaten
1 cup rolled oats
melted butter for brushing
loaves

*Glaze:*
2 tablespoons honey
2 tablespoons butter

*This attractive loaf recipe came from Tennessee. A longtime supporter of my bread baking, Josephine Pitcock, shared this energy-packed molasses recipe with me early in my bread baking journey.*

To prepare the bread: In a cup, dissolve yeast in lukewarm water and set aside to proof.

Combine in a large bowl the milk or hot water-nonfat dry milk mixture, ¼ cup honey, salt, melted butter, and molasses. Stir and cool to lukewarm.

Stir in 1 cup flour and beaten egg. Beat 200 strokes with a wooden spoon, or 2 minutes with an electric beater, or 1 minute in a food processor. Stir yeast mixture with a whisk and then add to flour and egg mixture. Stir in oats and let stand for about 5 minutes.

Then stir in enough additional flour to make a soft dough. Turn out onto a lightly floured surface and knead until smooth, about 8 to 10 minutes. Form dough into a ball, place into an oiled bowl, turn to coat, and brush lightly with melted butter. Cover with wax paper or plastic wrap and let rise in a warm place until doubled in bulk, about 1¼ hours.

Punch dough down, cover again, and let rest for 10 minutes.

Turn out onto a lightly floured surface and roll into a 23 by 6-inch rectangle. Cut in half lengthwise. Then fold in half lengthwise, pinching edges together, to make a 23-inch rope. Repeat with second piece. Place 1 rope of dough, pinched-side down, around the outside edge of a buttered 8-inch (measured across the bottom) cast-iron skillet. Pinch ends together. Wind second rope into a coil in the center of the skillet, pinched-side down. Brush lightly with melted butter. Cover and let rise in a warm place until nearly doubled in bulk, about 1¼ hours.

Bake in a preheated 350°F oven for 30 minutes.

To prepare the glaze: Beat together the honey and butter in a small bowl until smooth. Brush half of the honey glaze over the bread and bake an additional 5 minutes. Brush with remaining glaze.

Cool 10 minutes and serve warm. (The loaf is also very good served cool.)

*I was in a pack horse camp at an altitude of 9,500 feet when I dined on these delicious whole wheat rolls. They were baked at 400°F in an old wood-burning stove/oven. The "secret" ingredient in this recipe, created by Dawn Temple Hetherington, is chicken stock. I test-baked them at "Mile High" (5,200 feet) and they came out lovely and tasty!*

# Winter Park Mountain Rolls

(18 to 24 rolls)

> 3 cups chicken stock
> ½ cup honey
> 2 tablespoons dry yeast
> ½ cup sesame seeds
> 2 cups nonfat dry milk
> 2½ cups rolled oats
> 6 to 7 cups whole wheat flour
> 1 teaspoon salt (optional, see page 22)
> ½ cup butter

In a medium-size saucepan, heat stock and then add honey. Stir to mix and cool to lukewarm. Then dissolve yeast in this mixture and set aside to proof.

In a large bowl, mix together the sesame seeds, nonfat dry milk, oats, 5 cups of the flour, and salt.

Add butter to yeast mixture. Then transfer mixture to a large bowl. Add the dry ingredients, 1 cup at a time, and beat until manageable.

Turn dough out onto a lightly floured surface and knead for 8 to 10 minutes. Add a little more flour, if necessary, and knead until dough is smooth and elastic. Place into an oiled bowl, turn to coat, cover with plastic wrap, and let rise in a warm place until doubled in bulk, about 1 hour.

Punch dough down, turn out onto a floured surface, and knead briefly. Cover and let rest at least 5 minutes.

Roll out dough into a rectangle ¾ inch in thickness. Cut into rounds with a 2½-inch biscuit cutter. Then pat each round out with your fingers and shape it into an oval. Draw up the edges into a pucker and pinch the puckered top together. Turn dough over, and pat it out gently onto a dry baking sheet. Cover with wax paper and let rise in a warm place until doubled in bulk, about 1 hour.

Bake on the top shelf of a preheated 400°F oven for 12 to 15 minutes.

Place on wire racks to cool or eat them hot from the oven.

Note: These rolls freeze well.

# Nisua (Finnish Coffee or Sweet Bread)

(2 medium-size loaves plus 12 rolls)

*Bread:*
2 cups milk
¾ cup butter
¼ teaspoon ground cardamom seeds
3 eggs, beaten
½ cup honey
1 teaspoon salt (optional, see page 22)
2 tablespoons dry yeast
¼ cup warm water
8 to 9 cups whole wheat flour

*Filling:*
¼ cup honey
1 tablespoon butter, softened
⅛ teaspoon ground cardamom seeds

*I discovered that this cardamom-accented recipe represented cultural pluralism. A new-found friend, Kris Johnson, presented me with her family's Finnish Sweet Bread recipe. Then, when I tested my good friend Marian Hanen's Swedish Cardamom Bread, it became apparent that, with one noticeable exception, the Finnish and Swedish breads were virtually the same! The Swedish bread is allowed to ferment overnight, giving it a pleasant, but not overwhelming sour fragrance.*

Unbleached white flour is commonly used for this bread, but this version is a sure crowd-pleaser. *Nisua* can be made as filled rolls or as a braided bread.

To prepare the bread: Scald milk in a large saucepan and add butter. Allow butter to melt and then let mixture cool to lukewarm. Then mix in cardamom, beaten eggs, honey, and salt.

In a cup, dissolve yeast in warm water and set aside to proof for about 5 minutes.

When milk mixture is lukewarm, add yeast mixture. Pour into a large bowl. Stir in 4 cups of the flour and beat at least 200 strokes with a wooden spoon, or 2 minutes with an electric mixer, or 1 minute in a food processor. Add 4 more cups of flour, 1 cup at a time, and beat until manageable.

Turn dough out onto a lightly floured surface and knead for 8 to 10 minutes, or until smooth and elastic. Place into an oiled bowl, turn to coat, cover with plastic wrap, and let rise in a warm place until doubled in bulk, about 1¼ hours.

Punch dough down, turn out onto a floured surface, and knead 4 or 5 times. Cover and let rest for about 10 minutes.

Divide dough into 3 sections. Two sections will be used to make the breads and 1 section will be reserved for the rolls. (Of course, you may make all breads or all rolls, but this way is more festive!)

To make the loaves, divide each section into thirds and then roll each third into strands. Braid them just as you would a *challah* and either place them into 2 well-buttered 8½ × 4½-inch loaf pans or on buttered baking sheets. Cover and let rise in a warm place until doubled in bulk, about 1 hour.

To make the rolls, take the remaining piece of dough and roll it out to a 12 by 14-inch rectangle.

To prepare the filling: Blend together in a small bowl the honey and softened butter, and spread over dough. Then sprinkle with cardamom. Roll up, starting at the 12-inch end, making a tight roll. With a sharp, floured knife, cut into 12 1-inch rolls and place them into buttered 9-inch pie plates. Cover with a tea towel and let rise in a warm place until almost doubled in bulk.

Bake the loaves in a preheated 350°F oven for 30 to 35 minutes, or until golden brown and loaves sound hollow when tapped on the bottoms. Bake the rolls for 25 minutes, or until they are golden brown.

Cool loaves on a wire rack. Cool rolls briefly in the pie plates and then turn them out onto a wire rack.

Most confusing to first-time bakers is the notion that the amount of flour given in a recipe is not exactly what is used. Day-to-day differences in temperature and humidity affect how well the flour absorbs the liquid ingredients. The resolution of this problem is simple: Just keep adding flour until the dough no longer sticks to your fingers.

Al Shanker

# Nancy Smith and Lauren Lakoff

*The Breads:*

**Carob Bread**
**Bagels**
**Spicy Banana Quick Bread**

*I frequently bake bread with my 16-year-old great-niece, Lauren. I guess you'd call us a family baking team. Lauren spent one and one-half years in the kitchen of The Caraway Restaurant, until the economy—not the food—did the place in. They served all natural foods there, and some of our breads were devised and baked at the restaurant.*

Nancy is a librarian who works in a public school in Philadelphia. She does calligraphy in her spare time, and she calls herself a "typical suburban middle class wife and mother." Lauren is still in high school, but she managed to get her recipes to me right on time in spite of final exams and a case of chicken pox.

Nancy's first baking experience was with Monkey Bread (page 207), a fairly complex bread for a new baker.

*The bread required three risings; consequently I devoted the entire afternoon to what I then thought was the "ultimate" baking experience. The bread was delightful to behold as it rose and it smelled divine. But when I took the loaf from the oven, cooled it slightly in the pan, and turned it out, I was appalled as the "balls," or "monkeys," scattered across the table. I never did figure out why they didn't stick together!*

# Carob Bread

(2 medium-size loaves)

This is another of the excellent breads that they once served at Lauren's now-defunct restaurant. They used a mixture of white and whole wheat flour, but the recipe below uses all whole wheat, getting the desired rise from a second tablespoon of yeast that was added. In this manner, we have at least saved a delicious souvenir of The Caraway Restaurant for posterity.

2 tablespoons dry yeast
1¾ cups warm water
3 tablespoons blackstrap molasses
2 tablespoons corn oil
½ cup honey
1½ cups raisins
3 tablespoons nonfat dry milk (non-instant)
3 tablespoons carob powder
½ teaspoon salt (optional, see page 22)
4 cups whole wheat flour melted butter for brushing loaves

In a small bowl, dissolve yeast in warm water and molasses and let stand for 15 minutes.

Pour yeast mixture into a large bowl. Add the oil, honey, and raisins.

In a medium-size bowl, mix together the nonfat dry milk, carob powder, salt, and flour. Then add mixture to the liquid ingredients. Stir well. If dough is too sticky, just add more flour.

Turn out onto a floured surface and knead for 8 to 10 minutes, or until dough is smooth and elastic. Shape into a ball, place into an oiled bowl, turn to coat, cover, and let rise in a warm spot until doubled in bulk, 1 to 1½ hours.

Punch dough down, turn out onto a floured surface, and shape into 2 loaves. Place into 2 buttered and floured 8½ × 4½-inch loaf pans. Brush tops with butter, cover, and let rise in a warm spot until almost doubled in bulk, 45 to 60 minutes.

Bake in a preheated 325°F oven for 50 to 60 minutes, or until the loaves test done.

Cool on a wire rack.

# Bagels

(about 15 bagels)

*Bagels:*
1 medium potato
2 cups water
1 tablespoon dry yeast
1 tablespoon honey
4 cups whole wheat flour
½ teaspoon salt (optional, see page 22)
1 egg
1 egg white
3 tablespoons vegetable oil
3 quarts water
1 tablespoon cream of tartar
2 tablespoons baking soda

*Glaze:*
1 egg yolk
1 teaspoon cold water
poppy seeds, chopped onions, or sesame seeds (optional)

Of all the breads in *Bread Winners,* the bagel recipe seemed to create the most interest as well as some of the most unusual problems. As I mentioned in my introduction, one caller complained that the bagels didn't stick together. (Wet your fingers thoroughly, I advised.) Nancy Smith first contacted me for another reason. *Her* bagels were fine until they hit the water, but when she took them out, they began to shrink. I suggested doing something that Sheryl and I had discovered when we wrote *Creative Cooking with Grains and Pasta:* Simply add 1 tablespoon cream of tartar and 2 tablespoons baking soda to the boiling water to prevent shrinkage of the dough. A letter came back in the next mail:

> *It was the most exhilarating experience to bake bagels again. Positively orgiastic—more suitably described in a magazine like* Playboy *than in a serious book about bread baking. The addition of cream of tartar and baking soda did prevent the shrinkage!*

Here is Nancy and Lauren's variation for bagels, including the use of the ingredients to prevent shrinkage.

To prepare the bagels: Peel potato and cut into fairly thick slices. Place the slices in a medium-size saucepan and cover with enough water to give you 2 cups of liquid after the potatoes are cooked. (Some water will evaporate during the cooking.) Boil potato slices until soft. Measure 1 cup potato water into a small bowl and set aside to cool to 90° to 100°F. Reserve potatoes for another use.

Dissolve yeast in the potato water. Add about ½ teaspoon honey and set aside to proof. Place flour into a large bowl. Stir in the proofed yeast mixture, salt, and egg. Add the egg white, the balance of the potato water, the remaining honey, and oil. Blend with the flour to make a firm, workable dough, adding more flour if the mixture is too sticky.

Turn out onto a floured surface and knead for 8 to 10 minutes, or until dough is smooth and elastic and springs back when touched. Place into an oiled bowl, turn to coat, cover, and let rise in a warm spot until doubled in bulk, 1 to 1½ hours.

The next step is what makes a bagel a bagel. Bring the 3 quarts of water to a boil in a large pot or kettle. Then add cream of tartar and baking soda.

Meanwhile punch dough down and knead for 1 to 2 minutes. Pull off or cut dough into 15 pieces. Roll each piece between floured hands until about 7 inches long and about ¾ inch thick. Coil each length into a ring, moistening your fingers before bringing the 2 ends together to form a circle. Don't be afraid to press down on the dough to make the circle. Put the rings on a buttered baking sheet and let them stand for about 10 minutes while the water begins to boil.

Using a slotted spoon, *slide* each bagel into the boiling water, being careful not to crowd them. They will float. Boil for 2 minutes on 1 side and then gently turn them over with the spoon to boil for 2 more minutes on the other side. Remove with the spoon and return them to the baking sheet. They will be slippery.

To prepare the glaze: In a cup, mix egg yolk with cold water and coat each bagel using a pastry brush. Sprinkle with the topping of your choice and bake in a preheated 425°F oven for 20 to 25 minutes, or until golden brown.

Place on wire racks to cool.

When making bagels, try adding honey to the boiling water to improve the glaze.
Stanley Halbreich

# Spicy Banana Quick Bread

(2 medium-size loaves)

2½ cups whole wheat flour
1½ teaspoons baking powder
2 teaspoons baking soda
½ teaspoon salt (optional, see page 22)
1½ teaspoons ground cinnamon
¾ teaspoon ground nutmeg
⅔ cup butter, melted
½ cup honey
2 eggs, beaten
⅔ cup buttermilk
1½ cups mashed bananas
1½ cups chopped walnuts
1½ cups raisins

In a large bowl, mix together the flour, baking powder, baking soda, salt, cinnamon, and nutmeg and set aside.

In a medium-size bowl, blend together the melted butter, honey, beaten eggs, buttermilk, and bananas and then add to the dry ingredients, mixing with a wooden spoon. Mix in walnuts and raisins, making sure they are well distributed throughout the dough. Pour into 2 well-buttered 8½ × 4½-inch loaf pans and bake in a preheated 350°F oven about 50 to 60 minutes, or until the loaves test done.

Cool on a wire rack.

If you don't have the size bread pans called for, just use any containers you can find—cake pans, coffee cans, ceramic bowls, even dessert custard cups.

Mel London

# Albert Sayers

*In my ministry, I saw myself working for Him who called Himself "The Bread of Life." And often, my love for bread making has been worked into my preaching and teaching. To make a point, I have pulled out a loaf of my bread while in the pulpit. When we were concerned about the problem of world hunger, I gave bread to be auctioned off. One time, three loaves I made brought in $37!*

Albert Sayers is a retired Episcopal clergyman who lives in Roseburg, Oregon, and I first came to know him after seeing his picture in a magazine, surrounded by his home-baked breads. Now, several telephone conversations and letters later, we are long-distance friends. Recently, he sent one of his breads to New York with a young friend, Sarah Paulson, who delivered it to me still fresh. His bread baking began back in 1938 when he served as a missionary to the Eskimos at Point Hope.

*If we were to have bread, we would have to do our own baking. The flour, yeast, salt, and all our other supplies had to be ordered a year at a time. Our water came from a river some miles away, brought to us by dog team in the form of blocks of ice. We had no central heating system and the failures we experienced in baking bread were due largely to the difficulty of keeping the rising dough warm enough. We baked in a coal-fueled cookstove. Our "deep freeze" was right outside our kitchen door!*

I've loved my contacts with Albert, and just recently he told me that he had finally built an out-of-doors oven from scrap materials—broken pieces of concrete, angle irons, flat rocks from along the river, and some used firebrick. To top it off, it was built without plans. Though it's a crude creation, the oven does turn out delicious hard-crust rolls and breads.

*The Bread:*

**Russian Easter Bread**

Albert's bread baking is a cooperative activity with his wife, Thelma. If he is called away for a visit to a hospital, for example, she finishes the loaves. From both of them, then, comes an unusual bread with a story attached, and a final verse from the Scriptures (Eccl. 9:7): "Go thy way, eat thy bread with joy"—to which, Albert adds, "True. But let's not forget the joy of baking the bread plus the joy of sharing it with others."

# Russian Easter Bread

(3 or 4 loaves)

*Bread:*
2 cups warm water
⅛ teaspoon salt (optional, see page 22)
¼ cup vegetable oil
2 eggs
⅓ cup honey
2 tablespoons dry yeast
5½ to 6 cups whole wheat flour
¼ cup grated orange rind
½ cup raisins

*Icing:*
3 ounces cream cheese, softened
1 tablespoon butter, softened
¼ cup maple syrup

*My Russian Easter Bread baking came out of my ministry in Alaska. While I called on an old Russian woman in a nursing home, she told me how much she missed her Russian Bread at Easter time and then proceeded to tell me how she made it. I was able to follow her recipe, and she was delighted when I brought a loaf to her. Since that time, we've baked the breads each year and given them to friends as a "thank you."*

The breads are baked in small tins, about four inches deep. Albert suggests that ten-ounce peanut tins are perfect for the job. The finished product represents the King's Crown. The traditional bread is made with white flour, but it can be done quite successfully with whole wheat. The grated orange rind replaces candied orange peel and makes for a zestier, less sweet bread.

The traditional icing uses confectioner's sugar diluted with milk or water, then sprinkled with colorful sugar decorations. We have adapted the icing. You can decorate your breads with strips of orange rind and/or walnuts.

To prepare the bread: In a large bowl, combine the warm water, salt, oil, and eggs and mix well. Then stir in honey. Add yeast and 2 cups of the flour. Either beat with a hand mixer for 3 to 5 minutes or stir vigorously with a wooden spoon until well blended. Cover and let rise in a warm spot until doubled in bulk, 45 to 60 minutes.

Stir dough down. Add the orange rind, raisins, and the remaining flour. Mix well.

Turn out onto a floured surface and knead for 8 to 10 minutes, adding more flour if necessary until dough is no longer sticky. Place into an oiled bowl, turn to coat, cover, and let rise in a warm spot until doubled in bulk, 45 to 60 minutes.

Punch dough down, turn out onto a floured surface, and form into 3 or 4 balls, each 3 to 4 inches in diameter. Let them rest a few moments and then place them into 3 or 4 well-buttered round tins. (As mentioned, the 10-ounce size peanut tins are perfect.) A ball of dough should half-fill a tin. Cover and let rise in a warm spot until dough comes over the top (the King's Crown).

Bake in a preheated 350°F oven for 25 minutes.

Cool loaves on wire racks before frosting and decorating.

To prepare the icing: In a small bowl, beat together all ingredients until smooth. Frost cooled loaves with icing.

If your bread bursts in the oven, you probably let the second rise go too long. Remember, breads will expand during baking.

Sheryl London

# Carol Zeimann

*The Breads:*

**Crusty Butter-Herb Bread
Heidelberg Pretzels
Mushroom Bread
Cheesy Casserole Bread
Garden Batter Bread
Country Casserole Bread
Maple Wheat Bread
(No-Knead)**

It is no accident that both *Bread Winners* and this sequel have a remarkable representation from the state of Missouri. One of my most enthusiastic supporters in both endeavors has been Barbara Gibbs Ostmann, food editor of the *St. Louis Post-Dispatch*. Not only did she supply one of the funniest "Salt-Rising Bread" stories in *Bread Winners*, but she also introduced me to Suzanne Corbett and her 24 superb and unusual recipes. Barbara has not disappointed me this time either, for both Carol Zeimann and Etta Taylor (see Index) are her original discoveries and have been the subjects of feature articles in the *Post-Dispatch*.

Carol, originally a native of Minnesota, who now lives in Chesterfield, Missouri, is a free-lance home economist. Most of her work involves teaching cooking and baking at the Pampered Pantry Cooking School and at the Dierberg Cooking Schools in the St. Louis area.

> *My husband, Lyle, is an engineer/supervisor for the Monsanto Company. He loves bread—an inherited trait—and I used my bread baking talent to win his heart when we were dating. The old expression, "The way to a man's heart is through his stomach," seemed worth investigating!*

Carol and Lyle have two sons, Mike (six) and Matt (four), both of whom love playing with the dough, even eating it raw. At those tender ages, they already have their own set of kitchen utensils so they can pound, roll, and cut the dough as soon as Carol begins her baking. Though she is an experienced, professional baker, Carol still feels the way most of us do about making bread:

I think it's one of the most rewarding of culinary arts. I tell my students that they should make bread whenever they feel depressed or angry or unhappy about something. They can knead out all their frustrations and anger. Then when the dough bakes, it smells so good! (Few other aromas are so universally enjoyed.) Everyone gets happy and mellow. By the time the bread is served, even if it isn't the very best, it's a slice of heaven to those who receive it, and the baker is admired as a bit of a genius. No one can feel depressed after that!

# Crusty Butter-Herb Bread

(4 loaves)

*Bread:*
2 tablespoons dry yeast
2 cups warm water
2 teaspoons honey
¼ cup vegetable oil
2 teaspoons salt (optional, see page 22)
6 cups whole wheat flour

*Butter-Herb Filling:*
2 cloves garlic, minced
1 tablespoon grated onions
½ cup butter
½ teaspoon dried basil
½ teaspoon caraway seeds
¼ teaspoon dried oregano
⅛ teaspoon cayenne pepper
cornmeal for dusting pans
1 egg, beaten, for brushing loaves

To prepare the bread: In a large bowl, dissolve yeast in warm water. Stir in honey and then add the oil, salt, and 2 cups of the flour. Beat until smooth, about 3 minutes. Add enough remaining flour to form a soft dough.

Turn out onto a floured surface and knead until smooth and elastic, about 8 to 10 minutes. If dough is too sticky, add more flour. Place into an oiled bowl, turn to coat, cover, and let rise in a warm spot until doubled in bulk, 1 to 1½ hours.

To prepare the filling: While dough is rising, make the Herb-Butter Filling by combining all ingredients in a small bowl and mixing until well blended. Set aside.

Punch dough down, turn out onto a floured surface, and divide into 2 portions. Roll each portion into a 10 by 16-inch rectangle. Spread half of the Herb-Butter Filling on each rectangle, allowing a ½-inch margin on all sides.

Divide each portion in half to form 4 10 × 8-inch rectangles. Roll up each rectangle, beginning with the newly cut edge. Pinch and seal ends and seams. Place seam-side down in French bread pans which have been buttered and then sprinkled with cornmeal. Slash tops and let rise, loosely covered in a warm spot, until doubled in bulk, about 1 hour.

Brush tops of loaves with beaten egg. Bake in a preheated 425°F oven for 25 minutes. Remove from pans, turn loaves over, and return to oven (upside down in pans) for 5 minutes more.

Remove and cool on wire racks. Serve warm.

To steam the oven for a crisp crust, I use a plastic spray bottle filled with water.

Frank Howard

These are great fun to make. They should be served warm, since they become stale very quickly. In Heidelberg, white flour is traditionally used, but the whole wheat version is excellent.

Heat water in a small saucepan until warm (about 110°F). Then add yeast and molasses, stirring to dissolve. Pour mixture into a large bowl. Add the rye flour, caraway seeds, and salt and stir until smooth. Gradually add enough whole wheat flour to make a stiff dough.

Turn out onto a floured surface and knead until smooth, about 5 minutes. Place into a lightly oiled bowl, cover, and let rise in a warm place for 30 minutes.

Punch dough down, turn out onto a floured surface, and divide into 24 golf-ball-size pieces. Roll each piece into a rope about 15 inches long. Make a loop by picking up the ends and crossing them and then crossing the ends again to form a twist. Bring the ends over and down and press against the loop. Place on buttered baking sheets and brush with beaten egg. Bake in a preheated 450°F oven for 12 to 15 minutes. Serve warm.

# Heidelberg Pretzels

(24 pretzels)

1½ cups water
 1 tablespoon dry yeast
 1 tablespoon molasses
 3 cups rye flour
1½ teaspoons caraway seeds
 ½ teaspoon salt (optional, see page 22)
 1 to 2 cups whole wheat flour
 1 egg, beaten

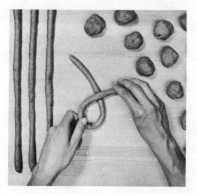
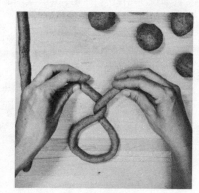

# Mushroom Bread

(2 medium-size loaves or 3 mushroom-shaped loaves)

2 tablespoons butter
¼ pound fresh mushrooms, minced
½ cup chopped onions
2 teaspoons salt (optional, see page 22)
¼ teaspoon black pepper
1 tablespoon dry yeast
¼ cup warm water
⅓ cup nonfat dry milk
2 tablespoons vegetable oil
2 tablespoons molasses
1 egg
½ cup toasted wheat germ
4½ to 5 cups whole wheat flour
1 egg, beaten with 1 tablespoon water

This is a bread that not only includes mushrooms as an ingredient, but it also can be baked in a mushroom shape. It can be baked in a standard loaf pan as well. The "bread-mushrooms" are perfect for dinner parties or for children's birthday celebrations. Both methods are described by Carol in the recipe that follows.

Combine the butter, mushrooms, onions, 1 teaspoon salt, and pepper in a medium-size skillet and sauté until onions are tender and the liquid has evaporated. Set aside to cool.

In a large bowl, dissolve yeast in warm water and set aside.

In a small saucepan, combine nonfat dry milk with enough water to make 1 cup liquid. Add oil and molasses to milk and heat until warm (about 110°F). Add to yeast mixture along with the remaining salt, egg, wheat germ, and 2 cups of the flour. Beat until smooth, about 2 minutes. Stir in the mushroom mixture and then enough of the remaining flour to make a workable dough.

Turn dough out onto a floured surface and knead until smooth, about 8 to 10 minutes. Place into an oiled bowl, turn to coat, cover, and let rise in a warm spot until doubled in bulk, 1 to 1¼ hours.

Punch dough down, turn out onto a floured surface, and shape into 2 loaves. Place each loaf into a well-buttered 8½ × 4½-inch loaf pan. Cover and let rise in a warm spot until almost doubled in bulk, about 1 hour.

Brush with egg/water wash and bake in a preheated 375°F oven for 30 to 40 minutes, or until loaves test done.

Cool on wire racks.

## To Bake Mushroom Shapes

Thoroughly butter a 1-pound fruit can and 2 soup cans (or other cans of similar size). Leave the bottoms intact. Then, using a heavy cardboard, cut 3 squares, each one 2 to 3 inches wider than the openings of the cans. Trace the can opening in the center of each square and cut out with scissors. Discard the circles, leaving 3 "collars" that will fit around the tops of the cans. Cover the cardboard rings with aluminum foil and place over cans so that they fit tightly around the openings. Butter the foil on top.

After the dough has risen, punch down and divide into 1 large piece and 2 smaller pieces. Shape each one into an oval and place into cans. Let rise, loosely covered, in a warm spot until doubled in bulk, 30 to 45 minutes.

The dough should come over the tops of the cans. With your fingertips, gently reshape the mushroom caps by pressing the lower edge of the caps down to meet the foil collars. Brush caps with egg/water mixture and bake in a preheated 375°F oven for 35 to 40 minutes.

To serve, slice crosswise into round slices.

This is a very easy bread for beginning bakers because it doesn't require kneading, shaping, or more than one rising. It's very attractive and it's great with soups or salads.

To prepare the bread: In a large bowl, dissolve yeast in warm water. Add honey and let stand 5 minutes.

In a small bowl, combine nonfat dry milk with enough water to make ¾ cup liquid. Then add the milk, 1½ cups of the flour, egg, softened butter, and salt to yeast mixture. Beat on high speed of mixer for 2 to 3 minutes, or until very smooth. Add cheese and enough of the remaining flour to form a soft dough. Turn dough into a buttered 2-quart casserole that has been sprinkled with cornmeal. Cover and let bread rise until doubled in bulk, 1 to 1¼ hours.

To prepare the topping: Combine all ingredients and spoon mixture over surface of loaf. Bake in a preheated 375°F oven for 35 to 40 minutes. Loosely cover loaf with foil during last 10 minutes of baking time if crust becomes too brown.

# Cheesy Casserole Bread

(1 loaf)

*Bread:*
  1 tablespoon dry yeast
  ¼ cup warm water
  1 tablespoon honey
  ⅓ cup nonfat dry milk
  2½ to 3½ cups whole wheat flour
  1 egg
  2 tablespoons butter, softened
  ½ teaspoon salt (optional, see page 22)
  ½ cup shredded sharp cheddar cheese
    cornmeal for dusting casserole

*Topping:*
  ½ cup shredded sharp cheddar cheese
  1 tablespoon cornmeal
  ½ teaspoon dry mustard
  ½ teaspoon sesame or poppy seeds
  1 tablespoon milk
  1 egg

# Garden Batter Bread

(1 loaf)

1 tablespoon dry yeast
¼ cup warm water
1 cup cold water
¼ cup molasses
2 tablespoons vegetable oil
½ teaspoon salt (optional, see page 22)
1 egg
3 cups whole wheat flour
1 cup toasted wheat germ
1 cup coarsely grated carrots
¼ cup minced fresh parsley
melted butter for brushing loaf

This is a quick, no-knead batter bread that tastes best when served warm with soups or salads.

In a large bowl, dissolve yeast in warm water and set aside.

Heat the cold water, molasses, and oil in a small saucepan until warm (about 110°F). Add to yeast mixture along with the salt, egg, and 2 cups of the flour. Beat until smooth, about 3 minutes. Add the wheat germ, carrots, and parsley and mix well. Gradually add the remaining flour and mix until well blended. Turn batter into a buttered 1½- to 2-quart casserole or soufflé dish. Cover and let rise in a warm place until doubled in bulk, 45 to 60 minutes.

Bake in a preheated 350°F oven for 50 to 60 minutes. Cover with foil near the end of the baking time if crust becomes too brown.

Brush crust with melted butter when bread comes out of the oven.

Get the children involved in your baking. They love helping to add the flour, stir the dough, or make dough figures and faces.

Andrea Brazer-Rush

In a large mixing bowl, dissolve yeast in warm water and set aside.

Heat the cold water, molasses, and butter in a small saucepan until warm (about 110°F). Add to yeast mixture along with 2 cups of the flour, salt, and egg. Beat until smooth, about 3 minutes. Beat in the remaining flour, and then stir in the granola and raisins or currants. Turn batter into a buttered 1½-quart casserole or soufflé dish. Cover and let rise in a warm place until doubled in bulk, 45 to 60 minutes.

Bake in a preheated 375°F oven for 50 to 60 minutes, or until loaf sounds hollow when tapped. Cover loaf with foil during the last 10 to 15 minutes of baking time if crust becomes too brown.

# Country Casserole Bread

(1 loaf)

1 tablespoon dry yeast
¼ cup warm water
1 cup cold water
3 tablespoons molasses
2 tablespoons butter
3 cups whole wheat flour
½ teaspoon salt (optional, see page 22)
1 egg
1 cup granola
½ cup raisins or currants

In a large bowl, dissolve yeast in warm water and set aside.

Heat the cold water, maple syrup, and butter in a small saucepan until warm (about 110°F). Add to yeast mixture along with the salt, 2 cups flour, and egg. Beat until smooth, about 3 minutes. Gradually add enough of the remaining flour to form a stiff batter. Cover and let rise in a warm place until doubled in bulk, 45 to 60 minutes.

Stir batter down and turn into a buttered 1-quart casserole or soufflé dish. Bake in a preheated 375°F oven for 40 to 50 minutes, or until loaf sounds hollow when tapped.

# Maple Wheat Bread (No-Knead)

(1 loaf)

1 tablespoon dry yeast
¼ cup warm water
1 cup cold water
⅓ cup maple syrup
2 tablespoons butter
½ teaspoon salt (optional, see page 22)
3 to 4½ cups whole wheat flour
1 egg

# Gage Walldren

*The Bread:*

**Whole Wheat Malt Bread**

Gage Walldren's letter postmarked "Crystal Falls, Michigan," arrived soon after *Bread Winners* was published. It told of a useful bread ingredient that was new to me.

> *I was and am surprised that your great book did not include at least* one *recipe using diastatic malt. As one who is interested in nutrition, I believe that any opportunity to eliminate sugar should be snapped up and used.*

I answered Gage quickly and asked him to send me the information about diastatic malt, feeling that I might write a sequel to *Bread Winners* one day. With his next letter, he included not only a recipe, but also complete instructions on how to make and use diastatic malt. The rest of this section is his.

> *Diastatic malt, despite its imposing name, is simply sprouted wheat or barley and is incredibly easy to produce. I have used both wheat and barley, but my wife, Sophie, prefers the taste of wheat malt.*

# How to Prepare Diastatic Malt

Place 1 cup wheat berries or unpearled barley into a 5-cup (or larger) jar, cover with tepid water, and let stand for 12 hours. Drain and save the water for soup or bread. Once they have been soaked, the grains must be rinsed and drained about 3 times a day to prevent molding. The sprouting takes about 2 days. When the rootlets are as long as the grain kernels, it is time to spread them on a baking sheet to dry. (I place mine in a warm gas oven overnight, with only the pilot light on.) Then finely grind the grains in a food mill or a powerful blender. (I use a Norelco coffee grinder, and it works quite well.) The malt should then be refrigerated in a tightly covered jar. One cup is sufficient for 150 loaves of bread! I use 1 teaspoonful for 4 loaves. Using more will only overpower the yeast and produce a sticky mess. The malt replaces any sweetener used in bread baking, such as sugar, molasses, honey, or sorghum.

Gage added in his letter that more than 90 percent of all European bread is made with diastatic malt. And, though the recipe that follows uses whole wheat flour, Gage notes, "I do occasionally use white flour—but I fortify it with bran, wheat germ, and lecithin!"

# Whole Wheat Malt Bread

(4 medium-size loaves)

5½ cups lukewarm water
4 tablespoons dry yeast
½ cup vegetable oil
1 teaspoon Diastatic Malt (see preceding recipe)
2 teaspoons salt (optional, see page 22)
¼ cup lecithin liquid (optional)
¾ cup whey powder or nonfat dry milk
13 to 14 cups whole wheat flour

Place all the ingredients plus 6 cups of the flour into a large bowl and beat with an electric mixer until smooth. Then stir in the remaining 7 to 8 cups flour, 1 cup at a time, until you have a workable batter.

Turn out onto a floured surface and knead for 10 to 15 minutes. Place into an oiled bowl, turn to coat, and let rise in a warm spot until doubled in bulk, about 1 hour.

Punch dough down, turn out onto a floured surface, and return to bowl. Cover and let rise again in a warm spot for 45 to 60 minutes, or until almost doubled in bulk.

Punch dough down, turn out onto a floured surface, and knead for 2 to 3 minutes. Shape into 4 loaves. Place into 4 8½ × 4½-inch loaf pans and let rise in a warm spot until dough is not more than 3½ inches in height, 20 to 30 minutes.

Bake in a preheated 350°F oven for 35 to 40 minutes, or until the loaves test done.

Remove from pans and cool on wire racks. Try to keep from eating the entire batch while it is still warm and tempting!

# Etta Taylor

*The Unleavened Breads and Crackers:*

**Honey Graham Crackers**
**Sourdough Dill Crackers**
**Whole Wheat Crackers**
**Buckwheat Crackers**
**Rice Crackers**
**Matzohs**
**Cornmeal Puffs**

Etta is another of the remarkable bread bakers that I've discovered through Barbara Gibbs Ostmann, the food editor of the *St. Louis Post-Dispatch* (see Index for recipes by Carol Zeimann). In fact, Etta is represented by *two* sections in this new book (see "Sourdough Serendipity," page 232), since both are so entirely different. She labels herself a "professional volunteer," though she is too modest. Trained as a medical historian and holding an M.A. in art history, Etta worked in the education department of the St. Louis Museum before and during her early years of marriage to Ted, a lawyer. She and Ted have three children, now 24, 22, and 20.

*All bake bread except the youngest, who is no slouch at eating it, however. Ted just began baking this past year when I developed "bread elbow" after baking some 60 loaves of French bread in three days!*

Etta gives bread baking demonstrations and classes in the St. Louis area, but I am particularly impressed with the reasons behind them.

*Since 1977, I've been active with our (Episcopal) Diocesan Hunger Task Force. We're actively engaged in learning about and doing something about hunger in the St. Louis metropolitan area. Fees charged for my bread baking sessions are turned over to the Diocesan Hunger Fund and used to buy food to stock the emergency centers. Along with bread baking techniques and information, my pupils are given a few world hunger statistics and they're told about the nutritional value of whole grains and the theory behind complementary proteins.*

This part of Etta's contribution to *Bread Winners Too,* deals with unleavened bread and crackers. I have "stolen" the title from Barbara Ostmann's excellent article in the *St. Louis Post-Dispatch* (April 29, 1980)—with permission, of course.

# Going Crackers

Etta claims, correctly, that unleavened bread came before leavened bread, and that there is an unleavened bread in every culture throughout history. She also points out that unleavened bread is not always a cracker, since crackers generally use some shortening. But whatever the genealogy of crackers, you'll find that most bread books and food articles are devoted almost entirely to yeast breads and quick breads, with very little time given to the simple process of making these delicious tidbits and snacks.

*Crackers are so easy. You can whip them up in no time, and they're economical to make. They're better tasting and more nutritious than the store-bought varieties. I find that, just as with bread, there are no commercial crackers that even taste good any more! They are either too salty, or have too many preservatives—or have no nutritional value whatsoever.*

The directions for baking crackers are simple. They call for little or no kneading, and the steps are quick and easy—mixing, rolling out the dough, cutting into shapes, and pricking. Etta describes the techniques as almost like working with "play dough."

• *The pricking is done to prevent air bubbles from forming. Prick the crackers with a fork or with a wooden meat mallet, first dipping the mallet in flour to prevent sticking.*

• *Bake crackers on a day when humidity is low, if possible.*

• *Store crackers in an airtight container. They'll keep for a week or two, if you can keep the kids from devouring them before that time.*

Crackers are great for snacks, helping to fight afternoon "letdown," for parties, served with dips or spreads, or for camping trips. And, above all, Etta says, "Why spend $1.09 for a box of crackers that you can make yourself in *15 minutes?*"

Some of the recipes that we've included here were originally made with some unbleached flour. They all converted easily to whole wheat flour; since they are unleavened, there's no need to worry about the rise.

# Honey Graham Crackers

*(24 crackers)*

*Crackers:*
3 cups whole wheat flour
1 teaspoon baking powder
½ teaspoon baking soda
½ cup butter
⅓ cup plus 3 tablespoons honey
1 teaspoon vanilla extract
½ cup milk

*Glaze (optional):*
3 tablespoons honey
1 teaspoon ground cinnamon

This recipe is a variation of the one that was listed among the top ten recipes for 1981 in the *Post-Dispatch* food section. Barbara Ostmann commented that they were so good that it was hard to stop eating them. Etta mentions that she usually chills the dough overnight to make it easier to handle. Here, then, is a monument to that pioneer of milling, Sylvester Graham, and the flour that carries his name.

To prepare the crackers: In a medium-size bowl, stir together the whole wheat flour, baking powder, and baking soda.

Cream together butter and 3 tablespoons honey in a large bowl and beat until smooth. Add ⅓ cup honey and vanilla and beat until fluffy. Add flour mixture to creamed mixture alternately with milk, beating well after each addition. Chill dough several hours or overnight.

Divide chilled dough into quarters. On a well-floured surface, roll each quarter into a 5 by 15-inch rectangle. Cut each rectangle crosswise into smaller rectangles measuring 5 by 2½ inches and place them on an ungreased baking sheet. Mark a line at the center of each rectangle and score a pattern of holes on each half with a fork or a floured meat mallet.

To prepare the glaze, if desired: In a cup, combine 3 tablespoons honey and cinnamon and spread lightly over the crackers. Bake in a preheated 350°F oven for 13 to 15 minutes.

Remove from baking sheet and cool.

See the section that I've called "Sourdough Serendipity" if you do not already have a sourdough starter bubbling in your kitchen.

Place the flour, salt, and dill into a large bowl. Cut in butter with a pastry blender or 2 knives until mixture resembles coarse cornmeal. Stir in sourdough starter. The dough should be firm enough to hold together.

Turn dough out onto a floured surface and roll out to a thickness of about ⅛ inch. Cut into squares, circles, ovals, or diamonds and place on lightly oiled baking sheets. Prick with a fork and bake in a preheated 375°F oven for 10 to 15 minutes, or until light brown in color.

In a large bowl, stir together the flour, honey, baking powder, baking soda, cream of tartar, and salt. Cut in butter with a pastry blender or 2 knives until the mixture looks like coarse crumbs. Add buttermilk all at once and stir with a fork just until dough follows fork around the bowl.

Turn dough out onto a floured surface, roll out to a thickness of ¹⁄₁₆ inch, and cut into shapes with a 2½-inch biscuit cutter. Place on ungreased baking sheets, prick with a fork, and bake in a preheated 350°F oven for 12 to 15 minutes, or until lightly browned.

# Sourdough Dill Crackers

(about 10 dozen crackers)

2 cups whole wheat flour
1 teaspoon salt (optional, see page 22)
1 teaspoon dried dillweed
½ cup butter
1 cup sourdough starter, room temperature

# Whole Wheat Crackers

(about 6 dozen crackers)

2 cups whole wheat flour
3 tablespoons honey
2 teaspoons baking powder
1 teaspoon baking soda
½ teaspoon cream of tartar
½ teaspoon salt (optional, see page 22)
½ cup butter
¾ cup buttermilk

# Buckwheat Crackers

(8 large crackers)

1 cup buckwheat flour
1 cup whole wheat flour
¼ teaspoon baking soda
¼ teaspoon salt (optional, see page 22)
¼ cup sesame seeds
¼ cup mayonnaise (do not use salad dressing)
½ cup yogurt
1 tablespoon honey

If you can't get buckwheat flour in your local supermarket or natural foods store, refer to the list of mail-order sources at the back of the book for information on how to order it.

In a medium-size bowl, stir together the buckwheat flour, whole wheat flour, baking soda, salt, and sesame seeds. With a pastry blender or 2 knives, cut in mayonnaise until mixture is well blended and resembles coarse crumbs. With a fork, stir in yogurt and honey. Then, using your hands, firmly press the dough into a ball and cut it into 8 equal pieces.

On a prepared pastry cloth, using a stockinet-covered rolling pin, roll out each piece to a thickness of about ¹⁄₁₆ inch. Each piece will be an uneven 8-inch round. Place them on an ungreased baking sheet and bake in a preheated 400°F oven until lightly browned, 6 to 8 minutes.

Using a wide metal spatula, remove the crackers to a wire rack for cooling. Store in a tightly covered container. If you wish, break the large crackers into smaller pieces before serving.

# Rice Crackers

(8 to 10 dozen crackers)

2 cups cooked brown rice
2 cups whole wheat flour
1 teaspoon salt (optional, see page 22)
¼ cup vegetable oil
½ cup water (approximate)
1 egg, slightly beaten with 1 tablespoon water

These easy-to-make crackers can be rolled right out on a lightly oiled baking sheet before they are cut and baked.

In a large bowl, stir together the cooked rice, flour, and salt with a fork. Add oil and stir thoroughly. Add water slowly until dough comes together in a moist, but not sticky, ball. Roll out on lightly oiled baking sheets until very thin. Brush with egg beaten with water and cut into squares with pastry cutter, pizza cutter, or sharp knife. Place in a preheated 425°F oven and immediately reduce the temperature to 350°F. Check after 20 minutes. If edges of crackers are crisp and dry, turn off heat and let crackers dry a little longer. If edges are not dry, bake about 5 minutes longer, then turn off heat, and let dry.

After baking, let crackers dry thoroughly on wire racks. Store in an airtight container.

Matzohs are the unleavened breads eaten by the Jews on the exodus from Egypt, and they are still eaten at Passover. After writing *Bread Winners,* it occurred to me that I might want to make a visit to New York's Lower East Side at the time of the Passover holiday, in order to watch the bakers make the traditional, perforated, crisp, flatbreads. Now that Etta Taylor has come my way, I have saved the trip—and besides, these are homemade.

In a medium-size bowl, mix flour with enough warm water to form a cohesive ball. It may be more than the ¾ cup called for or it may be less. Turn dough out onto a floured surface and knead for about 5 minutes, or until very smooth. Cover dough with a damp cloth and let rest for about 30 minutes.

On a floured surface, form the dough into a cylindrical roll about 18 inches long. Cut into 10 pieces. Roll each piece into a large, very thin wafer. When all are rolled, cover with a damp cloth and let rest for about 10 minutes.

Prick each one several times with a fork and then transfer to an ungreased baking sheet. (Commercially baked matzohs have very even and precisely perforated lines of punctures.) Bake 4 matzohs at a time in a preheated 475°F oven for 3 to 4 minutes on each side. Watch carefully to prevent burning.

Cool on wire racks.

These are great for snacks and/or appetizers, and like all the other recipes in Etta's section, they're very easy to make.

Place cornmeal and salt in a medium-size bowl. Add boiling water and stir well. Fold in beaten egg whites. Drop by the teaspoonful onto an oiled baking sheet and bake in a preheated 350°F oven for 20 to 25 minutes.

## Variation:

Add ¼ cup grated Parmesan or Romano cheese to mixture.

# Matzohs

(10 pieces)

2 cups whole wheat flour
¾ cup warm water
   (approximate)

# Cornmeal Puffs

(24 puffs)

½ cup stone-ground
   cornmeal
½ teaspoon salt (optional, see
   page 22)
½ cup boiling water
2 egg whites, stiffly beaten

# Paul Walsky

*The Breads:*

*Pain Complet*
*Challah*

One of my oldest and dearest friends, Eve Gentry, lives in Santa Fe, and I can always depend upon her to keep me informed of the goings-on down in New Mexico. For *Bread Winners*, she suggested several of the bakers who eventually appeared in print. She did not disappoint me when I told her that I was contemplating a sequel to the first book. By return mail, I learned about another talented bread baker in her area:

> *May I suggest my friend, Dr. Paul Walsky, a neurologist. His wife is a former dancer, a great beauty, named Nurit, born in South America, brought up in Israel. Fond friends. He acts in community theatre here. Recently did* Of Mice and Men. *A beautiful and sensitive job!*

Paul and I have been in touch ever since, and his favorite recipes are included here. When I asked him about his deepest feelings when he bakes bread, and serves the warm loaves to his family and friends, he answered:

> *From the way the question was phrased, I can see that you understand the joy from which the Hebrew word "nachas" comes—the simple deep joys from life's basic treasures: children, family, the baking of bread. My wife's face radiates when the loaves come from the oven. Our daughter, Oryan, is three years old, and I love to bring her into the process, show her the dough, have her touch it. And, when I bring the loaves to the table, Oryan says proudly, "Daddy made the bread!"*

Paul is a baker who uses a food processor for the initial mixing of the dough, but he does the final kneading by hand.

These are a variation on the traditional French loaves, and they're made with whole wheat flour. When you use white flour to make these breads, they become *baguettes,* with a slightly different texture and flavor. Some bakers raise the oven temperature as high as 400°F, or even hotter, in order to obtain a crusty loaf.

*The French bread is a delightful gift when we're invited to dinner, and it's a pleasure to serve to guests when they come to our house.*

Place the warm water, honey, and salt into food processor fitted with steel blade. Sprinkle yeast over water and honey mixture and let stand a few minutes to allow yeast to soften. Add about 2 cups flour and process by On/Off method until just combined. Continue to add flour, 1 cup at a time, processing by On/Off method, until dough is sticky and just firm enough to remove from the bowl.

Turn out onto a floured surface and knead the rest of the flour into the dough until it is smooth and elastic, 8 to 10 minutes. Place into a well-oiled bowl, turn to coat, cover, and let rise in a warm spot until doubled in bulk, about 1 hour.

Punch dough down, turn out onto a floured surface, knead a few times, and divide into 4 pieces. Roll each piece into an 18 by 5-inch rectangle with a thickness of ⅜ inch and roll up, jelly-roll fashion, into French loaves. Place on oiled baking sheets or in French loaf pans, slash tops obliquely, and brush with egg whites. Sprinkle with sesame seeds, if used. Cover and let rise in a warm spot until almost doubled in bulk, about 45 minutes. Bake in a preheated 350°F oven for 20 to 30 minutes, or until loaves are golden brown and sound hollow when tapped on the bottoms.

Cool on wire racks.

Note: These loaves freeze quite well. Simply cool and then wrap in heavy-duty aluminum foil before placing in freezer.

# Pain Complet

(4 long loaves)

2½ cups warm water
2 tablespoons honey
1 teaspoon salt (optional, see page 22)
1 tablespoon dry yeast
4 to 5 cups whole wheat flour
2 egg whites, well beaten, for brushing loaves
sesame seeds for topping (optional)

# Challah

(1 large loaf)

*Bread:*
1¾ cups warm water
2 tablespoons dry yeast
½ cup honey
¼ cup butter, melted
½ teaspoon salt (optional, see page 22)
4 eggs, beaten
7 to 8 cups unbleached white flour
melted butter for brushing loaf

*Glaze:*
1 egg yolk
1 tablespoon water
poppy seeds

*This challah is a very rich one and it always brings a great deal of pleasure. Not long ago, we were invited to the home of very good friends, and were accompanied by my mother-in-law who was visiting with us from Israel. Our hosts served some of the* challah *I had baked—and my mother-in-law was in a state of disbelief that I actually did it myself.*

To prepare the bread: Pour warm water into food processor fitted with steel blade. Sprinkle yeast over water and process with one brief burst to help dissolve yeast. (The entire recipe can be made using a standard mixing bowl and wooden spoon, if you like.) Add the honey, melted butter, salt, and beaten eggs and process again briefly. Add 2 cups flour and process by the On/Off method until just combined. Continue to add flour, 1 cup at a time, until dough is sticky and just firm enough to remove from the bowl.

Turn out onto a floured surface and knead in the rest of the flour until dough is smooth and elastic. The entire amount of flour (about 7 cups minimum) will probably be used, since the braiding will be more successful if the dough is on the firm side. Place dough into an oiled bowl, turn to coat, cover, and let rise in a warm spot until doubled in bulk, about 1 hour.

Punch dough down, turn out onto a floured surface, and knead a few times until smooth and elastic. The following instructions are for 1 very large loaf. If you prefer 2 medium-size loaves, just divide dough in half and proceed with each half as described. Take about two-thirds of the dough and divide into thirds. With your fingers, moving from the center of each third out toward the ends, roll dough into 3 18-inch lengths (shorter if you are doing 2 loaves). Pinch the 3 lengths together firmly at one end and braid a tight braid. Place on an oiled baking sheet. Cut the remaining third of the dough into 3 equal parts. Roll out, making them shorter and thinner than the first ropes. Braid them into a firm braid and place on top of the first braid. Brush with melted butter. Cover lightly and let rise in a warm spot until almost doubled in bulk, about 45 minutes.

To prepare the glaze: In a cup, beat together egg yolk and water and then brush over loaf. Sprinkle with poppy seeds and bake in a preheated 350°F oven for about 45 minutes, or until loaf is a rich brown.

Cool on wire rack.

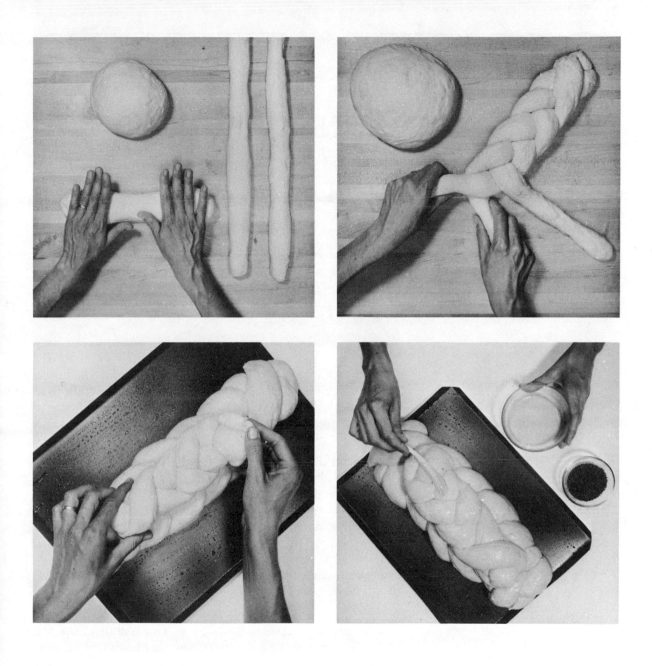

# BAKING BREAD AT VIOLI'S

When we work as filmmakers in America's cities and towns, the evening meal is the best way that we can unwind, tell "war stories" about our previous motion picture experiences, and most of all, get to know the local people. The custom is common among film crews.

A few years ago, we were working near the Canadian border, in Massena, New York, on a film for the Aluminum Company of America. We had scheduled about a week in the area. At the end of the day we generally had our dinner at the town's best restaurant, Violi's, where we soon became friends with the owners, Dominic, Ross, and Sue.

About the third evening, the discussion departed from the usual subject of motion pictures and turned to bread. We all agreed that most commercial breads served in restaurants were pale examples of what might be achieved for hungry diners. Egged on by my film crew, and in a jolly mood, I offered to bake bread for *the entire restaurant* the very next evening, if Dominic would supply the whole grain flour, the large kitchen ovens, and an occasional glass of white wine to keep the chef's throat from becoming too parched. He agreed.

The photographs show the results. I went right to the restaurant after work, and by dinner time we had baskets of Irish Brown Bread (page 41) on every table. I don't know how many loaves were baked, for I lost count after the first dozen, but the results of my efforts were devoured almost as quickly as the baskets of hot, crusty bread could be brought to the tables.

For me, the best part was baking in a commercial oven, where the temperatures were constant and reliable, quite unlike my Fire Island oven. By the end of the night I felt weary, but I had a glowing sense of achievement and some pride. The experience made Massena a very special place for me.

There was one additional bonus that came from the trip. The public relations manager at the ALCOA plant, Maggie Greenwood, turned out to be a bread baker in her spare time. Her story follows.

# Maggie Greenwood

*The Breads:*

**Trail Bread**
**Raisin Whole Wheat Bread**

It is not at all unusual for me to discover another bread baker while on my film trips. I smile each time I hear the words, "Oh, I bake bread too!" as I did from Maggie Greenwood. After the filming at Massena was completed, Maggie and I kept in touch with one another. She is now in Newburgh, Indiana, as the communications manager for the Aluminum Company of America, and her responsibilities include employee communications for a work force of 3,600 people, plus community and press relations. In addition, she's a downhill skier, a writer of fiction, a collector of antique dolls, and a bodybuilder. It's remarkable that she manages to bake bread too.

*I had my first experiences with baking bread at the age of ten, watching my favorite great aunt—her name was Aunt Mame—bake her beautiful breads. But, I started baking my own bread in graduate school at West Virginia University, while studying journalism.*

Like so many of us, Maggie likes to experiment, doing her own "enriching" with bran, molasses, wheat germ, and raisins.

*Though I like heavier breads—they taste and feel more nutritious to me, and I find that I eat less that way—my first breads were too heavy. I once tried baking bread with raw wheat germ, because it's a live, vitamin-rich food. The loaves would have been great cemented into a patio! I've learned to use toasted wheat germ or to simmer the raw germ in milk before using it in my breads.*

She has never been able to follow a recipe word for word, very much like our grandmothers, who baked with approximate amounts.

> *I put ingredients together just as I put characters together when I write, and I ask myself the question, "What makes the most unique, healthy blend?" I used to do my creative cooking with desserts, but now with my interest in body-building and nutrition, I do my concocting with natural ingredients. Adios to desserts!*

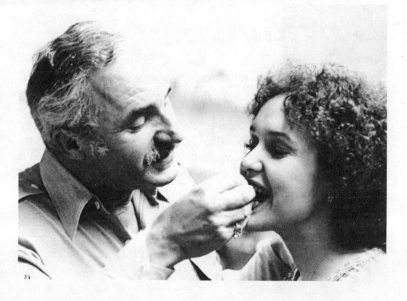

# Trail Bread

(1 medium-size loaf)

1½ cups whole wheat flour
1 teaspoon baking powder
1 teaspoon baking soda
1½ cups bran
1 cup hot water
¼ cup butter
1 cup maple syrup
2 eggs
1½ cups trail mix (about 2
    4-ounce packages)

Just as I bake breads for Christmas gifts, Maggie also bakes for holiday giving, generally using her own original recipes.

*I create recipes with my friends in mind and they do appreciate it. This Trail Bread, while not a yeast bread, is very popular, especially for camping and hiking. It's a meal by itself, but it's even better with some peanut butter between the slices. Maybe I should call it "Energy Bread" because that's exactly what it gives you.*

Maggie uses a packaged trail mix, made without preservatives or additives. There are several good ones on the market—combinations of sunflower seeds, pumpkin seeds, dry roasted peanuts and soybeans, raw cashew pieces, and raisins and other dried fruits.

In a small bowl, stir together the flour, baking powder, and baking soda.

In a large bowl, combine the bran, hot water, butter, and syrup. Mix until butter melts. Add eggs and beat well. Add the dry ingredients and stir until moistened. Stir in trail mix. Pour batter into a buttered 8½ × 4½-inch loaf pan and bake in a preheated 375°F oven for 1¼ to 1½ hours. If top becomes too brown, cover with foil after 1 hour.

Cool on a rack before slicing.

Note: "Trail mix" is one of those all-encompassing descriptions that includes a wide variety of seed/nut/dried fruit mixtures originally developed by hikers and campers to nibble on the march and climb. I always keep a package in my travel kit to make up for the low level of airline catering, and I buy it at my local sporting goods store or natural foods store. However, you can make your own trail mix by simply blending any of the following in the combination of your choice: sunflower seeds, raisins, sliced dried prunes or apricots, slivered dried coconut, dried pineapple, unsalted peanuts, almonds, pine nuts, pecans, or walnuts—and almost anything else that will keep without refrigeration, including figs, dried apples, and dates. Just use your imagination!

Sprinkle yeast over warm water in a small bowl, let stand for 5 minutes, and then stir to dissolve.

In a large bowl, combine the milk, honey, salt, and melted butter. Add 2 cups flour and beat until smooth. Stir in yeast mixture. Add raisins and cinnamon and stir again. Slowly blend in the remaining flour until dough leaves the sides of the bowl.

Turn dough out onto a floured surface and knead for 8 to 10 minutes, or until dough is smooth and elastic and does not stick to your fingers when you pinch it. Cover with wax paper and a towel. Let dough rest for 20 minutes.

Remove the covering, punch dough down, and then divide it into 2 equal portions. Shape into loaves, place into 2 buttered 8½ × 4½-inch loaf pans, and brush with melted butter. Cover pans with towels and let dough rise in a warm place until almost doubled in bulk, about 1½ hours.

Bake in a preheated 350°F oven for 50 to 55 minutes.

Place on a wire rack and brush again with melted butter while loaves are still hot.

# Raisin Whole Wheat Bread

(2 medium-size loaves)

> 2 tablespoons active dry yeast
> 1¼ cups warm water
> 1 cup milk, warmed
> ½ cup honey
> 1 teaspoon salt (optional, see page 22)
> 1 tablespoon butter, melted
> 5½ to 6 cups whole wheat flour
> 1½ cups raisins
> 1 tablespoon ground cinnamon
> melted butter for brushing loaves

If you accidentally add too much flour and the dough is dry and unmanageable, place the dough into a large bowl containing just enough tepid water to cover it. When the dough floats to the top (after about 15 minutes), remove it from the bowl, pat it dry with paper towels, and continue kneading.

Sam Kirk

# Theresa Bowler

*The Bread:*

**"Gramma Kaldahl's" Brown Bread**

If Carrie Price (see Index) is my youngest baker at 2½, then Theresa must certainly hold the record here for proving that this wonderful hobby of ours spans the generations with ease, for she is now 80 years old. I met her on my book tour for *Bread Winners* when she came into Famous-Barr Department Store in St. Louis to bring a sample of her bread and to chat about baking. She lives in Kirkwood, Missouri, and has been making bread for about 40 years.

*When people taste my bread and want to know how I learned to make it taste so good, I tell them that if you've been baking it for 40 years, it ought to taste good!*

*There is a story that I wrote when I was a child about coming home from school on a winter's day, opening the kitchen door, and smelling my mother's home-baked bread. That aroma I cannot forget, nor can I forget the fresh crust that mother cut for me to eat.*

# "Gramma Kaldahl's" Brown Bread

(4 loaves)

5 cups lukewarm potato water
½ tablespoon honey
2 tablespoons dry yeast
1 cup whole wheat flour
¼ cup butter, melted
1 cup graham flour
2 teaspoons salt (optional, see page 22)
1 cup rye flour
½ cup dark molasses
enough whole wheat flour to make a dough (about 8 to 9 cups)

This is a recipe that was handed down in Theresa's family. You'll note that the final ingredient just specifies "enough" flour to make the dough. Such a direction was typical of a generation that never measured anything, using terms such as "a bit" or "some" when describing ingredient amounts.

In a large bowl, combine potato water and honey and then stir in the yeast. Mix well and set aside to proof for 5 to 10 minutes.

Then add 1 cup whole wheat flour, melted butter, graham flour, salt, rye flour, and molasses and stir well. Add more of the whole wheat flour, 1 cup at a time, stirring it in after each addition. The dough should be moderately stiff yet soft enough to handle easily when you knead it.

Turn dough out onto a floured surface and knead for 8 to 10 minutes, or until smooth and elastic. Place into an oiled bowl, turn to coat, cover, and let rise in a warm spot until doubled in bulk, 1 to 1¼ hours.

Punch dough down, turn out onto a floured surface, knead for 1 to 2 minutes, and form into 4 free-form loaves. Place on an oiled baking sheet, cover, and let rise in a warm spot until almost doubled in bulk, 45 to 60 minutes.

Bake in a preheated 375°F oven for 45 to 50 minutes, or until the loaves test done. They should sound hollow when their bottoms are tapped.

Cool on wire racks.

Theresa adds a postscript to her recipe: "These are 4 loaves of the finest brown bread you have ever eaten!"

# Lori and Neil Meyer

They telephoned from Houston on Christmas of 1980, and I had just finished delivering my gift breads to the Fire Island neighbors. We had never met, but the idea of Christmas breads intrigued them and they had impulsively picked up the phone. Lori was in the midst of baking bagels that evening, while Neil, new to the craft, had a whole grain bread in the oven. In the winter darkness, we talked of bread and gifts and of the joys of making our own loaves for friends and neighbors and the people we love. Lori, a pharmacist, and Neil, an attorney, share their baking experiences.

*Neil first experienced homemade bread at his grandmother's ranch in southwest Texas, where freshly churned butter and local honey spread on top heightened the pure enjoyment of a warm slice of bread. So impressed was he with the experience, that his future wife (Lori), was persuaded to undertake the challenge of recreating those early memories.*

And so, the hobby became a mutual one. They write that it not only brought them closer to their friends, but it also affected their own relationship, bringing them closer to each other. As Lori says, "Who is to judge the effect and influence of baking bread?"

# Whole Wheat Croissants

(20 croissants)

1 tablespoon dry yeast
1 teaspoon honey
¼ cup warm water
2 cups lukewarm milk
¼ cup honey, warmed
2 tablespoons vegetable oil
1 teaspoon salt (optional, see page 22)
6½ to 7 cups stone-ground whole wheat flour
1 pound butter
1 egg
1 tablespoon water

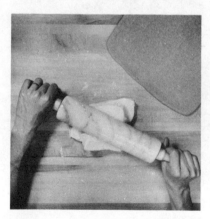

*This past year our "family" has been extended by the addition of Isabelle Gaume, a foreign exchange student from Nancy, France. Her comments and advice about French breads have expanded our knowledge, and her companionship has been the best aid and incentive to our hobby. These croissants were particularly inspired by her. They also reflect Neil's determination to bring whole grain nutrition to the highest form of the baker's art.*

Dissolve yeast and 1 teaspoon honey in ¼ cup warm water and set aside to proof.

In a large bowl, combine the milk, warm honey, oil, and salt. Add yeast mixture and stir in 2 cups flour. Blend in the remaining flour, 1 cup at a time, to achieve a soft dough.

Turn dough out onto a lightly floured surface and allow it to rest for 2 to 3 minutes. In the meantime, clean and lightly oil the mixing bowl. Knead dough about 3 minutes, or just until smooth. Place into the oiled bowl, turn to coat, cover with plastic wrap, and let rise for 3 hours at room temperature, about 70°F.

Turn dough out onto a lightly floured surface and roll out to a 10 by 16-inch rectangle. Fold it in thirds, as you would fold a letter, return to the bowl, cover, and let rise for 1½ hours.

Place dough on a lightly floured surface and roll out to a rectangle again, about 10 by 16 inches. Allow to rest for a few minutes. In the meantime, beat butter with a rolling pin right on your work surface, until it forms a cold paste. Then spread butter over the upper two-thirds of the dough, using a soft pastry scraper or a spatula. Leave about a ½-inch border at the edges. Fold the unbuttered bottom third over the middle third, then fold the top buttered third over the bottom portion, just as you would fold a letter. Lightly flour the dough and the work surface and turn dough clockwise one-quarter turn (the top folded edge will be on your right). Roll dough out to a 10 by 16-inch rectangle and fold into thirds again. It is the repeated folding technique that gives croissants their airy, flaky quality when they are baked. Place dough on a large plate, wrap tightly with plastic wrap, and refrigerate for 1½ hours.

Remove dough from the refrigerator and place on a lightly floured surface with the top folded edge on your right. Dust with flour and tap lightly with a rolling pin. Roll dough out to a 10 by 16-inch rectangle and then fold into thirds. Turn dough clockwise one-quarter turn, roll out again to a 10 by 16-inch rectangle, and fold again into thirds. Place dough on a large plate, wrap tightly with plastic wrap and a wet cloth, and return to the refrigerator for 2 hours or, preferably, overnight.

When you take the dough out of the refrigerator, place it on a lightly floured surface with the top folded edge on your right, tap lightly with a rolling pin, and roll out to a 10 by 26-inch rectangle. The dough will be about ¼-inch thick. Cut dough in half lengthwise to form 2 long strips, each measuring 5 by 26 inches. Fold one strip in half, cover, and return to the refrigerator. Cut triangles from the first strip with a pastry wheel. An easier method for measuring out triangles is to divide the dough crosswise into five equal squares and then cut the squares into triangles of 5 by 5 by 5 inches each. Gently enlarge each triangle with a rolling pin until it measures 7 by 7 inches.

Starting at the base of the triangle, roll it towards the top while stretching it gently by the ends. Shape the rolled triangle into a crescent with the tip of the triangle on the inside of the curve. Place the croissant on a lightly oiled rimmed baking sheet or jelly-roll pan. (The rim prevents the butter from spilling during the baking.) The tip of the croissant should just touch the baking sheet. Continue cutting and shaping the croissants until both strips of dough have been used.

In a cup, beat egg and 1 tablespoon water together and brush the croissants with mixture. Let rise for 1 hour at room temperature.

Brush the croissants again with egg mixture and bake in a preheated 425°F oven for 12 to 15 minutes, or until nicely browned.

Remove and cool on wire racks. Serve the croissants fresh, or freeze and reheat in 400°F oven for about 5 minutes.

(continued on page 162)

## Fillings for Whole Wheat Croissants

Any of these fillings may be placed inside the triangles of dough just before they are rolled into croissant shapes. Place about 2 tablespoons of filling at the base of the triangle and twist ends slightly to prevent leakage.

Nut Filling: Mix 2 cups chopped almonds, pecans, or walnuts with 1 teaspoon vanilla extract or ground cinnamon and ½ cup honey.

Dried Fruit Filling: Pour boiling water over prunes, raisins, or dried apricots. Allow to cool overnight, drain, and then puree in a blender or food processor. Add a small amount of honey.

Carob Filling: Add carob bits or chips.

## Pâte à Brioche (Basic Dough)

2 tablespoons dry yeast
¼ cup warm water
2 tablespoons honey, warmed
2 tablespoons nonfat dry milk
1 teaspoon salt (optional, see page 22)
4 cups whole wheat flour
5 eggs
1 cup butter, softened
1 egg yolk
2 tablespoons milk

From this basic dough, you can make several different breads, all of which are excellent for breakfast or as an accompaniment to fruits.

In a large bowl, dissolve yeast in warm water and then add warm honey. Add the nonfat dry milk, salt, and flour. Stir in 3 eggs and work mixture into a dough. Mix in the remaining eggs and softened butter and knead dough rapidly for 8 to 10 minutes. Place dough into a large, lightly oiled bowl, turn to coat, cover, and let rise in a cool place for 1½ to 2 hours.

Punch dough down, return to bowl, and let rise in a cool place for another hour.

Punch down again, return to bowl, cover tightly with plastic wrap and refrigerate overnight.

Remove dough from refrigerator and form into any of the shapes described below.

Divide dough into 16 to 24 pieces. From each piece, take a small piece of dough, then roll both the large and the small pieces into balls. Place the large piece into an oiled mold or buttered muffin tin. Then place the small piece on top of it, securing it into place with damp fingers. Repeat this procedure with each piece of dough. When the *brioches* are baked, they will have tiny "caps," or "heads," on them. For baking, follow the instructions at the end of this section.

## Petites Brioches à Tête

(16 to 24 small *brioches*)

Shape dough into one large ball. Then remove enough dough to form a smaller ball for the "head." (For 2 *brioches* divide dough in half and repeat the process.) Place into *brioche* mold making sure smaller piece of dough is firmly positioned on top of larger piece. Some bakers make a slit in the top of the large piece of dough with a floured knife, shape the smaller piece into a teardrop, and insert it into the cut. Then, with damp fingers, they close the sliced dough firmly around the cap. Bake as instructed at the end of this section.

## Brioche à Tête

(1 or 2 brioches)

Shape dough into a flat ball. Make a hole in the center and stretch dough into a ring. Bake as instructed.

## Brioche en Couronne

(1 *brioche*)

Divide dough into 10 to 12 pieces. Roll into cylinders and place across the bottom of 2  8½ × 4½-inch buttered loaf pans. Baking instructions follow.

## Brioche Parisienne

(2 brioches)

**To bake any style *brioche*:** Once you have shaped the dough into the *brioche* of your choice, cover with wax paper and let rise in a cool place for about 2 hours.

In a cup, beat together egg yolk and milk and brush *brioches* with this glaze. Bake in a preheated 375°F oven for 30 to 45 minutes, depending upon the size of the breads.

Remove from pans and cool on a wire rack.

# Tami Watson

*The Bread:*

**Teddy Bear Bread**

*I must tell you about my Teddy Bear Bread! You see, I'm a Teddy Bear collector and a member of one of the few teddy bear clubs. So, using one of my whole wheat or French bread recipes, I shape the loaf into a darling Teddy Bear that looks as spectacular as he tastes. And, he's guaranteed to get a warm smile out of even the grumpiest of critics!*

Tami wrote from Huntington Beach, California, sending along a photograph of herself and her Teddy Bear Bread. Though I have always maintained that breads can be made in any shape, as shown by my own creations using number forms or ten heels on one bread, it had never occurred to me that a bread might be molded in the shape of an animal.

Tami is 24 years old, the mother of two boys, age 2 and 3, and is married to a firefighter/paramedic for the city of Anaheim.

*I don't have to tell you what a hit my bread has been at the firehouse. My husband, Craig, and I grow our own vegetables and raise chickens for eggs; we have a pet rabbit named Sinbad the Sailor, a Dalmatian named Pirate (he has a patch over his left eye), and two cats named Seaweed and Abalone. We love to sail on our 22-foot sailboat, as well as surf and jog together.*

In her "spare" time, Tami is going to school to become a registered nurse. Still, she manages to find time for her bread baking.

*It's more or less therapy for me. With a couple of active little boys, I truly look forward to the calming effect that kneading the dough gives me. I wouldn't beat my kids, but I sure do beat the bread! It relieves all my frustrations.*

If there are any children around your house, you have a great excuse to try Tami's Teddy Bear Bread. If you have no children of your own, give a Teddy Bear Bread to a neighbor's kids.

# Teddy Bear Bread

(2 bears)

8 to 10 cups whole wheat
flour
1 teaspoon salt (optional, see
page 22)
2 tablespoons dry yeast
1½ cups milk
1½ cups water
½ cup honey
⅓ cup butter, melted

In a large bowl, blend 3 cups flour with salt.

In a medium-size saucepan, heat the milk, water, honey, and melted butter until lukewarm. Stir in yeast and set aside to proof for 5 to 10 minutes.

Slowly add yeast mixture to the dry ingredients. Beat with an electric mixer for about 2 minutes or beat by hand until well blended. Add 1 more cup of flour and mix with an electric mixer set at high speed or beat with a wooden spoon. Add the remainder of the flour, mixing until the dough is smooth and thick enough to knead.

Turn out onto a lightly floured surface. Let rest for 10 minutes and then knead for 10 minutes. (Tami usually counts to 300, which takes just about 10 minutes.) Place into a well-oiled bowl, turn to coat, cover with a damp cloth, and place in a warm spot until doubled in bulk, 45 to 60 minutes.

Punch dough down and turn out onto a floured surface. Divide dough in half and shape each half into a ball. Set one ball aside and cover with a dry cloth while you shape the first bear. Take about one-third or one-half of the dough (depending upon how chubby you want the bear to be) and form the tummy. Divide the remaining dough into enough pieces to form the head, 2 arms, 2 legs, and 2 small ears. Place a flat circle of dough on the face to form the snout, and then center a tiny round ball on the snout to form a little nose. Place 2 small eyes above the snout and then, of course, the finishing touch—the belly button! When you attach it to the tummy, blend the edges with your fingers. (Wetting your fingers helps to attach it firmly.) Place the bear on a well-buttered baking sheet and repeat the procedure with the second piece of dough. Bake in a preheated 375°F oven for 25 to 30 minutes, or until the bears are done.

Remove carefully and place on wire racks to cool.

# Andreas Esberg

In addition to his being an ardently committed, every-Saturday-without-fail bread baker, Andy is one of the most delightful people in our village. We met by chance. As he tells it:

*I was in the village store, looking for some ingredient which I needed but which wasn't there. I mentioned my problem to Carol, the owner, and she smiled, pointed to the man behind me, and said, "Ask Mel London. He just published a book called* Bread Winners.*"*

Our relationship has been a joy to me and not a Saturday seems to pass without the exchange of either a new recipe or some bread samples straight from the oven. As a senior partner in an accounting firm with a great many international clients, Andy has numerous opportunities for tasting the breads of Austria, Switzerland, and Germany, thus acquiring some fascinating recipes (and an occasional "Sorry, but that's our secret").

*I like to go for long walks on the beach, and I especially enjoy collecting items of interest to me as I stroll on the sand. But, unlike most people, who look for shells, beach glass, and other small lovely items, I look for and sometimes find red bricks. My collection is now large enough to line both my oven in Fire Island and the one in New York!*

The use of bricks in the oven is just one of the bread baking techniques that Andy favors. He prefers to use cake yeast, as I do, but sometimes finds it difficult to get. He also finds that he gets better results when he starts with the wet ingredients and then mixes in the proofed yeast, followed by the whole wheat flour. As you know, other

*The Breads:*

**Potato-Soya Bread**
***Zopf* (Braided Bread)**
**Berliner *Schusterjungen***
**Bran Muffins**

bakers reverse the procedure with equal success. No matter, Andy's *reasons* for baking bread are universal.

*It allows me the freedom to mix, knead, pound, add a little of this or that. The bread smells so good, tastes so delicious, even when it's not perfect. I treasure the enjoyment of getting up early in the morning and acting as master of the kitchen or relaxing by baking bread after working for hours—the physical expression it allows. And then I love to see the dough rise, watch the shaped loaf slowly turn a golden brown in the oven, and savor the excitement of tasting the first slice, still slightly warm!*

And, of course, Andy's family is appreciative?

*My family?* They're impossible! *My wife and two sons were very kind about my initial bread baking efforts, and even complimented me at times. Today, they are much less tolerant. They choose only certain of my breads. Their favorite is my Zopf, and they tolerate my simple whole wheat bread and sometimes my Berliner Schusterjungen.*

On the other hand, *I* greatly appreciate the breads baked by Andy Esberg, and so long as he keeps sending over samples every Saturday, I have no complaints.

You'll notice that each of Andy's breads contains some bran, one of the secrets of their excellent taste and their good nutrition. "I will not bake a bread without bran," Andy says. "It's my signature!"

In a medium-size saucepan, boil potatoes in their skins. Peel potatoes and mash enough to make 1 cup, and retain 1 cup of potato water. (Be certain potato water is lukewarm when you use it.)

In a small bowl, mix the yeast, ¼ teaspoon honey, and warm water. Stir and set aside.

In a large bowl, combine the potato water, milk, melted butter, and ½ cup honey and mix thoroughly. Add yeast mixture and stir. Then add the potatoes, soy flour, bran, and whole wheat flour, 1 cup at a time, mixing in each one thoroughly before adding the next.

Turn dough out onto a floured surface and knead for 8 to 10 minutes, or until smooth and slightly sticky. Place into an oiled bowl, turn to coat, cover with a towel, and let rise in a warm spot until doubled in bulk, 1 to 2 hours.*

Turn dough out onto a floured surface, knead again for a few minutes, and form into 2 free-form loaves. Place on a well-oiled baking sheet, make several slashes in the top of each loaf with a floured knife, cover, and let rise in a warm spot until doubled in bulk.

Bake in a preheated 375°F oven for 35 to 45 minutes, or until loaves test done.

Cool on wire racks before cutting.

*You will find that almost all whole grain breads vary in rising time. Some of them take as much as 2 to 3 hours to double in size. It depends upon the amount of whole grain flour, kitchen temperature, humidity, and altitude.

# Potato-Soya Bread

(2 loaves)

3 medium-size potatoes
2 tablespoons dry yeast
½ cup plus ¼ teaspoon honey
¼ cup warm water
1 cup lukewarm potato water
1 cup milk
¼ cup butter, melted
1 cup soy flour
1½ cups bran
6 to 7 cups whole wheat flour

# *Zopf* (Braided Bread)

(2 large loaves)

¾ cup plus 2 tablespoons
butter, melted
2 cups lukewarm milk
4 eggs, beaten
6½ tablespoons honey
2 tablespoons dry yeast
¼ cup warm water
8 cups whole wheat flour
(this would have to be
unbleached white flour to
result in the traditional
appearance of *Zopf*)
1 cup bran
1 egg yolk
1 tablespoon water
poppy seeds for topping

*Zopf,* which means "braid" in German, is simply Andy's grandmother's version of the traditional *challah* or twist. She came from a small village in Germany and Andy remembers her as a great cook and baker. Although the recipe is hers, Andy has added his signature again, 1 cup of bran.

In a large bowl, combine the melted butter and warm milk. Add beaten eggs and 6 tablespoons of the honey and let stand.

In a small bowl, mix yeast with the remaining ½ tablespoon honey and warm water. Let stand until foamy.

Gently stir yeast mixture into liquid ingredients. Add 4 cups of the flour, stirring in 1 cup at a time. Then mix in bran, and enough of the remaining flour to make a stiff dough.

Turn out onto a lightly floured surface and knead for 8 to 10 minutes, or until dough is satin-smooth. Place into a well-oiled bowl, turn to coat, cover, and let rise in a warm spot until doubled in bulk, 45 to 60 minutes.

Punch dough down, turn out onto a lightly floured surface, and knead for a few minutes, or until dough is firm and smooth. Divide into 6 equal parts and roll each part into a sausage shape about 18 inches in length. Pinch together the ends of 3 strands with your fingers. Then braid them to form a loaf, pinching the other ends together to seal tightly. If the ends seem to unravel once you've braided the loaf, just dampen your fingers and press down at each end to seal the dough. Follow the same procedure to make the second loaf. Place both loaves on a well-oiled baking sheet and cover lightly with a cloth or towel. Place in a warm spot and let rise until doubled in bulk, about 1 hour.

Mix egg yolk with water and brush loaves with the mixture. Sprinkle with poppy seeds and bake in a preheated 375°F oven for 50 minutes. (After 30 minutes, you might want to mist the loaves with water.)

*My grandparents lived in Berlin and I spent most of my vacations with them. They had a large household and meals were a special event for us children. One meal a week consisted only of dairy foods* (milchich), *which meant that my grandparents would serve delicious hot chocolate, cheeses, and the marvelous Berliner* schusterjungen *(translated as "cobbler's apprentice") rolls. When I was in Berlin recently, one of the things that I looked for were these rolls and their recipe.*

# Berliner Schuster-jungen

(12 rolls)

     2 tablespoons dry yeast
     2 tablespoons plus ¼
         teaspoon honey
2¼ cups lukewarm water
     1 egg, well beaten
     1 teaspoon salt (optional,
         see page 22)
     ¼ cup caraway seeds
     3 cups whole wheat flour
     3 cups rye flour
     1 cup bran

In a small bowl, combine the yeast, ¼ teaspoon honey, and ¼ cup lukewarm water and set aside to proof.

In a large bowl, blend together the remaining water, 2 tablespoons honey, beaten egg, salt, and caraway seeds. Stir in the yeast mixture. Add whole wheat flour 1 cup at a time, mixing as you do so. Then add rye flour and bran. Mix thoroughly with a wooden spoon or with your hands. The dough should be slightly sticky.

Turn out onto a floured surface and knead for 8 to 10 minutes. If dough seems too wet, add more whole wheat flour, but remember that whole wheat and rye flour make a stickier dough than unbleached white flour normally does. Place dough into a well-oiled bowl, turn to coat, cover, and let rise in a warm spot until doubled in bulk, 1 to 1½ hours.

Punch dough down, turn out onto a floured surface, let stand for a few minutes, and then knead just a few times. Divide dough into 12 equal pieces and form them into slightly elongated rolls. Place on a well-buttered baking sheet, cover with a towel, and let rise in a warm spot until almost doubled in bulk, 45 to 60 minutes.

Bake in a preheated 375°F oven for about 25 minutes. Then remove the rolls, brush with water, and return to the oven for another 5 to 7 minutes, or until done.

Cool on wire racks.

# Bran Muffins

(about 12 muffins)

3 tablespoons butter, melted
1 cup lukewarm milk
1¼ teaspoons baking soda
1 egg, beaten
½ cup honey
1 cup stone-ground whole
wheat flour
1½ cups bran
1 cup raisins

These are easy to make; you can complete the entire process in under an hour.

In a bowl, combine the melted butter, milk, and baking soda and let stand for a few minutes. Add beaten egg and honey and mix well. Then stir in the flour, bran, and raisins. Pour the mixture into a 12-cup muffin tin and bake in a preheated 375°F oven for 20 to 25 minutes.

When using raisins or dried fruit, dust them with flour to keep them from sinking to the bottom of the dough.

Nancy Eckert

# Kathy Skelly Gilmore

Kathy is a dear young friend who visits us both in New York and on Fire Island. When she asked *me* to take the photos of her wedding to Mark Gilmore last year, I must say that I worried for days until they came back from the laboratory. (They all came out!) She's a talented artist and illustrator (the drawings that accompany this chapter are hers) as well as a superb mechanic. Kathy and her husband spend part of their time revitalizing antique automobiles. She also bakes bread, samples of which she brings when she visits us.

> *Being an artist, I'm just not comfortable unless my hands are doing something. (I peel labels off bottles and tear up napkins!) So to me bread baking is both therapy and an art form. It's therapy in that it gives me a chance to punch something, to really take out my aggressions, but at the same time I feel that I'm being productive! Bread baking is an art form in that it is a way to create something very special and very beautiful, and you don't have to be an artist to sculpt a bread.*

Kathy feels very much as I do about the unwarranted mystique of bread baking, the treatment of the entire process with awe.

> *I think the biggest mistake the first-time bread baker makes is to treat the dough too gingerly. Good bread needs to be kneaded, not gently, but with real energy!*

*The Bread:*

## Dark Raisin Pumpernickel

# Dark Raisin Pumper-nickel

(2 loaves)

3 tablespoons dry yeast
1½ cups warm water
¾ cup dark molasses
1 teaspoon salt (optional, see page 22)
¼ cup carob powder
3 tablespoons caraway seeds (optional)
2 tablespoons vegetable oil
3 cups rye flour
2½ to 3 cups whole wheat flour
1½ to 2 cups raisins
cornmeal for dusting pan

This is one of the very best pumpernickel breads that I have ever tasted—the sample loaf that Kathy brought was devoured by all of us in less than a day. If you prefer a lighter colored bread, you can substitute light molasses for the carob. While you're munching on the pumpernickel, you might also entertain your guests with this bit of trivia, as Kathy did:

*Did you know that pumpernickel bread was developed in the fifteenth century in Germany by a baker named Nichol Pumper?*

In a large bowl, dissolve yeast in warm water. Add the molasses, salt, carob, caraway seeds, oil, and rye flour, and stir until smooth. Add raisins. Then stir in enough whole wheat flour to make the dough easy to handle. Turn out onto a lightly floured surface, cover, and let rest for about 15 minutes.

Knead until smooth, about 10 minutes. If dough is too sticky, add a bit more whole wheat flour. Place into an oiled bowl, turn to coat, cover, and let rise in a warm place until doubled in bulk, 1 to 1½ hours.

Punch dough down, turn out onto a lightly floured surface, and knead for 1 to 2 minutes. Then return to the oiled bowl, turn to coat, cover, and let rise in a warm place until doubled in bulk again, about 45 minutes.

Punch dough down, turn out onto a floured surface, and divide into 2 equal pieces. Press each piece into a flat shape about 12 inches square. This can be done roughly with your hands or with a floured rolling pin. Roll up the squares, jelly-roll fashion, and press on ends to seal. Then round out the ends and place both loaves on an oiled baking sheet which has been sprinkled with cornmeal. (Rolling up the dough distributes the raisins more evenly and gives the bread a lovely spiral texture when cut.) Cover loaves and let rise in a warm place until almost doubled in bulk, 45 to 60 minutes.

Bake in a preheated 375°F oven for 30 to 35 minutes, or until loaves sound hollow when tapped on the bottom.

Cool on wire racks.

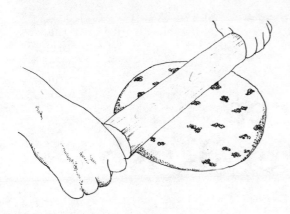

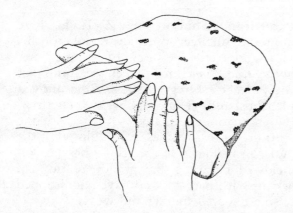

# Andrea
# Brazer-Rush

*The Bread:*

**Grandma's Butterhorns**

*Women in New Zealand don't bake bread(!)—at least the ones I've come across don't. It's considered taking advantage of a great American convenience to buy it at the store, like a lot of other American ideas.*

The letter came from Hamilton, New Zealand, where Andrea had promised to uncover some new recipes for this volume. The quote above tells the story. I first "met" her when she reviewed *Bread Winners* for a weekly column that she wrote for a newspaper in Oregon. She has since moved to Illinois with her husband, Geoff, and her two children, Susan and Drew, both of whom love to help with the baking chores. Andrea now teaches gerontology at the University of Wisconsin/Parkside and continues her research in the fields of fathering and grandparenting, in addition to working with parents who have handicapped infants. She is also a devoted spinner and weaver.

*I look at bread baking in the same way I might my entire process of making cloth. I pick the sheep before it's sheared, wash and dye my own wool in a "natural way," spin all my own yarn, and weave with my own handspun. Start to finish, I know what has happened and why. I think of bread baking in that sense. I decide on the ingredients, add "natural" materials like honey or molasses and fresh country eggs, use my own hands (as opposed to a dough hook) for kneading and shaping, and when I am finished I know that the product that we eat has been through a truly person-oriented process.*

Andrea adds: "The house smells terrific and it brings the bears out of the woods very quickly!"

As Andrea recalls it, making her grandmother's favorite rolls was the absolute goal of her first attempts at baking. However, the first batch turned out like "dog bones" and her second attempts were suitable for "using in the squash court"—and then she goes on with the story, finally succeeding, and bringing back memories of her childhood.

*Baking grandmother's rolls—the entire gustatory/olfactory/ cutaneous experience unlocks fond memories of dinners at grandma's house. I was allowed to help in the kitchen, and now that I've mastered the butterhorn technique, I can actually perpetuate the family tradition. My grandmother died four years ago, but I always make butterhorns for family dinners, and they help us all remember something precious about Gram: how much she loved us and how fantastic Sunday dinners were. And in a very quiet way, I can say, "Thanks Gram, you were right. I did learn and you knew I could do it all along!"*

# Grandma's Butterhorns

(24 rolls)

4 tablespoons buttermilk
powder
1¼ cups warm water
1 tablespoon dry yeast
2 tablespoons honey
½ teaspoon salt (optional, see
page 22)
2 tablespoons butter
2 eggs
3½ to 4 cups whole wheat
flour
2 to 4 tablespoons butter,
melted, for brushing
dough

In a large bowl, mix together buttermilk powder and 1 cup warm water. Sprinkle yeast over liquid and then add honey. Stir and let stand for about 5 minutes.

Add the salt, butter, and ¼ cup warm water to yeast mixture. Beat in eggs briskly. Add flour, 1 cup at a time, beating after each addition.

When dough begins to form into a ball, turn out onto a lightly floured surface and add approximately ½ cup flour to top of dough. Knead just enough to work in the added flour. The dough may still be a little bit sticky. Place dough into an oiled bowl, turn to coat, cover, and let rise in a warm place until doubled in bulk, 45 to 60 minutes.

Punch down, and turn out onto a floured surface. Divide dough in half and roll out each half into a circle, as for a pie. Brush each circle generously with melted butter and cut into 12 pie slices. Then, beginning with the outside edges, roll up pie slices and place on a buttered baking sheet 2 to 3 inches apart. The butterhorns can be formed into crescent shapes as they are placed on the baking sheet. Repeat process with second piece of dough. Cover lightly and let rolls rise in a warm place until doubled in bulk, about 45 minutes.

Bake in a preheated 350°F oven for about 15 minutes.

Cool on wire racks.

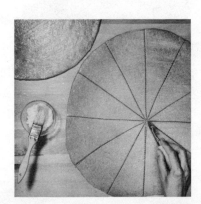

# Dave Ketchum

The photograph on this page was not taken on a street in New York City. Dave Ketchum and I are standing on the back lot at Warner Brothers Burbank Studios in California, where the film *Annie* was shot, and where Dave is a producer/writer/director in the television industry. He and his partner, Tony DiMarco, have written such shows as "Laverne and Shirley," "Happy Days," "Mork and Mindy," and "Fantasy Island."

*After a day of writing, talking to executives, worrying about how the kids are going to go to college, or if they're going to go to college, there's nothing like whipping up some bread dough and kneading it and beating on it until I'm a calm person again.*

Dave and his wife, Louise, and their two girls, Nikki and Wendy, live in Santa Monica. He loves to bake whole grain breads for his family, proudly presenting them . . .

*crunchy and warm as they come out of the oven. Unfortunately, my two children are still at the pasty, doughy, white bread stage. I'm getting a little tired of pulling a tasty, nutritious whole wheat loaf out of the oven and hearing, "That's gross!"*

While I was out in California, Dave and I lunched at the Warner Brothers commissary, and he visited the Rodale booth at the American Booksellers Association convention in Anaheim. In between, we spoke of bread, including some of our more spectacular failures.

*The Breads:*

**Griddle Scones**
**Jelly-Stuffed Bran Muffins**
**Whole Wheat**
  **Blueberry Muffins**

*My results now are good. But, believe me, they didn't start out that way. My first loaf never rose. It just lay there at the bottom of the bread pan as though it had died and were in its little coffin. My second loaf oozed over the edge of the pan. And the strangest thing was to find a pencil in my cheese loaf! One of my daughter's friends must have left it there.*

*When we parted, Dave said to me, "I just can't believe that you've asked me to be in your new bread book." Well, I did. And he is.*

# Griddle Scones

(about 12 scones)

1 cup rolled oats
2 cups whole wheat flour
1 teaspoon baking soda
½ cup butter
¾ cup milk
1 tablespoon vinegar
2 tablespoons honey
½ cup raisins

*Louise and I have these for breakfast, while the kids put some more sugar on their sugar frosted flakes!*

In a large bowl, mix together the oats, flour, and baking soda. Cut butter into small pieces and mix into flour mixture until flour gets crumbly. (This is one recipe for which I use an electric mixer.)

In a small bowl, combine the milk, vinegar, and honey and mix well. Add milk mixture to flour mixture and then stir in raisins.

With your hands, make the dough fairly firm and then form into little patties, a few inches in diameter and about twice as thick as a pancake. Cook over low heat on an electric griddle for about 10 minutes, or until they rise. (You can also cook them on a griddle over gas heat, but it's tricky keeping the right temperature.)

When the scones rise, raise the heat a bit and cook them until they are brown on the bottom. Then flip them over just like pancakes and brown the other side. Serve warm. They taste just great with honey.

# Jelly-Stuffed Bran Muffins

_I fool my kids with this one (until they read this book!). They think that the muffins are made with white flour and that it's the molasses that makes the dough so dark! If you're on a "hate-sugar" kick like we are, you can find jams and jellies that are sweetened with honey in natural foods stores. That's what we use._

(12 muffins)

    1 cup whole wheat flour
  ½ cup bran
2½ teaspoons baking powder
    1 egg
    3 tablespoons vegetable oil
    1 cup milk
    3 tablespoons molasses
      enough jam or jelly to
      stuff muffins

In a medium-size bowl, combine the flour, bran, and baking powder and mix with a wooden spoon.

In a large bowl, combine the egg, oil, milk, and molasses and mix well. Then add dry ingredients to liquid ingredients and mix just enough to wet the flour. Don't overmix. Fill a 12-cup muffin tin that has been lined with paper cups about two-thirds full. Drop about 1 teaspoon of jam or jelly into the center of each muffin. Bake in a preheated 425°F oven for about 15 minutes.

Cool in muffin tin for a few minutes before removing to wire racks.

# Whole Wheat Blueberry Muffins

_We live near the Pacific Ocean. On a bright, sunny day, we make a batch of these muffins and ride our bikes down to watch the waves—and eat._

(12 muffins)

  2 cups whole wheat flour
  2 teaspoons baking powder
  3 eggs
1¼ cups milk
  ¼ cup butter, melted
  ¼ cup honey
  1 cup blueberries

The trick with this recipe is to place all the ingredients into a large mixing bowl and just stir them together. Don't over-mix. Pour the batter into a buttered 12-cup muffin tin, filling the cups about two-thirds full, and bake in a preheated 425°F oven for 20 minutes, or until a cake tester comes out clean.

Cool in muffin tin for a few minutes before removing to wire racks.

# Cynthia Fox

I've lost count of the number of telephone calls between Fire Island and Bavon, Virginia, since I received the first letter from Cyndie:

*As I checked out your book for the fourth time at the library, I decided to write. . . . A recent move to rural Virginia has increased my baking and I've even purchased an old "Hoosier" cabinet with a pull-out enamel shelf, built-in flour bin, and sifter. Perfect for creating great breads. My favorite recipes are the bagels (unheard of here), George Meluso's Challah (also unheard of), and the pizza dough (the nearest Italian restaurant is 30 miles away).*

Cyndie assists her husband, George, in his home improvement business, and is one of his most efficient house painters. She also teaches Slimnastics, gardens, and works part time at the Mathews County Health Department. And, though she is a veteran bread baker, she has had her share of funny failures, just like the rest of us.

*The wildest was a batch of rolls that turned out rock hard. I had chickens at the time and used to feed them kitchen scraps. Well, they scratched and pecked at my rolls but couldn't manage to eat them—that's how hard they were. I never did find out what went wrong.*

One of the interesting tips that Cyndie has passed along to me is her use of bay leaves in the flour bin of her Hoosier cabinet. She finds that they keep the bin free of bugs and she can keep up to ten pounds of flour in it without worry.

In a large bowl, mix together the flour, baking powder, baking soda, and salt

In a medium-size bowl, blend together the egg, buttermilk, molasses or honey, and melted butter. Add to flour mixture, stirring until smooth. Mix in nuts and raisins. Pour batter into a buttered and floured 9 × 5-inch loaf pan and bake in a preheated 400°F oven for 45 to 50 minutes.

Cool on a wire rack.

# Whole Wheat Pecan Quick Bread

(1 large loaf)

2 cups whole wheat flour
1 teaspoon baking powder
1 teaspoon baking soda
½ teaspoon salt (optional, see page 22)
1 egg
2 cups buttermilk
3 tablespoons molasses or honey
2 tablespoons butter, melted
½ cup chopped pecans
½ cup raisins

# Sour Cream Wheat Germ Batter Bread

(1 bundt loaf or 2 medium-size loaves)

3½ cups whole wheat flour
½ teaspoon salt (optional, see page 22)
2 tablespoon honey
2 tablespoons dry yeast
1 cup milk
¼ cup water
3 eggs
1 cup sour cream
½ cup toasted wheat germ

Tucked inside a well-wrapped package that bore the Bavon, Virginia, postmark and four slices of this bread was a note from Cyndie:

*I've really got my doubts about mailing you these slices. I imagine you'll be able to use them for doorstops by the time they reach you. The Sour Cream Wheat Germ Batter Bread (the name is longer than the recipe) is very simple—a good bread for a beginner. It is light textured with a slightly sour taste.*

The bread, however, was still fresh—and delicious. My compliments to the United States Postal Service!

In a large bowl, combine 1 cup of the whole wheat flour, salt, honey, and yeast.

In a small saucepan, heat milk and water to 120°F. Blend warm liquid into flour mixture and beat with an electric mixer set at medium speed for 2 minutes. Add 1½ cups flour, eggs, and sour cream. Beat for 2 minutes at medium speed. Add the remaining flour and wheat germ and beat for 1 minute at same speed. The batter will be thick. Cover and let rise in a draft-free place until doubled in bulk, about 1 hour.

Punch dough down and place into a buttered and floured bundt pan or 2 8½ × 4½-inch loaf pans. Cover again and let rise in a draft-free place about 30 minutes.

Bake in a preheated 350°F oven for 35 minutes for medium-size loaves or 40 to 45 minutes for loaf baked in bundt pan.

Cool on a wire rack.

I have thoroughly enjoyed making breads that use whole wheat, rye, or triticale berries, but Cyndie writes that she has not been able to find wheat berries since first making this bread about a year ago. For bakers who can't find the berries in their local natural foods stores, I've included some sources in the back of the book from which they can be ordered by mail. They're well worth the trouble, since they're not only healthful, but they also add a remarkable texture to your loaves.

The night before baking, combine wheat berries with enough water to cover. Next morning, simmer berries in a small saucepan for about 45 minutes, or until tender. Drain, reserving the water. Measure out reserved wheat berry water, adding more very warm water, if necessary, to make 2½ cups of liquid.

Dissolve yeast in warm wheat berry water. Pour yeast liquid into a large bowl and add the nonfat dry milk, butter, and salt. Stir well. Add wheat berries and wheat germ. Gradually stir in flour to make a stiff dough.

Turn out onto a lightly floured surface, adding small amounts of flour, if necessary, to prevent sticking, and knead until smooth and elastic, 8 to 10 minutes. Shape into a ball, place into an oiled bowl, and turn to coat. Cover with a towel and let rise in a warm spot until doubled in bulk, about 1½ hours.

Punch down dough, turn out onto a floured surface, divide in half, and flatten each piece into a rectangular shape, about 8 by 12 inches. Sprinkle with nuts. Fold each piece in half to enclose nuts, kneading slightly to work nuts through dough. Shape each piece into a free-form loaf and place on an oiled baking sheet. Cover with wax paper and let rise in a warm spot until almost doubled in bulk, about 1 hour.

Brush loaves with melted butter. Using a floured knife or a razor blade, slash an "X" on top of each loaf. Bake in a preheated 350°F oven for 35 to 40 minutes, or until loaves sound hollow when tapped on the bottom.

Remove from baking sheet and cool on wire racks.

# Wheat Berry Nut Loaf

(2 loaves)

⅓ cup wheat berries
1 tablespoon dry yeast
½ cup nonfat dry milk
2 tablespoons butter, softened
1 teaspoon salt (optional, see page 22)
3 tablespoons toasted wheat germ
6 to 6½ cups whole wheat flour
2 cups coarsely chopped nuts (walnuts, pecans, or pistachios)
melted butter for brushing loaves

# BAKING BREAD ON TELEVISION ("NO TIME TO FAIL")

Over the centuries, our civilization has devised three superb methods of torture: the iron maiden, drawing and quartering, and the author book tour! The latter is an ingenious form of agony that sends a writer to *25 cities in 24 days*, has him appear on 75 television shows and 47 radio shows, as well as give 209 newspaper interviews, with no time to do laundry, eat a decent dinner, or even be sure which city he's in at a particular moment!

And so, for *Bread Winners*, I was sent across America (with a brief sally into Canada). I smiled a lot, appeared on too many television shows that started the day at 6:00 A.M., and flew on a lot of airplanes—and I baked bread, *live*, on TV.

An interesting characteristic of television, though, is that it is a "headline" medium. There is no time for expanding on a theme, no time to develop a demonstration. Psychiatrists have determined that the attention of the average American is about 30 seconds, and so a typical pre-show conversation might go something like this:

*"What would you like me to do?" I ask sleepily, this being the fourteenth day of the tour and I think I'm in Portland (or is it Seattle? It's raining, so it might be either one). "Well," the host or hostess answers, "We'd like you to tell us why you wrote the book, why it's different from any other, all about the bakers in the book . . . and we'd like you to bake a bread for us."*

*"Fine," I mumble. "How much time do I have?"*

*"Six minutes!"*

I learned to accomplish it all in six minutes, including the baking of the bread. It was, indeed, no time to make mistakes, no time to fail. Once again I used the reliable Irish Brown Bread (page 41), since it was the quickest of the breads to prepare.

However, even that quick bread takes longer than six minutes to bake, and so a completely baked bread was sent by air to each station, scheduled to arrive the day before my appearance, which I could show as the final result of my quick-mixing efforts. As a back-up, I also carried a finished bread in my overnight case, and several times it was rushed into service. In one instance, the television crew had *eaten* the bread when it was delivered on the previous day! I whipped out the spare, a little worse for the two weeks in a dark bag, brushed it off, and dusted it with flour—and it looked just fine in a close-up on the television screen.

On my way home, the blur of cities and shows still blending into one long loaf of bread, I read in the local paper that Erma Bombeck told an interviewer that she will never go on a book tour. It is exactly the statement that I made after my first tour, after my second tour, and after my third tour. As I prepare for my fourth trip around the country to publicize a book, I find that I have forgotten the pain, the loneliness, the bad food, the frustrations, the terrible hours, and somehow I am looking forward again to appearing on television, telling my life history, and baking bread—all in six minutes. But I swear that after this book tour, *I will never go on another one again!*

# Susan Manlin Katzman

*The Bread:*

**Granola Honey Bread**

*If your cup runneth over and your spoon spills, chances are you aren't measuring correctly. Careful measuring can make the difference between "wow" and "ugh" in some recipes.*

Susan Manlin Katzman is owner, manager, and teacher at a most unusual cooking school in Clayton, Missouri, a suburb of St. Louis. It's called "The Kitchen School" and its students range in age from 9 to 12 years old. The instructions, such as the one quoted above, are simple, direct, and leave very little to chance or the possibility of a kitchen accident:

*Pour sticky liquids (like honey) into a spoon; don't dip the spoon into sticky liquids. Scrape sticky liquids from the spoon with a rubber scraper.*

Each Saturday morning, the eager children try their hands at a variety of cooking adventures that include French, Italian, Mexican, and Greek dishes, a Thanksgiving feast— and, of course, freshly baked breads. Everything is cooked from scratch and the teacher stresses thorough cleanup as a part of the course.

*Parents won't let their kids cook at home unless they clean up afterwards. Kids are fun to teach. . . . They're inquisitive and they're wonderfully creative.*

The school has been so successful that Susan has collected her child-tested recipes in her own book, *For Kids Who Cook* (New York: Holt, Rinehart & Winston, 1977). Here is one of the favorite bread recipes from The Kitchen School.

This recipe uses whole wheat flour, which gives the bread the somewhat denser texture that I prefer. However, Susan says that the kids find the texture more to their liking when unbleached white flour, with a small addition of whole wheat is used. Either way, the result is scrumptious.

Place softened butter and honey into a large bowl. Beat with electric beater until smooth and fluffy. Add the egg, yogurt, and vanilla and beat until ingredients are well combined. Turn mixer off. Add the flour, baking powder, baking soda, cinnamon, and salt to mixture and beat until ingredients are well blended. Stir in granola and nuts, if desired. Spoon mixture into a buttered 8½ × 4½-inch loaf pan and bake in a preheated 350°F oven for 55 to 60 minutes.

Remove pan from oven and set on a rack until bread is cool. When cool, loosen bread from pan by running a sharp knife around the edge of the bread. Remove from pan and cool completely before slicing.

# Granola Honey Bread

(1 medium-size loaf)

½ cup butter, softened (To soften butter, let it stand at room temperature until it is easy to spread.)
½ cup honey
1 egg
1 cup yogurt
1 teaspoon vanilla extract
1½ cups whole wheat flour
1 teaspoon baking powder
1 teaspoon baking soda
1 teaspoon ground cinnamon
¼ teaspoon salt (optional, see page 22)
1½ cups granola
¼ cup chopped nuts (optional)

# Jason Stone

*The Bread:*

**Tofu Herb Bread**

*My occupation is librarian. When asked, "What do you do?" I venture the cautious reply, "I seek enlightenment and truth." I am strongly attracted to the East, my diet is vegetarian, with Greek, Middle Eastern, and Indian overtones, and my philosophy of life shares much with and is much beholden to Mohandas Gandhi and Hermann Hesse. I have lived the fast life of New York and have opted for a simpler place.*

I met Jay through Brenda Berger, who is in charge of the audio-visual department at the East Brunswick Library in New Jersey, where I have since lectured on a subject quite far from the baking of bread—middle age! My file contains Jay's descriptions of his life and his feelings about his philosophy, along with his view of baking as a form of *giving*, which indeed it is. For those of us who think of the New York area as a continual urban struggle, I present with relish Jay's description of where he lives—*facing* the big city:

*I live in a tiny house one mile from the ocean. . . . From the end of my street there is a panoramic view of the Verrazano-Narrows Bridge, lit up in garlands like a wedding-cake decoration, the Manhattan skyline, and the lights of Brooklyn and Staten Island stretching to the east behind Sandy Hook. It's a most precious place to me, the immensity of the ocean and the stillness of the bay waters, the relaxation of a tiny beach one and a half blocks from my home. Everything is here: beach, country, the city across the water— and peaceful solitude.*

Jay has been experimenting with substituting tofu for dairy products and with using herbs in place of salt. This fairly coarse, tasty, salt-free bread resulted.

To prepare the dry mixture: In a large bowl, mix together 1 cup flour with the rest of the dry ingredients.

To prepare the leavening: In a small bowl, dissolve yeast in warm water. Add honey, stir, and set aside to proof.

To prepare the wet mixture: Push tofu through a colander (or mash thoroughly) into a small heavy saucepan. Drain tofu and reserve ¼ cup liquid. Add the honey, butter, and reserved liquid and heat until very warm, 100° to 110°F. Remove from heat, stir in egg and yeast mixture, and add immediately to flour mixture. Beat about 3 minutes.

Add the remaining flour, ½ cup at a time, stirring thoroughly. Turn out onto a floured surface and knead only until the ingredients are well combined, 1 to 3 minutes. The dough will be very heavy, resilient, and a little sticky. Place dough into an oiled bowl, turn to coat, cover, and let rise in a warm place until doubled in bulk, 45 to 60 minutes.

Turn out onto a floured surface and punch down. The dough may have a broken outer surface, this is fine. Place dough in a well-buttered 1½- to 2-quart round casserole, cover, and let rise in a warm place for 15 to 30 minutes. The dough may not double in size.

Bake in a preheated 350°F oven for 35 to 40 minutes. The loaf will rise to only 2 to 3 inches in height.

# Tofu Herb Bread

(1 loaf)

*Dry Mixture:*
2½ to 3 cups whole wheat
 flour
 ½ teaspoon dried rosemary
 2 tablespoons grated
 Parmesan cheese
 1 tablespoon dried parsley
 1 teaspoon dried thyme,
 ground
 ¼ teaspoon baking soda
 ¼ teaspoon dried oregano

*Leavening:*
 1 tablespoon dry yeast
 ½ cup warm water
 1 teaspoon honey

*Wet Mixture:*
 1 cup soft tofu (about ½
 pound)
 2 tablespoons honey
 1 tablespoon butter
 1 egg

# Katherine Seem

*The Bread:*

**Yogurt Casserole Bread**

Katherine is, in a sense, a neighbor—not on Fire Island, but right next door to my publisher, Rodale Press, in Emmaus, Pennsylvania. Though she and her husband spent their working lives in agriculture, growing certified hybrid seed corn and small grains, they are now, as she puts it, "very busy retirees."

*We have two married sons and three grandchildren and all of them say nice things about my bread. I use home-ground, locally grown wheat that produces a flour somewhat different from the "store-bought" kind. And the whole process of creating a loaf of bread, from the grinding of the wheat, through the kneading, baking, and serving, makes me feel good. I do it with love!*

Out near an old summerhouse, right on her property, is an outdoor oven in which her great-grandmother used to bake bread.

*The one step I'd like to take in my bread-baking journey is to use that outdoor oven. If my great-grandmother could bake bread in it, I suppose I could too. So far I haven't been able to work up the courage to try it.*

Other readers who feel the same way about outdoor ovens might look at Suzanne Gosar's plans on page 280.

In a small bowl, dissolve yeast in warm water.

In a large bowl, combine all the remaining ingredients, except for the flour. Stir in yeast mixture. Add flour gradually, beating well. (Katherine says, "This won't be easy, but grit your teeth and do it. The texture will be coarse if your beating is half-hearted!") Cover and let rise in a warm place until doubled in bulk, about 1 hour.

Stir down and turn into a well-buttered 1½-quart casserole. Let rise, lightly covered, in a warm place for about 45 minutes.

Bake in a preheated 350°F oven for 35 to 45 minutes.

# Yogurt Casserole Bread

(1 loaf)

1 tablespoon dry yeast
¼ cup warm water
1 cup yogurt, heated to
   lukewarm
2 tablespoons honey
2 teaspoons minced onions
1 tablespoon vegetable oil
2 teaspoons dillweed
½ teaspoon salt (optional, see
   page 22)
1 egg, beaten
2¼ to 3 cups whole
   wheat flour

# Cathy Silverstein

*The Breads:*

**Muesli Bread**
**Jug of Wine and Thou Bread**

*I never use an apron. I bought one once—a Sweeney Todd complete with blood splatters—but I find that I always dust myself with flour from head to toe. Maybe it's a badge of baking, sort of like a painter's splotched pants.*

Cathy works in the New York area editing a newsletter for apartment managers and owners—doing production, promotion, circulation, advertising, and purchasing. She compares her job to baking bread:

*My job mixes a variety of ingredients—copy, typeface, paper, negatives, labels, envelopes, telephones, salesmen—to produce a full-risen/realized monthly newsletter. Lots of kneading necessary!*

In her bread baking, Cathy is still experimenting with finding the best ratios for sweetness and for texture, just like the rest of us. However, there's one area in which she has difficulties:

*I can't seem to manage sourdough starter. I keep forgetting to feed it!*

Note to Cathy: See the Index!

Cathy tells me that the original recipe for this bread came from her friend, Juliet Neidish, "dancer, cum telemarketer, extraordinaire." The recipe for her Muesli follows the bread recipe.

In a large bowl, cream butter and honey together until smooth. Add the beaten eggs, salt, lemon rind, rum extract, and milk. Stir in baking powder and then flour and Muesli. Mix thoroughly with a wooden spoon until well blended. Turn the batter into a well-oiled and lightly floured 9 × 5-inch loaf pan and bake in a preheated 350°F oven for 40 to 45 minutes, or until golden brown and the loaf tests done.

Cool in pan for 10 minutes and then turn out onto a wire rack to complete the cooling.

# Muesli Bread

(1 large loaf)

⅓ cup butter
1 cup honey
2 eggs, beaten
  pinch of salt (optional, see
    page 22)
  grated rind of 1 lemon
½ teaspoon rum extract
½ cup milk
1 tablespoon baking powder
2 cups whole wheat flour
½ cup Muesli (Familia), see
    page 196

## Muesli (Familia)

1 cup rolled oats
½ cup millet flakes
½ cup rye or wheat flakes
½ cup chopped dates, dried
apricots, or dried apples
½ cup toasted wheat germ
½ cup raisins
½ cup ground or slivered
almonds or hazelnuts
¼ cup sesame seeds
¼ cup sunflower seeds
¼ cup unsweetened shredded
coconut

Mix all the ingredients together in a large bowl.

The balance of the Muesli can be used as an excellent and tasty cold breakfast cereal, served with sliced bananas and milk.

# Jug of Wine and Thou Bread

(4 loaves)

4 cups milk
6 cups grated hard cheese
(cheddar, colby, or
Monterey Jack)
¼ cup butter
2 tablespoons dry yeast
1 cup warm water
⅓ cup honey
11 to 13 cups whole wheat
flour
2 teaspoons salt (optional, see
page 22)
melted butter for brushing
loaves
2 tablespoons chopped fresh
parsley
2 tablespoons caraway seeds
2 teaspoons curry powder

Cathy suggests that this bread be served with wine and fruit and a book of poetry—but she mentions that it's also great with tuna salad!

*In retesting the recipe, I was impatient and I poured the milk mixture in too soon. It killed the yeast! An hour and a half later, all I had was a piece of rock dough. In anger and desperation, I threw the dough on the table and dissolved two more tablespoons of yeast in water in the mixing bowl. Then I returned the dough to the bowl, squished the yeast mixture into it, waited another hour, and it actually doubled! Not only that, but the grain and texture of the finished bread was even finer than it had ever been before!*

In a large saucepan, heat the milk, 3½ cups cheese, and butter and stir until cheese melts. *Be sure to cool mixture to warm,* about 110°F. (See Cathy's comments at the beginning of the recipe!)

While milk mixture is cooling, dissolve yeast in warm water in a large bowl. Add honey and then add the cooled milk mixture and stir. Mix in flour, 1 cup at a time (use about 10 cups). Then add salt and the remaining cheese.

Turn out onto a floured surface and knead for 8 to 10 minutes, adding the remaining flour as needed to make a firm dough. Place dough into an oiled bowl, turn to coat, cover, and let rise in a warm spot until doubled in bulk, 45 to 60 minutes.

Punch down, turn out onto a floured surface, and knead for 2 to 3 minutes. Divide the dough into 4 portions, cover, and let rest for about 10 minutes. Shape loaves as desired. Place into 4 buttered 9 × 5-inch loaf pans, or use a black steel double Italian loaf pan and a baking sheet to make 2 long and 2 round loaves. Cover lightly and let rise again in a warm spot until almost doubled in bulk, 45 to 60 minutes.

Brush loaves with melted butter. Sprinkle with parsley, caraway seeds, and curry powder and bake in a preheated 375°F oven for 40 to 55 minutes, or until loaves test done. If the loaves brown too quickly, cover them with aluminum foil for the last 10 to 15 minutes of baking.

Cool on wire racks.

Solar Risen Bread: On a sunny day, place the bowl of dough under a south window, covered with plastic wrap, several layers of towels, and then a black cloth to absorb the heat.

Connie Hartland

# Kenneth Earhart Jack Reyne (Chemistry and Bread)

*The Breads:*

**Spicy Zucchini Whole Wheat Bread**
**Whole Wheat Papaya Bread**

The two men are most unusual bread bakers, and both have much in common. Kenneth Earhart lives in Allentown, Pennsylvania, Jack Reyne in Dunwoody, Georgia. So far as I know, neither one has been introduced to the other, yet both appear in this book as bread bakers who draw on their professional background in creating their recipes. They are retired chemists.

Ken, now 75 years old, is still active as a consultant at Lehigh University, but he's only been baking for about five years.

*Being a chemist, I still get a kick out of mixing any new formula which involves heating. When I retired in 1974, I began to dabble in cooking and then in bread. The formula (sic!) I am submitting involves the use of lecithin, an emulsifier in its own right. Lecithin is derived from the refining of soybean oil and contains important phosphorus derivatives.*

To put it in a nutshell, Ken likes to use his chemistry background to improve his art of bread baking. And, by strange coincidence, so does Jack Reyne. (And, by even stranger coincidence, Jack is a relative of mine by marriage.) For over ten years, I have tasted Jack's superb breads whenever I visited the South.

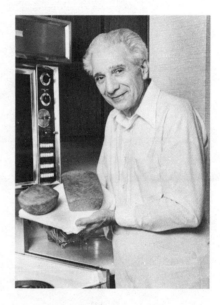

*I was an organic chemist doing research and development in the field of plastic polymers. I must say that my first breads reflected my professional background. They would have made excellent ceramic substitutes! There was even a time when the kitchen was declared off limits to me!*

Jack uses papaya enzyme in his breads, giving a distinctive taste to the results. In addition to enhancing flavor, he believes that papaya breaks up protein, producing a lower viscosity dough, which in turn is easier to leaven, and thus results in a lighter, more easily digestible loaf.

*Of course, that's what I believe takes place. Another biochemist might give you an entirely different idea!*

Both men prove to every bread baker among us that there is just no end to the imaginative and experimental opportunities that this craft provides. Jack's reaction is typical of the way we all feel:

*All bread to me is wonderful. As a boy, on the East Side of New York City, I lived over a bakery, and bread baking was the best smell in the world. However, when you want something really special, you bake your own.*

# Spicy Zucchini Whole Wheat Bread

(2 large loaves)

2 tablespoons dry yeast
¼ cup warm water
½ cup skim milk, warmed
2 teaspoons lecithin*
3 tablespoons butter, softened
2 tablespoons honey
6 cups whole wheat flour
¼ cup toasted wheat germ
1 teaspoon salt (optional, see page 22)
1 teaspoon grated orange rind
2 teaspoons ground cardamom
2 cups zucchini puree
¾ cup currants or raisins (optional)

Kenneth Earhart says that a mild sourdough version may be made using this same recipe by adding a cup of sourdough to the milk and yeast mixtures just prior to adding the flour mixture. The sourdough should be at room temperature, and slightly more flour may be needed at the end of the kneading process.

In a small bowl, dissolve yeast in warm water and set aside to proof.

In another small bowl, combine the warm milk, lecithin, butter, and honey and mix well. Stir in yeast mixture and blend. Place this mixture in a low oven to keep warm while carrying out the next step.

In a large bowl, mix together the flour, wheat germ, salt, orange rind, and cardamom.

Warm the large bowl of an electric mixer that has dough hooks and pour in milk/yeast mixture. Start the mixer at slow speed and slowly add about half the flour mixture. Then add zucchini puree and currants or raisins, if desired. Blend well. Then add the remaining dry ingredients 1 large spoonful at a time. Work dough with the hooks for about 8 minutes, or until elastic. (You may need additional flour if the zucchini puree is wet.)

Remove dough to a floured bread cloth and let rest while washing the mixing bowl with warm water. Dry thoroughly and oil bowl.

Work dough on the floured cloth for a few minutes, adding any flour necessary to remove tackiness. Place dough into oiled bowl, turn to coat, cover, and let rise in a warm place until doubled in bulk, about 1 hour.

Punch down, return to floured cloth, work for a few minutes, and divide into 2 portions. Place into 2 buttered 9 × 5-inch loaf pans. Cover and let rise in a warm place until dough reaches the tops of the pans, 45 to 60 minutes.

Bake at 325°F for 45 to 50 minutes from a cold start, or until breads test done.

Cool on wire racks.

*Lecithin concentrate may be obtained under the tradename ALCOLEC S 32-34 from American Lecithin Co., 61st Street, Woodside, NY 11377, or under the tradename STA-SOL UF-4 Lecithin Concentrate, from A. E. Staley Co., Decatur, IL 62525.

Jack Reyne is one New Yorker who made a lot of friends in Georgia when he began to share the recipe for this specialty with his southern neighbors.

In a large bowl, combine the flour, honey, yeast, and pulverized papaya enzyme tablets. Blend well. Add lukewarm water and mix thoroughly. At this stage, the mixture is tacky. Place butter into bowl, but do not mix in. Cover dough with towel and let stand for 30 to 45 minutes. The enzyme does its work at this point.

Knead dough in bowl for 8 minutes, working butter into mixture. If still tacky after kneading, add just enough whole wheat flour to eliminate the tackiness. Cover and let rise in a warm place until doubled in bulk, 45 to 60 minutes.

Punch dough down. Shape into loaf, place into a buttered 8½ × 4½-inch loaf pan, cover, and let rise in a warm place until doubled in bulk, 30 to 45 minutes.

Bake in a preheated 375°F oven for 35 to 40 minutes, or until loaf tests done.

Cool on a wire rack.

# Whole Wheat Papaya Bread

(1 medium-size loaf)

3 cups whole wheat flour
3 tablespoons honey
1 tablespoon dry yeast
3 tablets papaya enzyme (natural, 25 MC units per tablet), pulverized
1¼ cups lukewarm water
2 tablespoons butter

When using honey, try heating the spoon. A warm spoon cuts off almost all the threads when you drag it across the rim of the jar. I do the same for measuring cups by running hot water into them before pouring in the honey.

Andrea Brazer-Rush

# Elizabeth (Beti) Horvath

*The Breads:*

**Jaroslawa's Babka
–Jaroslawa's Filled
Crescents**

*Grandma Jaroslawa always made fancy breads for the holidays. After working in the Ukranian community in New York City, she and my grandfather retired to our rural community of Bloomingburg in the heart of the Catskills. There she became the operator of a boarding house where she cooked for "friends from the city."*

Though Beti Horvath is a recent convert to home-baked bread, the traditions of Grandma Jaroslawa continue to influence her efforts. The Jaroslawa Babka recipe that follows is a variation of the original. Not too long ago, in fact, independent filmmaker Dee Dee Hallack produced a short film that "starred" Grandma—naturally, it was titled *Jaroslawa*. In it, the techniques of making the babka were minutely detailed by Grandma as she prepared and baked her famous holiday breads.

Beti is a librarian at a community college in Loch Sheldrake, New York. Like all bakers, she has had her share of crises, such as the time she left the house to investigate the meowing of a cat marooned in a tree and locked herself out—with her dough set out to rise in the middle of the living room in the rays of the afternoon sun.

*But, when I bake bread, I feel creative, revolutionary, independent, strong, proud, earthy, clever . . . and that I'm carrying on a family tradition that started with Grandma Jaroslawa.*

Make sure that all ingredients are at room temperature. Scald milk in a medium-size saucepan and cool to room temperature.

In a large bowl, combine 3 cups of the flour with milk, setting aside a little milk in a cup in which to dissolve the yeast. Mix thoroughly. (Jaroslawa used a large enamel canning pot for mixing, and Beti continues to use it now.)

Dissolve yeast in the reserved milk and then add to flour/milk mixture. Stir in 2 cups of the flour and 1 teaspoon of the honey to make a sponge. Cover the bowl with a lintless towel and let rise in a warm spot until doubled in bulk, 1 to 2 hours.

In a medium-size bowl, beat together egg yolks and 4 of the eggs vigorously, adding the remaining honey, lemon rind, vanilla or mace, and salt.

Using a wooden spoon, stir down sponge and then blend in egg mixture. Add flour, 1 cup at a time, stirring after each addition. You will probably have to use your hands when the dough becomes too heavy to work with a spoon. The dough should be elastic and should hold together, even though it will still be soft. Add softened butter and continue to knead for 30 minutes more, adding flour as you need it, but being careful to keep the dough a soft mass.

Smooth a small amount of oil on your kneading board and make a circle with it about 10 inches in diameter. Encircle the oil with a "dam" of flour 1 to 2 inches high. Turn the very soft dough out onto the board and gently knead in more of the flour, kneading for another 30 minutes or more. Oil the bottom of the large bowl (or enamel pot), return the kneaded smooth dough to it, turn to coat, and cover with a towel. Let rise in a warm place until doubled in bulk, 1 to 1½ hours.

Punch dough down and knead briefly. Turn into 2 buttered 10- or 12-inch tube pans or cake pans, filling the pans about two-thirds full. If there is any dough left over, you can make Jaroslawa's Filled Crescents (recipe follows). Cover and let rise for about 1 hour.

Beat together the remaining egg and the water and brush this mixture over loaves. Bake in a preheated 375°F oven for 45 to 50 minutes.

Cool in pans before removing. Serve warm.

# Jaroslawa's Babka

(2 loaves)

4 cups milk
14 to 16 cups whole wheat flour
2 tablespoons dry yeast
¾ cup buckwheat honey (This honey has a strong flavor. You may use a lighter honey if you prefer.)
10 egg yolks
5 eggs
grated rind of 1 lemon
dash of vanilla extract or mace
1 teaspoon salt (optional, see page 22)
1½ cups butter, softened but not melted
vegetable oil for coating kneading board
¼ cup water

# Jaroslawa's Filled Crescents

(about 12 crescents)

Using the recipe that precedes this, you may make Jaroslawa's Filled Crescents as individual buns or filled shapes—or as a plain loaf for toasting at breakfast. The filled crescents or buns can be made with poppy seeds, prune filling, or apricot filling. Jaroslawa's recipes started with basic pieces of dough, 2½ to 3 inches square. She then filled them and rolled them into crescents and 4-cornered shapes.

To make the crescent shape: Fold in 1 corner. Continue rolling dough until pointed tube is formed. Then shape into a crescent.

To make the 4-cornered shape: Fold all 4 corners into center.

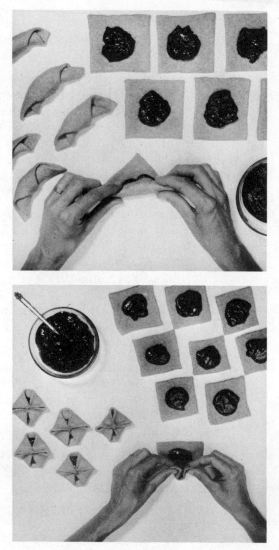

# BAKING
# BREAD AT
# THE ABA
# CONVENTION

We were told that it would be impossible. Baking bread on a convention floor was tantamount to trying the same thing in the parking lot at an NFL Super Bowl game. We were told that no one had ever attempted it before. We were told that it just would not work. So, we went ahead with the idea anyhow.

Each year, the publishing industry shows off its wares to the book world at the American Booksellers Association (ABA) convention, which is attended by as many as twenty thousand people who work in the field. Publishers, book retailers, chain store buyers, publicists—and hopeful authors—spend three full days displaying the most awesome aggregate of would-be "best sellers," most of them proclaimed as rivals to the Bible in terms of sales potential. It is, without a doubt, a most exciting time, and the competition is fierce. It was here that we were going to show off the new *Bread Winners* by baking bread in an oven set up on the convention floor. If we were going to publicize a bread book, what better way than to bake bread!

The results were remarkable. During the time that the breads were being formed, or were in the oven, we had the normal volume of traffic at the Rodale booth. But, each and every hour for three days, we took four fresh-baked breads from the oven. And each and every hour, we suddenly saw a mob of hungry people converging upon our small space. We called it "instant people." The aroma of fresh-baked loaves permeated the convention floor. The delegates lined up as soon as word got around the floor, "They're baking fresh bread at the Rodale Booth!"

I had chosen to bake my never-fail Irish Brown Bread because it's quick—I can get four loaves out within an hour from start to finish. Sheryl baked the more complicated Monkey Bread (recipe follows) and our friend, Stacie Hunt, one of the bakers in *Bread Winners* who lives right in Los Angeles where the convention was held that year, baked a brown bread in *flowerpots*. It's a baking method that dates back to the Etruscans.

The most wonderful result of baking at the ABA convention was the fact that so many people remembered what we had done. All around the country, I still meet booksellers who recall the aroma of fresh bread on the convention floor. And in 1982, almost three years later, when I attended the ABA convention in Anaheim to publicize *Second Spring* (dealing with middle age and having nothing to do with yeast and flour), people kept stopping at the Rodale booth to ask, "How come you're not baking bread this year?" Well, maybe next year if all goes well!

The recipe for the Irish Brown Bread is on page 41. If you'd like to try it in a flowerpot, rather than as a free-form bread, make sure you get a pot that has been heat tested or it may crack in the hot oven. It may also take a bit longer to bake on the inside. Just cover the top with aluminum foil if it's finished before the bottom and continue baking the bread. And, for those of you who want to try a most unusual bread, here is the original recipe for Monkey Bread that was included in *Bread Winners* and baked by Sheryl at the ABA convention. She calls it "tear-off-a-piece-of-bread bread" because it's baked in little pieces of ropelike dough—and it's already buttered!

In a large bowl, mix together 1½ cups flour, yeast, honey, and salt and set aside.

In a medium-size saucepan, heat milk and softened butter to 110°F, then pour over flour-yeast mixture. Add egg and, using an electric hand beater, beat 3 minutes at medium speed. Add another cup of flour and beat 3 minutes longer. Stir in the remaining flour and mix with a wooden spoon until completely blended. Place into an oiled bowl, turn to coat, cover, and let rise in a warm spot for about 30 minutes.

Turn out onto a lightly floured surface and knead for 10 minutes. Cover lightly and let rest for 10 minutes.

Divide dough into 2 equal parts. Roll out each piece into a 12 by 18-inch rectangle. Cut into strips ¾ inch wide and then divide each strip into pieces 3 inches in length. Using a large bowl or a deep saucepan, dip each of the strips into the melted, cooled butter and then haphazardly toss them into a 10-inch tube pan. Cover, place in an unheated oven, and let rise for about 1½ hours. (The pilot light in a gas oven will provide just enough heat to keep the temperature at about 100°F.)

Remove covering, then increase heat to 425°F and bake on bottom rack for 30 to 40 minutes, or until golden brown. If the top begins to burn before the bread is done, cover lightly with aluminum foil and continue baking.

Turn out onto a wire rack to cool slightly. Serve warm. The bread is *not* sliced; it is eaten by tearing off piece by delicious piece.

# Monkey Bread

(1 large loaf)

4 to 5 cups whole wheat flour
3 tablespoons dry yeast
2 tablespoons honey
½ teaspoon salt (optional, see page 22)
1½ cups milk
⅓ cup butter, softened
1 egg
¾ cup butter, melted and cooled to room temperature

Instead of regular water for proofing yeast, I use potato water. It makes for a delicious bread.
Tami Watson

# Bob Adjemian

*The Bread:*

**Cuban Bread**

*Our "family" consists of 15 to 20 monks, a neighborhood of members, and a convent. The nuns also make their own bread and I relied extensively on their advice in my early days of bread making. At one time, I used to cook for everyone; I suppose that no one else has shared the madness of baking 50 loaves of bread in one week.*

Bob and I met at the American Booksellers Association convention (see Index), when he brought me a slice of his home-baked bread to sample, and we spoke of his life as a monk, publisher of Vedanta Press, bookstore manager, advertising manager, and writer. As a monk, Bob also practices meditation according to Eastern philosophy. After the convention he wrote to me about his feelings.

*I was so delighted to meet another male who really enjoyed bread making and understood what it's all about. The day after you left, your booth was almost deserted. People love homemade bread. There was no bread, so there were no people!*

Bob believes that flour should be milled by the baker, since it imparts a special taste that is quite different from "store-bought" flour. He uses a flour mill that is 36 years old, yet still runs perfectly. He won't bake bread unless he can grind his own flour.

At the convention, we laughed and exchanged "failure" stories, discussing the classic problems of adding too much liquid, or using dead yeast. Bob related a delightful tale of forgetfulness:

*Once when I was doing a bread-making blitz for the monastery, I left a loaf of bread in the oven for 24 hours. Someone else had even used the oven. Imagine my surprise when I preheated the oven and saw the loaf from the previous day! However, it still made great toast. Bread is forgiving.*

When I received Bob's original recipe for the Cuban Bread, I noticed that the amounts of ingredients called for were enormous, such as 14 cups of hot water and 10 pounds of flour. Bob's answer to all that was, "Remember, I'm feeding 15 people at one time!" We adjusted the recipes for smaller groups, but Bob has also added the amounts needed for 10 large French breads (just in case *your* family is a big one).

# Cuban Bread

(2 or 3 loaves, or 8 to 10 loaves)

*For 2 or 3 loaves:*
1 tablespoon dry yeast
2 cups warm water
1 tablespoon honey
5 to 6½ cups whole wheat flour
1 cup cooked oatmeal
1 teaspoon salt (optional, see page 22)
1 tablespoon cornmeal
boiling water

*For 8 to 10 loaves:*
4 tablespoons dry yeast
8 cups warm water
¼ cup honey
2 cups whole wheat flour
4 cups cooked oatmeal
4 teaspoons salt (optional, see page 22)
8 to 10 pounds whole wheat flour
¼ cup cornmeal
boiling water

*This is a non-recipe. I don't necessarily follow the quantities listed. In fact, I don't even measure the flour, but add it until the dough is not sticky. I get the best results with freshly ground whole wheat flour, but this bread is extremely popular if I use about 30 percent unbleached white flour, in which case, I sneak in some bran or wheat germ.*

Bob also says that he bakes the bread until it *smells* like it's done. Although that method of testing may seem too simple, he maintains that it works beautifully.

In a large bowl, dissolve yeast in warm water. Add honey without stirring. Then, after 3 to 5 minutes, add ½ cup flour. Let yeast proof for 10 minutes.

Add oatmeal, blending in thoroughly, then add salt and remaining flour, 1 cup at a time, stirring after each addition. Do not knead. The mixture will become so thick that you will have to plunge in and mix it with your hands. When you have added just enough flour so that the dough is not sticky, form it into a ball, place into an oiled bowl, turn to coat, and cover with a wet cloth. Let rise in a warm spot until nearly doubled in bulk, 1 to 1¼ hours.

When dough has risen, do not punch down, but turn it out onto a floured surface and shape into round or long French loaves. Place them on a baking sheet, into 8½ × 4½-inch loaf pans, or into French loaf pans. Whatever shape you decide to use, sprinkle cornmeal generously on the surface of the baking sheet, loaf pans, or French loaf pans. Sprinkle tops of loaves with cornmeal if desired and slit with a razor blade or sharp, floured knife, so that the breads will expand evenly. Cover lightly and let rise in a warm spot for 20 to 30 minutes. Then place the breads in a cold oven and coat them with water. Place two pie plates full of boiling water at the bottom of the oven. Set temperature to 400°F and bake the loaves until crusty, about 50 minutes.

The bread tastes best within 24 hours after it's been baked. After that time, use it for toast or place into a shopping bag that has been moistened with water and warm in a 350°F oven for about 25 minutes. Serve immediately.

# Jane Praeger

You might be able to tell from the name of Jane's favorite muffins that she is an independent documentary filmmaker, just as I am. At the time of this writing, she is co-producing two films for public television, *The Cancer War*, a 60-minute documentary on the politics and economics of cancer research, and *The Frankie Lymon Story*, a film about the legendary 13-year-old singer.

> *I've been incredibly busy—you know how feast-or-famine this business is. I never bought a loaf of bread until I moved back to New York from California, and I began to miss my blissful days in the kitchen.*

And so, at present, the main beneficiaries of Jane's bread and muffins are her co-workers. She often disappears in mid-afternoon to bake up a batch:

> *So many things can go wrong during the making of a movie that it's important to do what you can to keep your spirits*

*high. I've found that a bowl of spicy, steaming, fragrant muffins is one of the best antidotes to the movie-making malaise. The frequency of my kitchen forays has turned my assistants into muffin gourmets—discerning critics equally devoted to helping me produce the perfect bran muffin as well as the perfect film!*

She confesses that, like many of us, her favorite part of the whole process of bread baking is eating the results:

*I especially love the first slice. No matter how many times you've made that particular bread, the first slice is a revelation of taste and texture.*

# "Take 2" Apple Cider Fruit Muffins

(12 muffins)

1 cup apple cider or apple juice
¼ cup currants or raisins
¼ cup finely chopped dates
1 cup whole wheat flour
1 cup bran
2 tablespoons toasted wheat germ
¼ cup rolled oats
1 teaspoon baking soda
1 tablespoon ground cinnamon
pinch of ground nutmeg
pinch of ground allspice
3 tablespoons honey
1 teaspoon molasses
1 egg
½ cup yogurt

In a small saucepan, simmer together the apple cider or juice, currants or raisins, and dates for 1 to 2 minutes. Remove from heat and set aside to cool.

In a large bowl, combine the flour, bran, wheat germ, oats, baking soda, cinnamon, nutmeg, and allspice.

In a small bowl, combine the honey, molasses, egg, yogurt, and cooled cider mixture. Add the liquid ingredients to the dry ingredients, stirring gently and only until the dry ingredients are moistened. Do not over-mix. Spoon batter into a generously buttered 12-cup muffin tin and bake for 30 to 35 minutes, or until muffins test done.

Allow muffins to cool for a few minutes before removing from tin.

## Coconut-Date Muffins

Substitute 2 tablespoons unsweetened shredded coconut for the wheat germ. Use ½ cup finely chopped dates instead of ¼ cup dates and ¼ cup currants or raisins. Substitute 1 teaspoon vanilla for the molasses.

Substitute ¼ cup chopped walnuts for the dates.

Currant-Nut
Muffins

# Banana Bran Bread

(1 large loaf)

This is a moist, dense, and cakey bread that Jane says tastes better on the second day. She adds a note about this bread which also applies to her other recipes:

> *Working on* The Cancer War, *which explores some of the alternative nutritional cancer therapies and diet as a cancer preventative in general, I've become more conscious of the way I eat. Not only does that mean using whole grains and natural sweeteners, but cutting down on fats and sugars in general. So I've devised recipes which rely more on fruits to sweeten, and ingredients like yogurt and juices to moisten.*

She goes on to point out that in this recipe she uses about half the amount of butter generally called for in banana breads. Instead, she uses lemon juice and Postum. Reducing fats is a principle that both Sheryl and I have followed in all of our cookbooks.

1½ cups whole wheat flour
½ cup bran
1 teaspoon baking soda
2 teaspoons baking powder
¼ cup butter
¼ cup honey
1 egg
3 small or 2 large bananas
1 teaspoon lemon juice
¾ cup yogurt
½ cup strong Postum
1 teaspoon vanilla extract
½ cup golden raisins
½ cup chopped walnuts
    (optional)

In a small bowl, combine the flour, bran, baking soda and baking powder. Set aside.

In a large bowl, cream butter and honey until fluffy. Lightly beat egg and add to the butter/honey mixture. Mix well and set aside.

In medium-size bowl, mash bananas with lemon juice. Add the yogurt, Postum, vanilla, raisins, and nuts, if desired, and mix well.

Starting with flour mixture, alternately add flour mixture and yogurt mixture to butter/honey mixture, stirring only enough to combine the ingredients. Pour batter into a well-buttered 9 × 5-inch loaf pan and bake in a preheated 350° F oven for 1 hour, or until a wooden pick inserted in center comes out clean.

Cool for 10 minutes in the pan before removing to a wire rack. Wrap any leftover bread tightly in aluminum foil to store.

Note: For an even "dessertier" bread, Jane substitutes rum for the Postum and adds ¼ cup of unsweetened shredded coconut.

# Stanley Halbreich

Stan Halbreich's letters and telephone calls began soon after publication of *Bread Winners*. His stories were filled with humor and wit, and bread lore. He also included some valuable introductions to other bakers, most notably Ed Feiner (see Index), and that led to the eventual, uproarious "Little League Bake-off" in Toms River, New Jersey.

I have detailed the famous event (accompanied by a photograph) in the section on Ed Feiner. But it was Stanley who arranged the event in his own inimitable way, traveling all the way from his home in a suburb of Buffalo, New York, with his wife, Adele, to join us in Toms River.

Stan has been involved with real estate and equipment finance and has served as consultant to the pharmaceutical industry. While still a novice baker, he entered some of his breads in the Amherst County Fair, and to his surprise, won *first, second, and third prizes* for his entries!

> *Like most of us when we fantasize about our youth, I remember the joy of eating my aunt's fresh bread, or the warmth of a fresh bagel, the aroma enticing me as I rushed home on Sunday from the neighborhood deli. But the quickening pace of time, the demands of modern grocery distribution, and our concern with hygienic packaging in our stores, all served to change the character, taste, and nature of our breads . . .*

Stan says that he has never been an artistic person, cannot draw a straight line, cannot read his own handwriting (his letters are typed), and suddenly—by baking bread—he began creating something that was not only good to eat, but something his wife, Adele, was willing to use as a centerpiece for her table! He writes:

> *Bread baking is, frankly, a disease! When you analyze some of the symptoms of the syndrome, there is a common thread running through most of the sufferers:*
>
> *Insomnia: Who but us "driven souls" would stay up all hours of the day and night to see that our creations don't chill and are constantly caressed?*
>
> *Masochism: We drive ourselves in cruel and incredible ways. We will run hither and yon for some exotic flour, seed, or spice. With all of the conveniences available in our supermarkets, we make it a point to pass up these neighborhood stores in order to patronize some out-of-the-way hole-in-the-wall that carries a special ingredient.*
>
> *Exhibitionism: It's a form of show biz and each of us is very proud of his or her act. Friends, neighbors, strangers— all of them applaud us. As they say in my favorite San Francisco massage parlor, "It's nice to be kneaded!"*

The breads that Stan has given to me for this volume are prizewinners from the Amherst County Fair. He baked the original with some unbleached white flour, but, as you will see, they turn out beautifully when made entirely with whole wheat flour.

# High-Fiber Honey Whole Wheat Bread

(2 large loaves)

5½ to 6 cups stone-ground
whole wheat or graham
flour
1 teaspoon salt (optional, see
page 22)
1 cup milk
1 cup water
½ cup honey
2 tablespoons butter
2 tablespoons dry yeast
1 egg
½ cup toasted sunflower
seeds
½ cup bran

This high-fiber bread makes an excellent all-purpose family loaf. It keeps well, is marvelous for sandwiches, and makes exceptional morning toast.

In a large bowl, stir together 3½ cups flour and salt.

In a medium-size saucepan, combine the milk, water, honey, and butter and warm until butter begins to melt. It does not have to liquify completely. Dissolve yeast in liquid ingredients and set aside to proof for 10 minutes. Add yeast mixture to flour mixture and work it in until you have a soft dough. Add egg and mix thoroughly with an electric hand mixer or wooden spoon for about 2 minutes. Slowly add 1 cup flour, working it in as you do so. Then work in sunflower seeds and bran.

Turn dough out onto a floured surface, add 1 cup flour to dough, and knead until smooth and elastic, 8 to 10 minutes, adding more flour as needed. Place dough into a well-oiled bowl, turn to coat, cover, and let rise in a warm place until doubled in bulk, 1 to 1½ hours.

Punch down, turn out onto a floured surface, and knead for a few moments. Cut dough in half. Roll out each half, then roll up jelly-roll fashion, sealing the ends as you go. Tuck under toward seam. Place loaves into well-buttered 9 × 5-inch loaf pans. Cover the pans with a cloth and let loaves rise in a warm place until doubled in bulk, 45 to 60 minutes. The crown should be above the edge of the pan.

Bake in a preheated 375°F oven until golden brown, 40 to 45 minutes, or until loaves test done. If the crust seems to be browning too quickly, cover with a foil tent and continue baking until the bottoms are done.

Cool on wire racks.

This is a whole grain variation of pumpernickel bread. It uses carob to make the bread even darker and richer looking. I suppose that most of us also find something romantic about the designation, "Old World."

In a small bowl, dissolve yeast in ½ cup lukewarm water.

In a large bowl, combine the molasses, the remaining lukewarm water, salt, and caraway seeds. Add the rye flour, carob, yeast mixture, butter, and 1 cup whole wheat flour. Beat until smooth. Spread 1 cup whole wheat flour on a board or countertop. Turn dough out onto floured surface and knead in the remaining flour. Knead dough until firm, smooth, and elastic, 8 to 10 minutes, adding more flour if necessary. Place into a well-oiled bowl, turn to coat, cover, and let rise in a warm spot until doubled in bulk, about 2 hours.

Punch dough down, turn out onto a floured surface, shape into a loaf, and place on a buttered baking sheet that has been sprinkled with cornmeal. Cover and let rise in a warm spot for 40 to 50 minutes.

Glaze loaf with beaten egg yolk and sprinkle with sesame seeds, if desired. Bake in a preheated 375°F oven for 35 to 40 minutes, or until loaf tests done.

Cool on a wire rack.

# Old World Black Bread

(1 large loaf)

2 tablespoons dry yeast
1½ cups lukewarm water
½ cup molasses
½ teaspoon salt (optional, see page 22)
2 tablespoons caraway seeds
2 cups rye flour
½ cup carob powder
2 tablespoons butter
2½ cups whole wheat flour
cornmeal for dusting pan
1 egg yolk, beaten, for brushing loaf (optional)
sesame seeds for topping (optional)

If your free-form loaves seem to flatten out when they're baked, you may not have enough flour in the mixture. You can try baking them in pans of various shapes, including pie pans, to keep the dough in check.

Howard and Agnes Arns

# Mary Anne Gross

*The Breads:*

**Carrot Sunflower Seed
Bread
Semolina Bread**

*When I'm not cooking, cleaning, shopping, changing diapers, baking bread, gardening, tutoring, taking care of the needs of my two-year-old son, Daniel, my six-year-old daughter, Antonia, and my husband, Angelo, I try to find some time to work on a few books that I'm writing . . . which is to say that every now and then I find a rare five minutes to write!*

In spite of her schedule, Mary Anne has written one of my favorite bread books (*Baking Bread the Way Mom Taught Me,* $3.25, from Mary Gross-Ferraro, Yesterday's Village, Highland Mills, NY 10930. Cost includes postage and handling). We began our telephone and mail correspondence right after *Bread Winners* was published, and we have continued ever since.

*Making bread is in my blood, or should I say, in my hands. My mother made bread once or twice a week and I learned the art from her. She came from a large midwestern Norwegian farm family where bread baking was a necessary skill. And my paternal grandmother, Mary Gross, came to America from Italy and opened the first Italian bread bakery in Newburgh, New York. So you might say that I've inherited this fondness for good homemade bread from both sides of my family.*

She also bakes her own bread because she finds it so difficult to find decent, chemical-free loaves, and because it's a lot cheaper to bake her own. She agrees with the rest of us who bake bread that doing it yourself has the extra advantage of allowing you to add your own nutrition in the form of yogurt, whole grains, brewer's yeast, or nuts

and seeds. Versions of both recipes given here are included in her book, which, incidentally, carries a charming dedication:

> . . . to my mother, Anne Buckneberg Gross, who taught me how to make bread;
>
> to my daughter, Antonia Anne Ferraro, who loves bread and butter;
>
> and to my husband, Angelo Ferraro, who complains about buying flour, but loves to eat my bread!

# Carrot Sunflower Seed Bread

(2 large loaves or 3 medium-size loaves)

2 tablespoons dry yeast
½ cup lukewarm water
3 tablespoons honey
1½ cups low-fat ricotta
cheese
½ cup water
½ cup plus 2 teaspoons corn
oil
2 tablespoons brewer's yeast
1 teaspoon salt (optional, see
page 22)
6 eggs
1 cup raw, unsalted
sunflower seeds
2 cups grated carrots
9 cups stone-ground whole
wheat flour
1 egg, slightly beaten
raw sunflower seeds for
topping

A delicious, high-rising, nutritious 100 percent whole wheat bread full of sunflower seeds and grated carrots. The texture is soft and smooth, yet crunchy.

In a small bowl, dissolve yeast in lukewarm water. Add honey, stir, and set aside until foamy.

Combine ricotta cheese and water in a small saucepan and heat until warm. Pour into a large bowl and stir in ½ cup oil, brewer's yeast, salt, eggs, sunflower seeds, and carrots. Mix well. Add foamy yeast and then flour, 1 cup at a time, mixing well after each addition. Knead the last 2 cups of flour into dough on a floured surface and continue kneading until dough is smooth and not sticky, 8 to 10 minutes. In another large bowl, roll ball of dough in 1 teaspoon corn oil. Cover with towels and let rise in a warm place until doubled in bulk, about 1½ hours.

Punch dough down in the bowl, and roll it in the remaining teaspoon of corn oil. Cover and let rise in a warm place about 1 hour.

Turn out onto a floured surface, form into 2 or 3 loaves, place into 2 buttered 9 × 5-inch loaf pans or 3 buttered 8½ × 4½-inch loaf pans, cover with paper towels, and let rise in a warm place until doubled in bulk, about 45 minutes.

Brush beaten egg on top of risen loaves and sprinkle with sunflower seeds. Bake in a preheated 350°F oven for 60 minutes. If you are making smaller loaves, the baking time will be reduced 10 to 15 minutes.

Cool on wire racks.

The bread that follows is traditional and thus uses unbleached white flour. Mary Anne discusses Semolina Bread in her book:

*The Italian bakers in Brooklyn make a wonderful semolina bread in their huge brick ovens. I buy my semolina flour from them, but they won't give me their recipe. So I experimented and came up with this one. It's crusty and very much like the bread baked on Knickerbocker Avenue, despite the fact that I don't have a brick oven—yet.*

In a small bowl, dissolve yeast in lukewarm water. Add honey, stir, and set aside in a warm place until foamy.

Pour hot water into a large bowl, add salt and ¼ cup corn oil. Blend in 2 cups semolina flour and then 2 cups white flour. Add foamy yeast, mixing well. Add the remaining flour, alternately, starting with 1 cup semolina and then ½ cup white, kneading in the last cup to make a workable dough. Turn out onto a floured surface and knead for 15 to 20 minutes, or until dough is smooth, firm, elastic, and not sticky. In another large bowl, roll ball of dough in 1 teaspoon corn oil, cover with a hot damp towel, and let rise in a warm place until doubled in bulk, about 1½ hours.

While dough is still in the bowl, punch down and roll in the remaining teaspoon of corn oil. Cover with a hot, damp towel and let rise in a warm place for 1 hour.

Punch dough down, turn out onto a floured surface, and divide into 4 equal portions. Form 4 small, round loaves and place them on buttered, dark baking sheets that have been sprinkled with cornmeal. Place loaves far enough apart so that they don't touch while rising. Cover with a dry cloth and let rise in a warm place until doubled in bulk, 25 to 30 minutes.

Slash the tops of the loaves with a sharp knife or razor blade to form a cross on each. The cuts should be no more than ½ inch deep or the loaves may fall. Brush the tops with lukewarm water and sprinkle with sesame seeds.

Place a pan of hot water on bottom shelf of oven. Bake the loaves in a preheated 400°F oven for 15 minutes. Reduce heat to 350°F and brush loaves with water again. Bake 15 minutes longer. Brush once more with water and bake a final 10 minutes. The total baking time is 40 to 50 minutes. Tap the bottoms of the loaves. They should be crusty and have a hollow sound when tapped.

Cool on wire racks. To crackle the crust, place under a fan. Store loaves in a brown bag in the refrigerator. Plastic will soften the crust.

# Semolina Bread

(4 small loaves)

2 tablespoons dry yeast
½ cup lukewarm water
1 teaspoon honey
2 cups hot water
1 teaspoon salt (optional, see page 22)
¼ cup plus 2 teaspoons corn oil
4 cups semolina flour
3 cups unbleached white flour
cornmeal for dusting pan
sesame seeds for topping

# Elaine Burke

*The Bread:*

**Whole Wheat
Banana Muffins**

I met Elaine Burke at the American Library Association convention in New York (along with the other librarians who are included in this volume). She is head of Adult Services at a suburban public library near Highland Park, Illinois. Though her job is primarily administrative, she does some work in the areas of reference and book selection:

*One of my favorite subject areas is cookbooks. Choosing and ordering books is like having a charge account at Marshall Field and never having to pay the bill!*

Elaine began baking bread over 28 years ago, when her husband—then a relatively young man—had a serious coronary and it appeared that there was some connection between his diet and his heart trouble, a relationship that has since been thoroughly explored by the medical profession, and one in which most of us now believe.

*I bake my own bread because I believe it is necessary to control the ingredients in our diet, not for fun or therapy. However, I do enjoy a challenge, and bread baking certainly is that!*

Elaine mentioned in her last letter that her husband is still going strong and feeling better than ever 28 years later. "I think my care in cooking has helped—it certainly hasn't hurt him!"

In a medium-size bowl, combine the buttermilk or sour milk, bananas, beaten egg, oil, and molasses.

In a large bowl, combine the flour, bran, baking soda, and salt. Stir in banana mixture. Add raisins and blend. Spoon batter into a buttered 12-cup muffin tin. (Do not use paper cups.) Bake in a preheated 375°F oven for 25 minutes.

# Whole Wheat Banana Muffins

(about 12 muffins)

¾ cup buttermilk or sour
    milk
½ cup mashed ripe bananas
 1 egg, beaten
 2 tablespoons safflower oil
¼ cup light molasses
 1 cup whole wheat flour
¾ cup bran
 1 teaspoon baking soda
¼ teaspoon salt (optional, see
    page 22)
¾ cup raisins

When baking muffins, fill one center cup with water instead of dough. This will keep the muffins moist during baking.

Jane Praeger

# Ed Cullen and Carolyna Smiley-Marquez

*The Breads:*

**Whole Wheat Crunch Bread
Red Corn Loaf**

Ed Cullen and I met some years back in New York, when he was working for a filmmaker friend of mine, Gene Searchinger. Ed sent a homemade Irish Soda Bread over to me by way of introducing himself. For an avid bread baker, there is no greater form of introduction, and the bread was devoured by me and my staff in about 30 seconds flat!

We met again some years later, after Ed had moved to Longmont, Colorado, and he worked as part of my film crew when we were producing a documentary in the Denver area. By that time, he had become almost a "native" Coloradan, and had met Carolyna Smiley-Marquez, a remarkable young woman who traces her Native American background to her Pueblo Indian forbears in New Mexico. Soon after the film was completed, Ed and Carolyna were married, and both are now living and working in the Longmont area. We have kept in touch over the years, partly due to our friendship and partly because both are avid bread bakers.

*I'm working now for the Colorado Council on the Arts and Humanities, making films and tapes. Carolyna is forging ahead with her Ph.D. dissertation on the legislative changes in Colorado's bilingual laws . . . and we are both very happy and enthralled and busy(!) with our new daughter, Sarah Mariah.*

Both Ed and Carolyna have a "victory garden" filled with corn and beans, watermelon and canteloupe, and both grind their own flour and cornmeal for their breads. Carolyna relates her Pueblo grandmother's directions for mixing up dough for *tortillas*:

> *First you make a hole in the ground, a big hole, and then you take a 100-pound bag of flour and empty it into the hole. Then you take a bucket of lard . . . and a bucket of water. . . .*

Ed comments that this is a "clan-size recipe"—you merely divide it in half if only the extended family is coming for beans and corn!

This is a hearty bread submitted by Ed Cullen, and it requires some grinding of your own grains, either in a mill or in some substitute such as a spice grinder. The bread is crunchy and holds together well.

In a large bowl, mix together warm water and yeast. Add the honey, oil, eggs, and 1 cup of flour. Beat with a wooden spoon for about 100 strokes. Cover and set aside for about 45 minutes.

Stir the sponge to blend any uneven rising and to mix in the foam. Then add 2 to 3 cups of the flour (depending upon the fineness of the grind). The dough should be wet. If it seems too dry, add another ½ to ¾ cup warm water.

In a small bowl, mix together the barley, light buckwheat, oat groats, rye berries, and whole wheat berries. Grind these together *coarsely* and then add to dough. Mix with a wooden spoon.

Turn out onto a floured surface and knead for 15 minutes, adding flour as needed to make a workable dough. Place into an oiled bowl, turn to coat, cover, and let rise in a warm spot until doubled in bulk, 1 to 1½ hours.

Punch dough down, turn out onto a floured surface, and shape into a loaf. Place into a well-buttered 9 × 5-inch loaf pan or a buttered 7-inch round pan, if you want a round loaf. Cover and let rise in a warm spot for about 1 hour.

Bake in a preheated 350°F oven for about 1 hour, or until the bread tests done.

Cool on a wire rack.

# Whole Wheat Crunch Bread

(1 large loaf)

2 cups warm water
2 teaspoons dry yeast
3 tablespoons honey
¼ cup vegetable oil
2 eggs
3 to 4 cups freshly ground
   whole wheat flour
3 tablespoons barley
3 tablespoons light
   buckwheat
3 tablespoons oat groats
3 tablespoons rye berries
3 tablespoons wheat berries

On our trips out to Colorado, Carolyna Smiley-Marquez introduced us to a variety of Indian corn, including the blue corn that we've used in our own recipes (see Index). Carolyna describes the history and the preparation of Pueblo Indian breads, in her own words.

*Sitting on the dry, brown earth under the turquoise New Mexico sky, the women would grind corn—blue, red, and yellow—between two worn rocks. The Spanish, who battled with and married among the native Indian peoples of the Southwest, named these* metate *(a large flat stone worn into a bowl like hollow that holds much dried corn) and* mano *(a smaller stone that is hand held for grinding). The* metate, *usually a metamorphic rock, may have added iron and other elements to the food.*

*The ground corn would be mixed with water, animal fat, and salt and kneaded, then rolled or pressed into a flat round shape with skilled hands that danced as quietly as the desert breeze. It was baked on a hot stone over an outdoor fire.*

*Brown beans, squash, red chili gravy, and perhaps mutton, rabbit, or deer meat would be served with this corn* tortilla, *providing a meal surprisingly high in vitamins, minerals, protein—and ritual.*

*Later, however, and almost without notice, the arrival of processed, bleached wheat (white flour), canned shortening, and white sugar at the trading centers changed the look, taste, and feel, as well as the nutritional content, of the traditional Indian and Spanish supper. The tortilla and bean combination that had provided a marvelous protein source was now principally carbohydrates. The Indian body became more and more round and, like our white neighbors, more and more addicted to sugars in their many forms.*

*Even with the addition of vegetables, where they could be afforded (a refrigerator is necessary for storing fresh vegetables) on* Indian Tacos *(pillowlike fried* tortillas), *the packaged food would never have the same simplicity and power of the early meals.*

*This recipe is like a little song that I am writing in honor of the old ways.*

This is a basic red corn loaf based upon the Pueblo Indian recipes, but blue or yellow corn can be substituted. Carolyna reminds us:

*Remember to use all the kernels from the dried ears of corn that you choose, since they are all children of one mother and should not be separated!*

In a large bowl, combine yeast, warm water, 1½ cups flour, and honey. Stir to blend and set aside to proof, about 15 minutes.

Add the egg, softened butter, oil, and salt and mix well. Mix in ground corn, and then add the remaining flour, ½ cup at a time, until the mixture holds together for kneading without stricking to your hands. The differences in the wheat berries and corn will determine how much of the moisture they will absorb.

Knead well until dough is smooth and elastic, 8 to 10 minutes. Be careful to return all the little runaway "corn children" to the dough. Place into an oiled bowl, turn to coat, cover, and let rise until dough is 1½ times the original size, 1 to 1½ hours.

Punch dough down and let rise for a second time (this rise is not absolutely necessary). Divide equally and form into 2 loaves—either adobe (brick) shapes or medium-size loaves. Place adobe shapes on an oiled baking sheet, or place loaves into 2 well-buttered 8½ × 4½-inch loaf pans. Let rise 15 to 20 minutes. Bake in a preheated 400°F oven for 35 to 45 minutes, or until the loaves test done. The crust should be a delicate brown.

Cool on a wire rack.

# Red Corn Loaf

(2 medium-size loaves)

- 2 tablespoons coarse dry yeast
- 2 cups warm water
- 5½ cups whole wheat flour, finely ground from fresh wheat berries
- ¼ cup wild or alfalfa honey
- 1 egg
- ¼ cup butter, softened
- ¼ cup corn oil
- 1 teaspoon salt (optional, see page 22)
- 2 cups whole red corn kernels, coarsely ground from dried corn

If the yeast was proofed and the dough didn't rise, the problem may be with flour that was too cold or a liquid that was too hot. All ingredients should be at room temperature.

Yvonne Rodahl

# Bethami Auerbach

*The Breads:*

**Corn Rye Bread**
**Corn Bread**

It had been a great many years since I'd seen Beth, but her name leaped out at me from a small book of poetry called *Women Poets Rising.* I had known her parents since I met them in Berlin, Germany, in the days after World War II, and my renewed contact with her made me realize again how quickly the time had passed.

*I'm now a lawyer, though I am not practicing at this time. At present, I'm a graduate student in the Writer's Workshop at the University of Iowa, writing fiction. And, I've also been teaching Environmental Law and Resource Planning at the College of Law.*

When I read her poetry (reprinted here with Beth's permission), I realized that she must surely be a bread baker, and indeed she is.

*I like to knead to music—maybe this is on the same level as talking to plants, which I don't do—because I somehow*

*got it into my head that music gets the yeast creatures moving
around, particularly if they like what's on the stereo!*

Her first attempts, like those of most bread bakers,
were with simple breads like whole wheat with no
embellishments.

*I remember being a little disappointed that my first loaf
didn't have the characteristic shape of store-bought bread,
but it tasted a lot better and I had made it. Those were the
things that counted with me.*

Here, then, are both the poetry *and* the breads of Beth
Auerbach.

## The Search for the Perfect Rye Bread

The perfect rye bread
is a light-colored rye,
missing the molasses and bran
of the pumpernickel
(I've already found the perfect pumpernickel);
it hasn't the orange scent of the limpa,
its character is caraway and cornmeal.
It's a cosmopolitan Jewish rye,
immigrating constantly,
its fragrance makes me feel welcome
in my own home.

The search is for something
I know does not exist
at the start, cannot exist
until I create it
and which then
—by that creation—
is guaranteed
found.
In this search the quarry
is the creature of the detective
so it's helpful
in the experience column
to have been a poet.

How much
(if any)
        flour
            (white/wheat/rye/cornmeal)

```
liquid
        (water/milk/potato water/buttermilk)
shortening
        (oil/butter/vegetable)
etc
        (yeast/sugar/honey/salt/caraway)
```
and in what combination?
Breadmaking
affirms with every bite
the infiniteness
        (butter/cream cheese/preserves)
of possibility.

The perfect rye bread
has not been found
but every near-miss,
every changeling
emerging from my oven
is savored;
nothing I make
with my own hands
can be all that bad.

It's a long time to be housebound
        researching
        organizing
        measuring
        mixing
        kneading
        rising
        baking
        cooking
        tasting
4 hours at least,
sometimes 6
But these are hours
when something is going on in my life,
hours when I might be home
staring at my hands
in terror that nothing is going on in my life.

These are hours of ferment
when, after washing my spoon,
I might grab my pen;
hours of waiting
for a sign
that I can make something
out of nothing.

In a small bowl, dissolve yeast in warm water. Stir in honey.

Pour hot water over butter in a large bowl. Add salt and caraway seeds. Let cool to lukewarm and then add yeast mixture. Stir in cornmeal.

In a medium-size bowl, blend together rye and whole wheat flours and gradually add to cornmeal mixture, stirring as you do so, until a stiff dough forms.

Turn out onto a lightly floured surface and knead until satiny and elastic, 8 to 10 minutes, using additional whole wheat flour if necessary. Place dough into a large buttered bowl, turn once to coat, cover, and let rise in a warm place until doubled in bulk, about 1 hour.

Punch down, turn out onto a floured surface, and form into 2 loaves. Place each loaf into a buttered 8½ × 4½-inch loaf pan that has been dusted with cornmeal. Cover and let rise for about 45 minutes.

Bake in a preheated 375°F oven for 30 to 40 minutes, brushing loaves with water every 15 or 20 minutes.

When loaves test done, turn them out of the pans and cool on a wire rack.

# Corn Rye Bread

(2 medium-size loaves)

2 tablespoons dry yeast
1 cup warm water
2 tablespoons honey
1 cup hot water
2 tablespoons butter
1 teaspoon salt (optional, see page 22)
2 tablespoons caraway seeds
1 cup yellow cornmeal
2 cups rye flour
3 cups whole wheat flour
cornmeal for dusting pans

---

This is another of those simple, easy-to-do recipes for people who have no time to wait for the yeast to do its work.

Using a fork, mix the dry ingredients in a large bowl.

In a small bowl, combine the eggs, milk or buttermilk, honey, and oil. Add the liquid mixture to the dry ingredients, stir briefly, and pour into a buttered 9-inch pie plate or an 8 × 8-inch baking pan. Bake in a preheated 425°F oven for 20 minutes.

Cool in pan before slicing into squares. Serve warm.

# Corn Bread

(1 flat loaf)

1 cup yellow cornmeal
⅓ cup toasted wheat germ
⅔ cup whole wheat flour
2 teaspoons baking powder
½ teaspoon baking soda (if buttermilk is used)
2 eggs
1 cup milk or buttermilk
2 tablespoons honey
3 tablespoons vegetable oil

# Sourdough Serendipity

*Possibly the most popular use for sourdough other than baking, was as a form of libation. With warmth and time, a clear liquid rises to the top of all starters. To the prospectors, this was* hooch. *With an alcoholic content of 15 percent and a devilish smell and taste, it wasn't much competition for the store-bought variety. But to a frontiersman snowed-in in a cabin in the middle of the wilderness, it was ambrosia. . .* (Barbara Gibbs Ostmann, *St. Louis Post-Dispatch,* March 21, 1979. Used with permission)

Possibly no form of bread baking carries with it more of a sense of American history and more of a mystique of difficulty than the making of sourdough loaves. It has, through the years, developed its own terminology, such as *sponge, wild yeast,* and *sweeten the pot* (a term borrowed by poker players); but, at the same time, its literary and folkloric popularity has served to create a "fear of trying" in the new baker, and even among some of my friends who have been baking bread for ten years or more.

Sourdough breads are, in fact, quite easy to make. The care and nurturing of a starter does not require a master's degree in chemistry. A cup of starter borrowed from an old friend, a freshly made brew that follows the directions on page 236, or even the simple, dry sourdough starters in packages that can be purchased in almost any tourist shop in San Francisco, will do nicely to put you on your way.

The origins of sourdough bread, of course, are quite well known. The miners and the frontier trappers could not purchase yeast as we do, and had no way to keep the yeast alive on the trail, even if they could purchase it. Thus the starter that was ever ready to perform became the means by which they were able to bake their daily breads

and replenish the leavener easily. These pioneers understood even then that this was a living organism that had
to be fed and nurtured with love, warmth, and care. I read
in Barbara Ostmann's article that some families passed on
starters as wedding gifts and others gave them pet names,
and I smiled with the recollection that my own starter was
called "Melvin" by my Fire Island neighbors because of
the love and attention that I showered upon it—until one
day it "died" through inadvertent neglect and I felt a deep
and abiding sadness! Another sourdough story that Barbara
related in her article shows the importance of starter to the
frontier people:

> The sourdough crock that most miners and trappers carried,
> was loved not only for the bread and other baked goods it
> made possible, but also for many unlikely uses. It was used
> as medicine—from healing poultices for all sorts of wounds,
> aches, and pains to raw starter taken internally for stomach
> distress. A little starter applied to brass fittings on rifles and
> allowed to sit for a minute or two did a fine job as a metal
> polish. Sourdough starter also made a great glue for paper,
> wood, cloth, leather, and anything porous. Even log cabins
> were chinked with starter, or so they say.

At our Fire Island home, we have found another use
for starter. Our garden is inundated with slugs, as is any
damp location. We find that bottle tops filled with starter
attract the garden pests, which then climb over the tops
and promptly drown!

In this section of the book, however, we shall limit
ourselves to the use of sourdough starter as a bread leavener, a taste enhancer, a chance to make some of the most
exquisite of breads, as well as an opportunity to meet some
of my other Bread Winners and share in their recipes.
Remember, the making of starter is really quite simple.
Just follow the directions and then abide by the simple
rules. And one day, if "Melvin" dies again, I may come
knocking at *your* door to borrow a cup of your sourdough
starter.

# Sourdough Starters

One sunny day on Fire Island, my next-door neighbor, Margaret Peabody, introduced me to Shirley Sparr, a baker who actually had a 112-year-old starter! I was, of course, fascinated, since "Melvin" had died only a few days before. She, in turn, also had a name for her starter. She called it "The Thing."

*It was about 12 years ago that I purchased "The Thing" at a church fair. I was told that it was a sourdough starter originated on the East Coast over 100 years ago and carried by wagon train out to Minnesota. I decided to buy some and soon discovered that it was certainly alive and growing. In fact, before I could walk all the way home, it was coming up over the top of the plastic butter container and I had to run the rest of the way to get it safely to my kitchen.*

*Little did I know what I was in for. It proved to be both incorrigible and incontinent. It was like having a new, narcissistic baby in the house who assumed that life centered around it. It took control. It required constant care and feeding. I used to get up in the middle of the night to check its activity.*

Luckily, someone gave Shirley a large glass cookie jar with a loose-fitting lid and from that day on, her life has been much easier.

No matter how you obtain your starter—whether bought or borrowed, or made from the beginning as a wild or "tame" starter—there are certain rules of which you should be aware:

• It is not necessary to give your starter a name, though most bakers do. It is, after all, a living organism that requires care. However, if the starter should die, it is that much more difficult to accept. Starters with a name seem to leave an indelible mark after they're gone.

• Make certain that you use a large enough container to allow the starter to expand. *Do not use metal,* since it throws off acids that will affect the leavener. The best materials are either ceramic containers or large glass cookie jars.

• The lid should fit loosely. The gases in the container must be allowed to expand.

• Always use a wooden spoon to stir the starter.

- Keep the starter in a cool spot. If you use it constantly, say, several times a week, it can stay in a cool spot in the kitchen.

- If you use the starter only occasionally (as most of us do), it should be kept in the refrigerator, lightly covered.

- Each time you use the starter, replenish it with equal amounts of flour and warm water. Then stir the mixture. Lumps will form but that's O.K. Just leave them alone and they'll smooth out by themselves.

- If the starter is in the refrigerator and has not been used for two or three weeks, take it out, pour off half, refill the crock or jar with equal amounts of flour and warm water, and stir down. This is known as *sweetening the pot*. Let the starter begin to bubble again (I leave mine out overnight, lightly covered) and then put it back in the refrigerator.

- If a clear liquid forms on top of the starter, just stir it down.

- The starter can be frozen too. However, after about four to six months, take it out of the freezer, thaw it, pour off half, and replenish with flour and water. Leave it out long enough to begin bubbling again and then refreeze.

Since the air is filled with wild yeast organisms, grandmother used the traditional method of making a starter. Some of our more adventurous friends still do the same.

Pour low-fat milk into a ceramic or glass container, cover with cheesecloth, and leave at room temperature for 24 to 48 hours. It should smell sour.

Add flour and honey and stir to blend well. Cover the container with cheesecloth and place it outdoors in a warm spot (but not directly in the sun) where the yeast will be "captured" and the starter will be activated. Leave it outdoors for 2 to 3 days. However, if the nights are quite cool, you might want to take the starter indoors and leave it in a warm spot overnight. Then return it outdoors in the morning. When the starter becomes bubbly, it is ready to use. You have actually captured the wild yeast!

# Traditional Wild Yeast Starter

2 cups sweet acidophilus low-fat milk (regular low-fat milk may be substituted)
2 cups whole wheat flour
1 teaspoon honey

# A Simple Sourdough Starter

1 tablespoon dry yeast
2 cups warm water
2 cups whole wheat flour
1 tablespoon honey

Some of us have called this the "tame" starter. It's quite easy to make.

Place all ingredients in a large crock or glass jar, cover lightly with a cloth or towel, and let stand at room temperature for 2 to 3 days. Several times during this process, stir down the mixture. When it's bubbly and smells sour, it's ready to use. Place it in the refrigerator until baking time.

# Yogurt Sourdough Starter

1 cup skim milk
¼ cup yogurt
1 cup whole wheat flour

The remarkable qualities of this starter came to light recently. I first made yogurt sourdough starter as a test for the book, *Bread Winners;* and that Christmas, my gifts to my Fire Island neighbors were the breads baked using that starter and a traditional Finnish recipe. When the tests were completed and the gift breads delivered, I poured the starter into a ceramic crock and placed it far back on the bottom shelf of the refrigerator.

For three years, the lightly covered crock was pushed from side to side and from front to back, with little care that it might be long dead; I was too lazy to take it out and throw it away. Finally—*three years* old and never replenished—the starter was removed from the dark reaches of the bottom shelf and idly placed in a warm spot in the kitchen. When I had time, I planned to get rid of it.

The next morning, I awoke to smell something familiar and yet stronger and more pungent than I had ever smelled before. I traced it to the crock that now stood on a kitchen counter—and there, in all its glory, *the yogurt starter was actually bubbling away!* It was not only alive, it was quite well! And ready for a bread, I thought. The results—two Yogurt Sourdough Bran/Rye Breads (see Index)—were probably the best, most delicious sourdough breads that I have ever baked.

I cannot guarantee that the same thing will happen to you if you put this starter away for three years. However, I do think that it's one of the most unusual bread starters that I have ever come across. In case you don't have *Bread Winners,* let me take the liberty of repeating the recipe here.

Be certain, however, that you use yogurt that is a *live* culture. You can check this when you buy your yogurt. If you are in doubt, check the manufacturer or your distributor for the information.

*Bread Winners Too*

Pour warm water into a 1- or 2-quart ceramic or glass container and let it stand for several minutes.

Heat milk to a temperature of 95°F. (Either use a thermometer or judge by putting a drop on your wrist, as in warming a baby's milk.) Remove from heat and stir in yogurt. Pour water out of the container and pour milk/yogurt mixture in. Cover tightly and place in a warm spot. I use the gas oven with only the pilot light providing the heat.

After about 24 hours, the starter will have formed a curd, possibly covered with a clear liquid. Stir the liquid back into the starter. (If the liquid is pink, discard the entire starter and begin again. The most common error here is the use of a yogurt that is not made from a live culture.)

When the curd has formed, stir in flour, blending with a wooden spoon until smooth. Cover tightly and let stand again in a warm place for 3 to 5 days. It should be bubbly and should have a superb, sour smell. Cover the starter and store it in the refrigerator. The older it gets, the better it seems to be—even after 3 years.

# Some Starters from Ed Feiner

A few years ago, during a busy morning at my office, the receptionist came into the room holding a package at arm's length with one hand while the other clutched firmly at her nose. She dropped the neatly wrapped box on my desk and fled the room. I had to admit it did indeed smell sour, but I thought it was a "good" sour; she obviously disagreed. Opening it, I took out a firm plastic bag in which a superb, fairly thick liquid sloshed—a gift from Ed Feiner (see Index), his pungent, forceful, exquisite, useful sourdough starter. Over that weekend, it formed the base for a starter which I still use, and still feed according to his instructions.

Though the preceding pages have discussed the standard forms of starter, its preparation and use are areas where imagination also comes into play, just as in the actual baking of bread or the choosing of unusual ingredients. Ed's recipes can be found in this chapter, but his basic philosophy is very much like mine:

*Generally, I start off with a starter somehow. I think its effect on the flavor and the structure of the bread is worth the extra time. For me, it works better because I can sneak the starter in before I go to bed, add the flour during lunchtime, let the dough rise while I see patients (Ed is an optometrist, as you will find out), and after dinner it's ready for the oven.*

# Basic Starter

1 cup whole wheat flour
1 cup warm water
1 tablespoon dry yeast

Combine ingredients in a large bowl and mix well. Cover with plastic wrap and let stand for 12 to 24 hours.

## Variations:

Add ½ cup more water plus ½ cup cornmeal, or ½ cup triticale, or 1 cup cooked or soaked bulgur, or a combination of the three.

Add ½ cup stone-ground rye flour.

# Basic Starter II

1 cup whole wheat flour
1 cup water
1 tablespoon dry yeast
1 tablespoon vinegar

Combine ingredients in a large bowl and mix well. Cover with plastic wrap and let stand for 12 to 24 hours.

## Variations:

Add ½ cup buttermilk after yeast proofs.

Add ½ cup rye flour or ½ cup cornmeal.

*There are many "themes and variations" in the making of sourdough starters. I use our leftover baked potatoes, skin and all, blended with water—the breads then have freckles and taste great!*

Combine ingredients in a large bowl and mix well. Cover with plastic wrap and let stand for 3 to 5 days, or until well blended and fermenting. If the starter is used fresh within a week, the bread will have a sweet aroma. As with all sourdough starters, refrigerate after 4 to 5 days. The night before using the starter, add 1 cup flour, 1 cup water, and a bit of honey and leave in a warm spot to rise until doubled in bulk. Be sure to use a large enough container.

Just one final note about sourdough starters. For purists, the starter itself is quite sufficient to act as the leavening, though rising time may be increased. Some bakers (such as the author) use what I call "belt and suspenders," utilizing the starter for some rising of the dough, but adding yeast to insure the rise and to cut down on the time needed to double the bulk of the dough. Both methods are quite acceptable.

# Basic Starter III

1 cup unbleached white flour
1 cup nonfat dry milk
1 tablespoon honey
1 large potato, peeled, grated, and mixed with 1 cup water, or 1 large potato, baked and blended with skin, or 1 cup mashed potatoes, blended with potato water
1 tablespoon vinegar
1 tablespoon (or more) yeast starter or pinch of yeast (optional)

---

Keep the kitchen timer in a cabinet when you set the dough aside to rise. The eye is a better guide than the clock for judging when the dough has doubled in bulk.

Bobbie Leigh

---

# Shirley Sparr

### The Bread:

## Basic Sourdough Bread

*I originate from a farm in Ohio and my roots are there where I learned how to bake bread from my Aunt Goldie. I subsequently brought home blue ribbons from the Hardin County Fair, where I entered my breads as a 4-H project.*

Now a psychiatric social worker on Long Island, Shirley is the proud "mother" of the 112-year-old starter (page 234). She describes her baking skills in professional terms:

*I strongly believe that each person is capable of creating his or her unique loaves. Baking bread is a creative process; it incorporates numerous skills and touches all the senses. It's therapeutic. It can be used to alleviate tension, aggression, anxiety, and depression—and beholding the finished product can do wonders for the ego.*

Shirley gives bread baking demonstrations in her off hours; she encourages novice bakers to attempt to create their own loaves, tries to dispel the myths of bread baking (a woman after my own heart!), and generally fosters pursuit of the process without abiding by the rigid rules and regulations called for in so many recipes and books.

Her basic sponge and sourdough bread that follows is just such an example of her serendipitous baking philosophy. For that reason, I have included it in this section—to give encouragement to first-time bakers of sourdough loaves, as well as to convince them that they not only have the talent, but can make the time to turn out their own creations. Shirley has even broken down the recipe to allow for a busy work day in the baker's schedule.

In baking sourdough breads, you will come across the word "sponge" as a description of an element in the preparation process. This is merely a mixture of sourdough starter, other ingredients, and a liquid, all of which blend for a period of time, usually overnight, to begin the process and to create what looks just like a "sponge." This mixture is then incorporated with the other ingredients to make the dough.

To prepare the sponge: Early in the day, spend 5 minutes assembling the sponge by combining all the ingredients in a large bowl with a wooden spoon and 5 minutes beating it. Leave it uncovered on a counter or in a gas oven with the pilot light on. Remember, the sponge can even wait until the next day, or it can be prepared the night before baking. You are in control. If time is short, just cover it lightly and refrigerate. Then take it out and bring it to room temperature when *you're* ready to continue baking.

To prepare the dough: Late in the day, spend another 10 to 15 minutes beating salt and flour into the sponge. Then knead vigorously on a floured surface for 5 minutes. Divide dough into 2 or 4 pieces, roll each one out into a fat roll, and place into buttered 9 × 5-inch loaf pans or long French loaf pans. Cover and let rise in a warm spot for about 1½ hours.

Sprinkle with seeds of your choice, place the loaves into a cold oven, set the temperature at 350°F, and bake for 45 to 50 minutes for regular loaves and 30 to 35 minutes for long French loaves.

Cool on wire racks.

# Basic Sourdough Bread

(2 to 4 loaves)

*Sponge:*
  2 cups sourdough starter
  2 cups liquid (any combination of ¼ cup vegetable oil, plus ¼ cup maple syrup, or honey, or molasses, plus 1½ cups water or milk, or potato water, or vegetable water)
  ¼ cup seeds (caraway, millet, dill, or anise)
  ¼ cup meal (cornmeal, bran, toasted wheat germ, or soy grits)
  1 cup whole wheat flour

*Dough:*
  2 teaspoons salt (optional, see page 22)
3½ cups whole wheat flour or a combination of rye, barley, and whole wheat flours
  seeds for topping (sesame, caraway, or poppy)

# Ed Feiner

Ed is, without doubt, the best bread baker that I know. He is innovative, easy, serendipitous, unafraid, and remarkably productive. I met him through Stan Halbreich (see Index), who decided from all the way up in Buffalo, New York, that he and I and Ed and our families should have a gathering—the so-called Little League Bake-off—down in Toms River, New Jersey, where Ed is a Doctor of Optometry, a superb trumpet player, and a carver of decoy ducks.

Over the weeks of winter, the plans were made—plane schedules from Buffalo to Newark for Stan and Adele, driving instructions to Toms River for Sheryl and me, and great excitement closely approaching that of the high school prom days when we were kids. It was, to say the least, exhilerating! Ed and Judy Feiner had prepared a wonderful lunch, Stan had actually made aprons for each of us, reading "Upper Crust," with individual names embroidered on them, and best of all, Ed had baked *nine* different, exquisite, aromatic, tasty breads for the feast.

Without doubt, I knew that he had to be a part of any new book that might follow *Bread Winners,* but he, like most good bakers, does not work by specific recipes:

> *The worst thing I can tell a bread book author is that I don't use recipes, and that to translate the various types of bread I make into rigid formulas is sheer torture.*

Over a two-year period, letters and packages arrived and telephone conversations hummed with requests for further explanation. It was during that time that Ed's pungent starter also made its way to my kitchen with the aid of the United States Postal Service (see the section on sourdough starters), and his recipes mounted in number, always with notes that complained about my putting him in a straitjacket:

> *For someone who doesn't use recipes, it's been hard to translate "feel" into amounts, but you asked for it and you got it—if you want more, how about sourdough* challah, *sourdough pita, and a section on sourdough Chinese dumplings?*

In one of his letters, Ed included a few sheets of notes scrawled on hotel stationery from Atlantic City. He titled them "Random Notes." I include them here as a free-thought list of instructions from a baker whom I admire greatly and whose breads rank right at the top:

- *I always make fresh starter for every batch of bread.*

- *I always use cool water.*

- *Since I don't really use any measurements when I bake and go by the "feel" of the dough, my measurements are always approximate and are based on a 2½ or 3 to 1 ratio of flour to water.*

- *I always add the flour to the liquid. I find that when I add the liquid to the dry ingredients, the dough never seems to have the right feel.*

- *I never use sweeteners in my starters or in my breads, with the exception of some honey for a change of flavor in whole wheat bread.*

- *I always let the first rise go to at least double and sometimes to triple the bulk.*

- *When I use salt, I use only the coarse Kosher kind.*

- *I always let bread rise in cool areas. It's slower but it works for me.*

- *I always bake in a very hot, wet oven; and since oven temperatures vary, I merely use temperature as a guide. If breads brown too quickly, I reduce the temperature or put a tent over the loaves. I start my oven at 500°F with a pan of water on the bottom and let it steam before I put the breads in.*

- *I keep the oven at 500°F for the first 5 minutes and then reduce the temperature to 450°F. After 15 minutes, I remove the pan of water.*

- *I change the flavor of my breads by using different seed toppings: caraway, sesame, poppy, and so on.*

- *I always apply the seeds by dipping my hands in water, picking up the seeds, and pushing them vigorously into the bread. Otherwise, they just don't adhere.*

- *When using whole egg wash or yolk and cream wash, do not use too much; the crust will be too dark and eggy.*

Over all, Ed comments that he has always tried to mimic the taste and consistency of the breads that he and Judy have eaten in Europe:

> *No matter where we were—in Spain, Italy, England, Germany, Austria, or Hungary—we could always count on decent and varied breads, the kind that didn't stick to the roof of your mouth. Most of these breads were based on water, flour, yeast, and salt, but if you want to change the consistency and taste, substitute milk, eggs, or oil (no wine) for the water. In fact, I use potato water for most of my breads.*

Ed adds one final note for bakers who do not have a sourdough starter, are currently out of their favorite starter, or are too lazy to make one. The breads in this section can also be made with yeast instead of using a starter as a leavener.

> *However, even though you can substitute from three to four tablespoons of dry yeast for the starter, you will have then reduced the total amount of liquid, so remember to also reduce the total amount of flour.*

# Basic Sourdough Bread Recipe and Procedure

(3 large loaves)

2 cups sourdough starter
3 cups cool water
1½ teaspoons coarse salt
    (optional, see page 22)
9 cups flour
    cornmeal for dusting
    pans
    glaze for brushing loaves
    (optional)
    seeds for topping
    (optional)

By learning this basic sourdough recipe, all the rest of the breads can become your own creative playground. It is the fundamental "European" recipe of which Ed speaks in his introduction to this section. Everything else in bread baking—variety of flour, seeds and nuts, oils, butter, eggs—is all "icing on the cake."

Pour starter into a large bowl. Add cool water and mix well. Then add salt and mix well. Stir in flour, 1 cup at a time, reserving 1 cup for the final kneading. Beat the mixture with a large spoon or spatula. When dough is too hard to handle in the bowl, transfer to a floured surface and knead by hand. The dough will always be on the wet side, but sticky. Avoid adding too much flour. Knead for 5 minutes; if dough feels too wet, dust on ¼ cup flour and knead a bit more. The dough should feel like cool, soft flesh. Dust a deep bowl with flour. Roll dough in flour, dust with more flour, cover with plastic wrap or a towel, and let rise in a cool place until doubled in bulk. This can take 1, 2, 3, or 4 hours, depending upon the temperature of the room and the leavening effect of the starter.

Punch dough down with floured hands. Let rest for a few minutes. Then either let rise a second time or form into 3 loaves. Place on oiled baking sheets sprinkled with cornmeal or into 3 buttered 9 × 5-inch loaf pans dusted with cornmeal. If you like, the formed loaves may be glazed with any mixture that you prefer—egg white and water, beaten whole eggs, cream, or milk. Or, you can dust the tops with flour. Slash the loaves with a sharp razor blade and coat with seeds, if desired.

Place a pan of water on the bottom of the oven and preheat oven to 500°F. Bake loaves for 5 to 10 minutes. Then reduce heat to 450°F. After 15 minutes' baking time, remove pan of water from oven. Continue to bake until loaves test done when tapped on bottoms. If bread is browning too quickly, reduce heat still further or cover with foil. The size of the bread will determine the baking time. *Baguettes,* for example, should bake for 25 to 30 minutes or less. Large round loaves should bake for 40 to 50 minutes.

Cool on wire racks.

# Sourdough *Brioche-* Type Bread

(2 or 3 loaves)

2 cups sourdough starter
3 cups milk or mixture of ½
milk and ½ water
3 large eggs, separated
2 tablespoons honey
1 teaspoon coarse salt
(optional, see page 22)
10 to 11 cups whole wheat
flour
1 cup butter, softened
cornmeal for dusting pans
1 egg yolk, beaten, for
brushing loaves

This rich bread can be shaped in a variety of ways—like a traditional *challah*, a *brioche*, or as free-form loaves. The preparation process can also be divided into two days if time is a problem. After the dough is kneaded, refrigerate overnight in a plastic bag. Then, next morning, remove the dough from the refrigerator, let it stand until it returns to room temperature, let it rise, and continue with the recipe.

In a large bowl, combine starter with milk or milk/water mixture. Beat egg yolks in a small bowl and add to sourdough mixture. Then add honey and salt. Beat in half the flour.

In another small bowl, beat egg whites until fluffy and then fold into dough. Add the remaining flour slowly and knead well. If dough seems too wet, slowly add more flour.

Turn out onto a floured surface and knead well, 8 to 10 minutes. Place dough into a floured bowl, cover, and let rise until doubled in bulk, 2 to 4 hours.

Punch dough down and work in softened butter. Dough will be ropey, but keep kneading until all the butter is absorbed. Form dough into desired loaf shape, or braid dough as if you were making a *challah*. Place loaves on baking sheets dusted with cornmeal. Brush with beaten egg yolk, slash with a razor blade, cover loosely, and let rise until doubled in bulk, 2 to 3 hours.

Place a pan of water on the bottom of oven and preheat oven to 500°F. Reduce heat to 450°F and place breads close to the middle of the oven. After 15 minutes' baking time, remove pan of water. Watch carefully. Breads glazed with egg yolk tend to brown quickly. If this happens, just reduce the heat or place a foil tent over the loaves and continue baking. Baking time will vary depending upon the shapes of the loaves. It usually takes 35 to 40 minutes. Test for doneness by tapping on bottoms.

Cool on wire racks.

Note: Make sure that the breads are allowed to rise fully before baking, otherwise the combination of eggs and milk will make a bread that is too dense.

*Bread Winners Too*

Ed has based this recipe on a bread that he and Judy tasted in Switzerland.

In a large bowl, combine starter with cool water and mix. Gradually add rye flour, 1 cup at a time, stirring after each addition. Add rye and wheat flakes and bran. Then stir in graham flour, 1 cup at a time. The dough will be sticky, but it should knead easily. If it is too sticky, add more flour, but do not make dough too dry.

Turn out onto a floured surface and knead for 8 to 10 minutes. Then place into a floured bowl, dust with flour, cover, and let rise in a cool place until doubled in bulk, 2 hours or more.

Turn out onto a floured surface and roll out either with your hands or roughly with a floured rolling pin. Sprinkle nuts over surface of dough and roll up like a jelly roll. Form loaf into any shape that you like, seal the ends, and brush with a glaze of your choice, or dust the top with graham or rye flour. Cover and let rise in a cool place until doubled in bulk, 30 to 40 minutes.

Slash loaf with a razor blade, and bake as directed in the Basic Sourdough Bread Recipe and Procedure (page 245).

# Sourdough Coarse Whole Grain Walnut Bread

(1 large loaf)

> 2 cups sourdough starter
> 3 cups cool water
> 4 cups coarse rye flour
> ¼ cup rye flakes
> ¼ cup wheat flakes
> ¼ cup bran
> 4 to 5 cups graham flour
> ½ pound walnuts, shelled and kept whole
> glaze of your choice for brushing loaves

Heavy mixed-grain breads, especially sour-doughs, may look done and sound done, but still be gummy inside. Insert a bamboo skewer into the bottom of the loaf and if it comes out clean, the bread is done.

Art Hartman

# Sourdough Round French Bread

### (2 to 4 loaves)

2 cups sourdough starter
3 cups cool water
1 teaspoon coarse salt
(optional, see page 22)
½ cup toasted wheat germ
(optional)
½ cup coarse cornmeal
(optional)
1 cup mashed potatoes
(optional)
7 to 8 cups whole wheat
flour
cornmeal for dusting pans
beaten egg, cream, or milk
for brushing loaves
poppy seeds, caraway seeds,
or sesame seeds for coating
loaves (optional)

You have probably noticed by now that Ed does not have a standard method, nor does he use a standard shape, for any of his breads. Eventually, most bakers come to his conclusion that each bread is an adventure.

In a large bowl, combine starter and cool water and blend well. Add the salt. If desired, add wheat germ, cornmeal, or mashed potatoes. Then gradually add 6 to 7 cups flour, 1 cup at a time, beating well after each addition with a large rubber spatula or a wooden spoon. Reserve remaining cup of flour for kneading. (The dough should be light and sticky and on the soft side. Do not make dough too dry.) Knead for only about 1 minute to incorporate flour and to induce the gluten build-up. (Ed says, "As in all non-recipe recipes, you must learn to judge the feel of the dough.") Dust a bowl with flour and then dust dough. Place dough into bowl and cover with plastic wrap, a towel, or wax paper. Let rise in a cool place until doubled in bulk.

Punch down and let rest for a few minutes. At this point you can either shape dough into loaves or let dough rise a second time in a bowl dusted with flour.

To form dough into loaves, cut dough into as many pieces as you like. Dust each with flour to facilitate handling.

To make the round loaves, grasp ends of dough and tuck underneath, keeping your hands dusted with flour. Repeat several times in order to stretch the gluten and firm up the crust.

To make the coil loaves, roll out dough into long loaves, just as you would if you were making *baguettes*. Each rope should be about 2 inches thick and approximately 24 inches long. Starting from the center, wind dough around to form a coil.

When loaves are formed, place them into baking pans or on baking sheets dusted with cornmeal. (You can use an 8-inch nonstick round pan, a pie plate, a ceramic dish, a baking sheet, a sheet of iron, or a ceramic tile—anything that makes a firm, ovenproof base.) Brush the breads with beaten egg, cream, or milk. Slash with a razor blade and, if desired, coat with poppy seeds, caraway seeds, or sesame seeds. Bake as directed in the Basic Sourdough Bread Recipe and Procedure (page 245) for 20 to 30 minutes, depending upon the shape of the breads, or until loaves test done when tapped on bottoms.

Cool on wire racks.

Use the Sourdough Round French Bread recipe to make the basic dough. Then, after the first rise, divide dough into pieces about the size of tennis balls or smaller, form into desired shapes, and arrange on a baking sheet dusted with cornmeal. Cover and let rise in a cool place until doubled in bulk.

Slash rolls with a razor blade (single horizontal for small Italian; triple diagonal for small French; quadruple swirls for Kaiser), brush with your favorite glaze, add seeds (poppy, caraway, or sesame), and bake according to the directions in the Basic Sourdough Bread Recipe and Procedure (page 245).

# Sourdough Rolls

(12 to 24 rolls)

# Sourdough Boiler Plate (5-Pounder)

(1 very large loaf)

3 cups sourdough starter
5 cups cool water
14 cups whole wheat flour
(1 to 2 cups coarse rye
or graham flour may
be substituted)
cornmeal for dusting pans
glaze of your choice for
brushing loaf (optional)
¼ to ½ cup caraway or
black caraway seeds or
sesame seeds

*Some years ago, I traded a loaf of bread for a thick piece of boiler plate iron. I've baked my breads on it ever since. Black and well seasoned, it produces a thick bottom crust. When I'm lazy and I don't want to bother with the shaping of loaves, I make very large breads and then cut them up into smaller individual breads for freezing.*

In a very large bowl or tub, mix starter with cool water. Stir in flour, 1 cup at a time, reserving 1 to 2 cups for kneading.

Turn dough out onto a floured surface and knead for 8 to 10 minutes. Place into a floured tub or large bowl and cover. Let rise in a cool place until doubled in bulk, 2 to 3 hours.

Punch dough down, turn out onto a floured surface, and form 1 large, round loaf. Place it on a baking sheet dusted with cornmeal. Brush with glaze, if desired, and then sprinkle on seeds, working them into dough so that they won't fall off during baking. Cover and let rise in a cool place until doubled in bulk, about 2 more hours.

Bake according to the directions in the Basic Sourdough Bread Recipe and Procedure (page 245). Because of its size, the baking time will probably be quite long—well over an hour. Watch to see that the loaf does not burn on top. If it browns too quickly, cover with a foil tent and continue baking. Test the bread for doneness by tapping on the bottom.

Cool on a wire rack.

It is, to say the least, a most spectacular loaf!

In a large bowl, combine starter and cool water. Add the salt, bran or wheat germ, and mashed potatoes, and stir well. Add ¼ cup sesame seeds and mix. Reserve balance of seeds for coating. Gradually beat in flour.

Turn dough out onto a floured surface and knead for about 10 minutes. Place into a floured bowl, cover, and let rise in a cool place until doubled in bulk, 2 hours or more.

Punch dough down, turn out onto a floured surface, and divide into pieces the size of ping pong balls. Roll each one out into a long stick of any convenient size. Then roll each stick in the remaining seeds. Place on a baking sheet coated with sesame seeds, cover, and let rise for about 2 hours, or until the sticks are about doubled in bulk.

Bake in a preheated 375°F oven as directed in the Basic Sourdough Bread Recipe and Procedure (page 245), but keep in mind that the baking time will be very short, about 15 minutes in all. If you prefer crispier sticks, continue baking in a low oven 5 minutes longer.

Cool on wire racks.

# Sourdough Sesame Sticks

(about 12 sticks)

1 cup sourdough starter
1 cup cool water
½ teaspoon coarse salt
    (optional, see page 22)
¼ cup bran or toasted wheat
    germ
½ cup mashed potatoes
1 cup (or more) sesame
    seeds
3 cups whole wheat flour

---

If you can't complete a recipe all at one time, wrap the dough in plastic wrap, place it in the refrigerator, and bring it to room temperature when you're ready to continue baking.

Corinne Wastun

# Etta Taylor

*The Bread:*

**Sourdough English Muffins**

Etta also has her own section in another part of the book containing some unusual recipes for crackers (see Index). This sourdough recipe originally appeared in the *St. Louis Post-Dispatch* (used with permission) in an article written by Barbara Gibbs Ostmann. As a result, I have left the ingredients just as they were, though bakers may want to vary the amounts of flour with the use of more whole grains rather than the unbleached white flour that Etta calls for. Either way, they taste just great.

These muffins can be cooked all at one time and then either frozen or stored in a plastic bag in the refrigerator. Or, part of the dough can be cooked and the remainder placed in the refrigerator to be made later in the week.

In a large bowl, combine the starter, honey, milk, whole wheat flour, and 2 cups unbleached white flour. Cover with wax paper and a towel and let stand in a warm place overnight.

The next morning, add baking soda and salt. The dough should be moderately stiff.

Turn out onto a floured surface and add more unbleached white flour as needed (and, Etta adds, as kneaded). You will probably need an additional 1 to 2 cups. Knead about 5 minutes, or until dough is stiff enough to roll out. Roll out dough to about ½-inch thickness. Cut with a round 3-inch cutter (a washed tuna can is perfect) or cut into any other shape you desire. Place cut muffins on a baking sheet that has been dusted with cornmeal, sprinkle more cornmeal over the tops of the muffins, cover, and let rise in a warm place for about 30 minutes, or until about ¼ inch higher than before.

Heat a griddle or electric skillet to medium high heat, or until a drop of water skitters on the surface, about 325°F. Butter griddle or skillet very lightly and only once. Lift the muffins onto the griddle or into the skillet with a spatula, cooking only as many as will fit comfortably without crowding. Cook each side for 5 to 7 minutes, or until browned. If muffins puff up too much, gently flatten them with a spatula after turning. Turn only once, just as with pancakes. Cool, then split with a fork and toast. If the muffins should be slightly gummy in the center, the toasting will take care of it.

# Sourdough English Muffins

(about 20 3-inch muffins)

1 cup sourdough starter
2 tablespoons honey
2 cups milk
2 cups whole wheat flour
3 to 4 cups unbleached white flour
1 scant teaspoon baking soda (optional)
1 teaspoon salt (optional, see page 22)
cornmeal for dusting pans and muffins

# Mel London

The Breads:

**Yogurt Sourdough
Bran/Rye Bread
Sour Rye Berry Rye Bread**

Since I like to keep my starter active and working, I find that a great percentage of my baking uses the sourdough method. Here are just two tasty examples.

## Yogurt Sourdough Bran/Rye Bread

(2 loaves)

*Sponge:*
1 cup Yogurt Sourdough
Starter
1 cup rye flour
1 cup whole wheat flour
*Dough:*
1 tablespoon dry yeast
1¼ cups warm water
1 teaspoon honey
1 cup rye flour
1 cup bran
1 tablespoon honey
1 teaspoon salt (optional, see
page 22)
3½ to 4½ cups whole wheat
flour
white cornmeal for dusting
pan
black caraway, caraway, or
sesame seeds

This is the bread that was such a great and tasty surprise when I used a "dead" starter that was three years old (page 236). It was baked one damp afternoon at Fire Island, and I was delighted with the sour smell, the fact that the yogurt starter had kept so well all that time, and the anticipation of a surprise in flavor when it came out of the oven. It's hearty, unusual, and great when toasted!

To prepare the sponge: About 8 to 12 hours before baking, or the night before, make the sponge by combining the yogurt starter, rye flour, and whole wheat flour in a medium-size bowl. Cover and let ferment in a warm spot, or in a gas oven with only the pilot light on.

To prepare the dough: When you're ready to bake, proof the yeast by combining it with ¼ cup warm water and 1 teaspoon honey in a small bowl. Stir and wait for bubbles to form.

In the meantime, pour the sponge into a large bowl. Stir in 1 cup warm water, rye flour, and bran, mixing well. Then add proofed yeast mixture. Stir well and add the 1 tablespoon honey and salt. The mixture will be watery and very loose. Add whole wheat flour, 1 cup at a time, mixing as you do so. You should use about 3 cups flour before dough begins to pull away from the sides of the bowl. Add flour until you can turn dough out onto a floured surface, reserving the remainder of the flour to add to dough and to your hands as you knead. As with all rye breads, dough will be very sticky—you will need to add more flour as you knead.

Knead for 8 to 10 minutes. The dough will become smooth and wonderful to handle, though still a bit sticky. By this time, you will probably have used almost 4 cups flour and possibly a bit more. Place into an oiled bowl, cover, and let rise in a warm spot until doubled in bulk, about 1 hour.

Punch dough down a few times and turn out onto a lightly floured surface. Knead for 1 to 2 minutes. The dough will be damp but smooth. Form into 2 oval or round loaves and place on a well oiled baking sheet that has been sprinkled with white cornmeal. Cover lightly with a towel and set aside to rise in a warm spot until almost doubled in bulk, about 45 minutes.

Slash the loaves lengthwise with a razor blade, or make 2 or 3 cuts across the width. The design is up to you. Spray with water from a plant mister and sprinkle with seeds of your choice. Lightly run your hand along the loaves to set seeds more deeply into dough. Bake in a preheated 375°F oven for 35 to 40 minutes, or until the loaves test done. About 15 minutes into the baking time, mist the tops of the loaves again.

Cool on wire racks.

I use a heating pad wrapped in a heavy towel to provide constant warmth for fermenting a sponge and raising dough.

Art Hartman

# Sour Rye Berry Rye Bread

(1 large loaf or 2 small loaves)

*Sponge:*
1 cup sourdough starter
1½ cups whole wheat flour
1 cup pumpernickel or dark
rye flour
1 teaspoon honey

*Dough:*
½ cup rye groats or rye
berries
1½ cups water
2 tablespoons dry yeast
½ cup warm water
½ teaspoon honey
½ teaspoon salt (optional, see
page 22)
2 cups rye or pumpernickel
flour
3 to 4 cups whole wheat
flour
caraway seeds for topping

I made this delicious bread one lazy day, scribbled the recipe on some note paper, and found the quite unintelligible scrawl just as I started to get my recipes together for this new book. Baking as I do, for the most part without written recipes, it is not unusual to find my notes on half-torn scraps of paper. I have finally deciphered words such as "remove any bad ones." I used some unbleached white flour in the dough to let the rye berries become more dominant in taste, color, and texture.

To prepare the sponge: Mix all ingredients together in a medium-size bowl, cover, and let ferment in a warm place overnight.

To prepare the dough: Pick over rye groats or berries, removing any bad ones, place into a small bowl with the water, and soak overnight.

The next morning, transfer rye groats or berries and their soaking water to a medium-size saucepan and simmer until soft, 10 to 15 minutes. (If water is absorbed by the grains before the end of the cooking time, just add a bit more.) A few of the grains will pop just like popcorn, but the shape of most will be retained.

Drain groats or berries, reserving 1 cup water to be used in the dough. Cool groats or berries and water to room temperature, drying groats or berries on paper towels.

In a small bowl, combine the yeast, warm water, and honey. Stir and let stand for 5 to 10 minutes to proof.

Meanwhile, add simmered rye groats or berries to the sponge, stirring in well. Pour sponge into a large bowl. Add salt and the reserved water from rye groats or berries, stirring as you do so. Add rye or pumpernickel flour, 1 cup at a time, stirring after each addition, and then add 3 cups whole wheat flour, reserving the rest for kneading.

When dough is workable, turn it out onto a floured surface and knead for 8 to 10 minutes, or until smooth and elastic. If you need more flour, add it during this process. Place dough into an oiled bowl, turn to coat, cover, and let rise in a warm spot until doubled in bulk, about 1 hour.

Punch down, turn out onto a floured surface, knead 1 to 2 minutes, and shape into 1 large or 2 small free-form loaves. Place on a buttered baking sheet, cover, and let rise in a warm spot for about 45 minutes.

*Bread Winners Too*

Slash a cross on top of each loaf with a razor blade, spray with water, and sprinkle with caraway seeds, working them in with your hands. Bake in a preheated 375°F oven for 50 to 60 minutes. After the first 15 minutes of baking time, spray again with water.

Cool on wire racks.

# Andreas Esberg

*The Bread:*

**Flemish Peasant Bread**

## Flemish Peasant Bread

(3 loaves)

1 tablespoon dry yeast
1½ cups lukewarm water
2 tablespoons honey
1 cup Yogurt Sourdough
Starter (see page 236)
½ cup buttermilk
1½ cups bran
1 teaspoon salt (optional, see
page 22)
1 cup rye flour
4 to 5 cups stone-ground
whole wheat flour
½ cup sesame seeds

Many of us have gotten some of our best recipes from our family, passed down from generation to generation. Andy Esberg, my Fire Island friend (page 167), traces this one back to Europe.

*My favorite uncle, who lives in Ghent, Belgium, is now 96 years old. I have always classified him as a gourmet, no small accomplishment in a country where food is important, prepared with care, and in many instances better than the French cuisine. Even at his age, he still insists upon doing his own shopping at the local market down the street, where he buys this marvelous bread. On my last trip, I accompanied him, and convinced the local baker to let me have the recipe. I make it with whole wheat flour instead of the white flour he uses, and I like the result very much. I think my uncle would say it's delicious . . . "but it's not my bread." Try it both ways and make up your own mind.*

In a large bowl, dissolve yeast in ½ cup lukewarm water. Add ½ tablespoon honey, mix, and set aside for 5 minutes to proof.

Add the remaining honey, the remaining lukewarm water, starter, and buttermilk. Then add the bran, salt, and rye flour. Stir in enough whole wheat flour, 1 cup at a time, to make a pliable dough. Sprinkle sesame seeds over dough and work in well.

Turn out onto a lightly floured surface and knead for 8 to 10 minutes, or until dough is smooth and satiny, adding more flour, if necessary. Place into a well-oiled bowl, turn to coat, cover, and let rise in a warm spot until doubled in bulk, about 1 hour.

Punch dough down, turn out onto a floured surface, and knead for 1 to 2 minutes. Form into 3 loaves. The traditional shape is an elongated oval, but any shape will do—you can form 3 different shapes if you like. Place them on a well-buttered baking sheet, cover, and let rise in a warm spot until doubled in bulk, about 30 minutes.

Slash 2 lines on top of each loaf with a sharp single-edge razor blade. Bake in a preheated 400°F oven for 30 minutes and then reduce the heat to 350°F for the last 20 minutes of baking time, or until loaves test done.

Cool on wire racks.

Coat your loaves with egg glaze *before* slashing them. The bread will come out of the oven with two shades of brown on top to emphasize the design.

Suzanne Gosar

# Art Hartman

I've called Art a "gold mine," and indeed he is. One of his basic breads and his Mexican repertoire appear on page 96. Here are some of his superb sourdough creations preceded by special notes on how he feels about this fresh adventure in bread baking.

*I am a newcomer to sourdough baking, but the first loaves that I baked made me a believer. They were the first non-commercial sourdough breads I had ever tasted and the flavor was fabulous. Of course, success on the first try is always most gratifying.*

*I feel that when baking sourdough breads, I'm involved with a joint effort—a collaboration of the sour, the leaven, and the baker. The baker must be in tune with these other living organisms, their needs, their characteristics, and their rhythms, in order to produce a successful bread. It is satisfying in a way that I find hard to explain.*

*I have not yet captured and developed my own wild sourdough culture, but that will come. My starter was made from a commercially available San Francisco sourdough culture, following directions on the package. It produces a clean, sour taste and has excellent leavening power. I don't use any yeast with my starter.*

*This is the first sourdough bread I made, and the only change in the recipe is the addition of baking soda. The bread is one of Mary Ann's favorites.*

To prepare the sponge: Place starter into a large warmed bowl. Add warm water and honey. Stir in flours until well mixed. Cover with plastic wrap and let ferment in a warm place for 8 to 12 hours or overnight.

To prepare the dough: Sprinkle salt and baking soda over sponge. In a small bowl, beat egg and oil together and then add to sponge. Stir in whole wheat flour and enough triticale flour to form a dough that pulls away from the bowl.

Scrape dough out onto a floured surface and work in more triticale flour. The dough should be somewhat moist and not too stiff. If dough is still sticky after using the 2 cups of triticale flour, add more whole wheat flour. Knead for 10 minutes. Place into an oiled bowl, turn to coat, cover with plastic wrap, and let rise in a warm place until doubled in bulk, about 1 hour.

Punch dough down, turn out onto a floured surface, and knead again for 1 to 2 minutes. Cover and let rest for 5 minutes. Shape dough into 2 loaves, place into 2 buttered 8½ × 4½-inch loaf pans, cover, and let rise in a warm place until nearly doubled in bulk, about 1 hour.

Slash tops of loaves in several places and bake in a preheated 375°F oven for 45 minutes, or until loaves test done.

Remove from pans and cool on a wire rack.

# Sourdough Triticale Bread

(2 medium-size loaves)

*Sponge:*
1 cup sourdough starter
2 cups warm water
1 tablespoon honey
2 cups triticale flour
2 cups whole wheat flour

*Dough:*
1 teaspoon salt (optional, see page 22)
¼ teaspoon baking soda (optional)
1 egg
¼ cup corn oil
2 cups whole wheat flour
2 cups triticale flour (approximate)

---

A Sourdough Note: Though Art uses loaf pans for these breads, any sourdough recipe can be made in the shape of the long French-type loaves, either using the long loaf pan or shaping aluminum foil as a holder. In that case, you would bake the breads between 25 and 35 minutes, depending upon the thickness of the loaves.

# Sourdough Buckwheat Bread

(2 medium-size loaves)

*Sponge:*
1 cup sourdough starter
2 cups warm water
4 cups whole wheat flour

*Dough:*
1 teaspoon salt (optional, see page 22)
2 eggs, beaten
¼ cup butter, melted
⅓ cup maple syrup
4 cups stone-ground buckwheat flour
additional whole wheat flour as needed

*When I first tried this bread, I put the buckwheat flour into the sour sponge and let it ferment overnight. The next day it had developed a fiercely pungent aroma that carried into the baked bread as a strong flavor. Though not too bad, it was not appetizing, and it was just not what I wanted. The next time, I followed the same procedure, using a buckwheat flour from a different source—but with the same results. I finally figured out that the strong aroma and flavor came from the souring of the buckwheat, and the solution was to use only wheat flour in the sponge.*

To prepare the sponge: Place starter into a large warmed bowl. Add warm water and stir in flour until well mixed. Cover with plastic wrap and let ferment in a warm place for 8 to 12 hours or overnight.

To prepare the dough: Sprinkle salt on the sponge. Stir in the beaten eggs, melted butter, and maple syrup. Mix in buckwheat flour until dough is no longer sticky. If more than 4 cups flour are needed, add whole wheat flour. Knead dough for 10 minutes. Place into an oiled bowl, turn to coat, cover with plastic wrap, and let rise in a warm spot until doubled in bulk, about 1½ hours.

Punch dough down, turn out onto a floured surface, and knead again for about 5 minutes. Return to bowl, cover, and let rise again in a warm spot until doubled in bulk, about 1¼ hours.

Punch dough down, turn out onto a floured surface, and knead for a few minutes. Cover and let rest for 5 minutes. Shape into 2 loaves, place into 2 buttered 8½ × 4½-inch loaf pans, cover loosely, and let rise in a warm spot until nearly doubled in bulk, about 45 minutes.

Bake in a preheated 400°F oven for 40 minutes, or until loaves test done.

Cool on a wire rack.

# *Postscripts*
# Whatever Happened to . . .

The years since the publication of *Bread Winners* have not only brought forth a veritable inundation of letters and telephone calls from new bakers, but they have also meant a continuing relationship with many of the friends who filled the first book with their warmth, their stories, and their recipes.

On my trips to Minnesota, Kentucky, California, New Mexico, and Texas, I have managed to visit with my old friends, and during the author book tour, they visited me at the department stores and had breakfast with me after the early morning television shows. It was my chance to thank them all in person for the success of the book, and generally I was sent on my way with at least half of a home-baked loaf as insurance against airline food.

I learned that almost every one of our bakers was interviewed on local television right after the book was published. Newspapers all across the country, proud of their home-grown talent, printed feature articles. In Amarillo, Bangor, Mason Valley, Glen Cove, St. Louis, Minneapolis and St. Paul, Burlington, Raleigh, and Louisville, newspapers reported on local *Bread Winners*. I was pleased.

To our new readers this chapter may sound like a classic Christmas update from friends not heard from in twenty years. However, those who attempted the breads described in the first book got to "know" some of the people who contributed them, so let me just recap briefly. What follows, too, is more specific information about those *Bread Winners* alumni, plus their new recipes.

All of us complain that "time sure does fly" and I agree when I find that my youngest bread baker, Amy Seltzer, 16 years old when *Bread Winners* was in progress, is now a senior at Princeton University. Our "cover people" are as active as ever. Noelle Braynard is still dancing and designing costumes with the Battery Dance Company, and she's had her second art show, at which she sold 21 of her 30 paintings! Suzanne Gosar still bakes bread in her outdoor oven and has contributed the plans for the structure, at the request of many readers (page 280). The Holsapples are still trekking though Alaska and baking breads at 14,000 feet.

Our Honey Queen, Pam Anderson, had become engaged at the time of this writing and is probably married by now, while Sylvia Moore, Stacie Hunt, and Judy Slinden (the daughter of Joyce and Don) were all married during the past few years. Howard and Agnes Arns celebrated their fiftieth wedding anniversary. And, our ex-mayor of Fargo, North Dakota, Dick Hentges, is now deeply involved in real estate as the owner and developer of a $2.5 million office condominium called Agassiz Square.

So, even if you've never met the people who populate the next few pages, I think you'll find them interesting, provocative, and pretty darned good bread bakers. And, if you do know them from the earlier book, you may have wondered: Whatever Happened to . . .

# Sheryl and Mel London

The Breads:

**Blue Corn Sausage and**
 **Cheese Loaf**
**Blue Corn Blueberry**
 **Orange Tea Bread**
**American Indian**
 **Blue Corn Puffs**
**Apple Bran Spice Muffins**
**Kasha Whole Grain Bread**
**Whole Wheat Raisin**
 **Apple Bread**
*Khachapuri* **(Russian**
 **Cheese Bread)**
 **–Individual Tarts**

And what have *we* been doing in the years between the publication of *Bread Winners* and this new volume? The film work on our documentaries has continued. We worked in Ecuador for some time, producing a series of films on breast feeding and immunology for the Pan American Health Organization, aimed at an eventual audience of Quechua Indians. We just returned from Hong Kong and Japan. And before that we completed a documentary in California for Sunkist Growers on the subject of citrus.

But, over the past two years, our major project has been the development and testing of recipes—as well as the publication of a new book for Rodale Press, *Sheryl and Mel London's Creative Cooking with Grains and Pasta.* When we were not traveling to check out growers and grain mills, we were at Fire Island testing hundreds of recipes for breakfast, lunch and dinner dishes—soups, salads, appetizers, entrees, side dishes, desserts, *and 38 breads,* ranging from Finnish Hardtack to Green Peppercorn Pones. For bakers who would like to try some of the unusual breads in that book, we suggest that you check the book out of the library and add them to your recipe files.

Because Sheryl and I have been working together so closely since the publication of *Bread Winners,* we have decided that this portion of the Postscripts should be one in which we combine our recipes in a single section. Anyway, it is difficult to decide which recipe was created by whom, at this point in our baking lives.

# About Blue Corn

Blue cornmeal is ground from Indian blue corn and it's a regional southwestern specialty. Until now, it has been quite difficult to find, so very few recipes have surfaced for those of us who like to try new things. However, it can now be ordered by mail (Casa Moneo—see Mail-Order Sources—carries it) and we have even found it in a New York department store.

The flavor is much more intense than other cornmeals and the color is, of course, most unusual. In one of our recipes, blueberries enhance the color of the cornmeal, and all the breads are unusual dinner party conversation pieces among guests who are unfamiliar with blue corn. If you can't get blue corn or if you prefer not to order it by mail, the recipes will work just as well with yellow cornmeal, but the taste will be somewhat different and not as distinctive.

This is a festive, layered bread that when sliced reveals a rainbow of blue cornmeal, flecked with yellow corn kernels, orange cheddar cheese, and the green of the hot peppers. A colorful party loaf that can be prepared ahead, it's a spectacular conversation piece. If you like the bite of hot peppers, use the ½ cup suggested. However, if you prefer a milder flavor, just use half the amount.

In a medium-size skillet, cook the sausages in one layer, turning with tongs to cook the other side. Remove and drain on paper towels. Spoon out 1 tablespoon pan drippings and reserve.

In a medium-size bowl, mix all the dry ingredients together.

In a large bowl, beat together the eggs, melted butter, sour cream, yogurt, and reserved pan drippings. Beat well and then stir in corn kernels. Add the dry ingredients and blend. Spoon half the batter into a buttered 9 × 5-inch loaf pan. Arrange layers of sausage, shredded cheese, and hot peppers over batter. Then spoon the remaining batter over the layers and smooth with a spatula. Bake in a preheated 375°F oven for 60 to 70 minutes.

Cool for 10 minutes on a rack before loosening and removing from pan. Serve warm.

# Blue Corn Sausage and Cheese Loaf (with Jalapeño Peppers)

(1 large loaf)

3 Italian or Spanish
   sausages, thinly sliced
1 cup blue cornmeal
1 tablespoon baking powder
1 teaspoon salt (optional, see
   page 22)
⅛ teaspoon baking soda
2 eggs
⅓ cup butter, melted
½ cup sour cream
½ cup yogurt
2 cups cooked yellow corn
   kernels, fresh or frozen
½ pound sharp cheddar
   cheese, shredded
¼ to ½ cup jalapeño
   peppers, finely minced

If the baked loaves have moist centers, the oven temperature may be too high or the baking time may be too short.

Andy Esberg

# Blue Corn Blueberry Orange Tea Bread

(1 medium-size loaf)

1½ cups blue cornmeal
½ cup whole wheat flour
1 tablespoon baking powder
¼ teaspoon salt (optional, see page 22)
¼ teaspoon ground cinnamon
2 eggs, beaten
1 cup milk
¼ cup butter, melted
2 tablespoons grated orange rind
1 cup fresh blueberries

In a medium-size bowl, combine all the dry ingredients.

In a large bowl, mix together the beaten eggs, milk, melted butter, and orange rind. Add dry ingredients to egg mixture, then stir in blueberries. Pour batter into a buttered 8½ × 4½-inch loaf pan and bake in a preheated 400°F oven for 1 hour.

Cool on a wire rack for 10 minutes before removing from pan.

Note: Frozen blueberries can be used, but the amount of liquid may make the bread somewhat damp. Make certain that frozen blueberries are thawed and dried thoroughly on paper towels. Then add another ½ cup flour to dry ingredients before combining with egg mixture.

# American Indian Blue Corn Puffs

(about 10 puffs)

¾ cup blue cornmeal
1 cup milk, scalded
3 eggs
¼ teaspoon salt (optional, see page 22)

These little corn puffs—a cross between crisp spoon bread and popovers—are absolutely delicious. We made some when we had dinner guests and they disappeared almost as soon as they were taken from the oven and placed on the table. Like all other blue corn recipes, they can also be made with yellow or white cornmeal and they'll taste wonderful.

In a large bowl, stir cornmeal into scalded milk and stir until mixture thickens. Beat with a wooden spoon.

In a medium-size bowl, beat eggs with a wire whisk until foamy and slightly thick. Add to cornmeal mixture and blend. Pour mixture three-quarters full into a generously buttered popover pan or custard cups and bake in a preheated 400°F oven for 30 minutes. Loosen and serve at once.

In a medium-size bowl, beat together the honey, melted butter, vanilla, beaten egg, and buttermilk.

In a large bowl, mix together the flour, baking powder, baking soda, salt, and pumpkin pie spice. Then stir in bran.

Place apples into a second medium-size bowl and sprinkle with lemon juice. Add raisins and currants and stir in well.

Combine egg mixture with dry ingredients and then add apple mixture. Mix with only a few strokes. As with all muffin recipes, do not over-mix. Pour batter into a buttered 12-cup muffin tin, filling the cups to the top, and bake in a preheated 350°F oven for 20 to 25 minutes.

Cool muffins in the tin on a wire rack before removing. Serve warm.

# Apple Bran Spice Muffins

(about 12 muffins)

¼ cup honey
¼ cup butter, melted
1 teaspoon vanilla extract
1 egg, beaten
½ cup buttermilk
¾ cup whole wheat flour
1½ teaspoons baking powder
½ teaspoon baking soda
¼ teaspoon salt (optional, see page 22)
¼ teaspoon pumpkin pie spice
½ cup bran
1½ cups finely chopped, peeled apples
½ teaspoon lemon juice
¼ cup golden raisins
¼ cup currants

It's easy to do your own "enriching" with bran, blackstrap molasses, wheat germ, or raisins, even if the recipe doesn't call for them.
Maggie Greenwood

# Kasha Whole Grain Bread

(2 loaves)

1 cup medium kasha
1¼ cups hot water
¾ cup warm water
2 tablespoons dry yeast
1 tablespoon honey
1 cup yogurt
1½ teaspoons salt (optional, see page 22)
¼ cup peanut oil
1 cup light buckwheat flour
4 to 5 cups whole wheat flour*
cornmeal for dusting pan
1 egg white
¼ cup cold water
sesame seeds

We have found that people fall into two distinct groups in their attitudes toward buckwheat—those who don't like the strong, assertive flavor and those who are just crazy about it. We are among the latter and so is our Fire Island friend, Herb Schlosser. The roasted variety of buckwheat groats is called kasha, and if your grandparents came from eastern Europe, you are probably quite familiar with it. The process of roasting gives it an even nuttier flavor, a dark color, and a very distinctive aroma. You'll find buckwheat groats—both roasted and unroasted—in most supermarkets. However, kasha and buckwheat flour can also be ordered from Birkett Mills (see Mail-Order Sources). If you number yourself among us buckwheat lovers, you'll love this bread.

In a medium-size bowl, mix kasha with hot water and let stand for about 30 minutes. Since kasha is already roasted, it will absorb most of the water.

In the meantime, combine warm water with yeast and honey in a small bowl, stir, and set aside to proof.

In a large bowl, combine kasha (and any water left over after soaking), yeast mixture, yogurt, salt, and oil. Slowly stir in buckwheat flour, mixing as you do so. Then, add whole wheat flour, 1 cup at a time, stirring after each addition until dough is workable.

Turn out onto a floured surface and knead in additional flour with your hands until dough is quite firm and handles with some difficulty. Place into a well-oiled bowl, turn to coat, cover, and let rise in a warm spot until doubled in bulk, about 1½ hours.

Punch dough down, turn out onto floured surface, and knead for 1 to 2 minutes. Divide dough into 2 pieces, pat each piece out flat with your hand, and then roll up jelly-roll style until you have formed 2 loaves. Firmly pinch the ends to seal the loaves and then place on a baking sheet that has been dusted with cornmeal. Allow enough room between the loaves. Cover and let rise in a warm spot for another 1 to 1½ hours, or until almost doubled in bulk.

In a cup, beat egg white with cold water, and brush the tops of the loaves with this mixture. Sprinkle with sesame seeds and rub seeds in lightly with your fingers so that

*Because of the bulk of the kasha, some bakers prefer to use white flour to keep the bread lighter and more manageable.

they do not fall off during baking. Then brush on the remainder of the egg white glaze, covering seeds. Using a sharp knife or razor blade, cut the loaves with several slashes or with a cross to allow for expansion during baking. Bake in a preheated 375°F oven for 40 to 50 minutes, or until the loaves test done when tapped on the bottoms.

Cool on wire racks.

Apply seeds by dipping your hands in water first and then rubbing seeds into the dough. It will keep them from falling off during baking.

Ed Feiner

# A Book Tour Postscript

There is a treasure trove of new bakers with new recipes all across the country, and one of the side benefits of a book tour (page 186) is that I get to meet many of them face to face. Many times these colleagues are performers or production people hidden away in the back offices of television and radio stations on which I am lucky enough to appear. These next two recipes were given to me by just such people—Jim Belles, who was News Director of WHK-AM in Cleveland, Ohio, and Carol Storey, producer of "Morning Exchange" in Cleveland, who has, by this time, become an old friend. (I have appeared on that program four times.) The recipes were put in my files and tested in due time. They are printed here as an exchange from one medium to another.

# Whole Wheat Raisin Apple Bread

(1 loaf)

2 tablespoons dry yeast
½ cup warm water
3 tablespoons honey
½ teaspoon salt (optional, see page 22)
1 cup milk, scalded and cooled to room temperature
1 egg, beaten
½ cup cracked wheat
1 cup golden raisins
1 cup chopped tart apples
3 to 4 cups whole wheat flour
1 egg yolk
1 teaspoon milk
cracked wheat for dusting loaf

Jim left this recipe at the station for me, along with a very complimentary note about *Bread Winners* and this comment about the bread:

*This recipe makes a two-pound loaf. I have tried several times to make two one-pound loaves, but the texture never seems quite the same. If you figure out a solution, I'd appreciate a line. Bon appetit!*

He is quite right. The texture is not the same. Thus, the recipe for one two-pound loaf follows.

In a small bowl, dissolve yeast in warm water.

In a large bowl, combine the honey, salt, and milk. Stir in beaten egg and add yeast mixture. Stir in cracked wheat, raisins, apples, and 2½ cups flour, reserving the balance for the kneading.

Turn out onto a floured surface and knead for 8 to 10 minutes, or until dough is smooth and elastic. Knead in ½ cup flour and any additional flour that might be necessary. Place into an oiled bowl, turn to coat, cover, and let rise in a warm spot for about 1 hour, or until almost doubled in bulk.

Punch dough down and knead on a floured surface for 1 to 2 minutes. Shape into a loaf and place in a buttered 8½ × 4½-inch loaf pan. Cover and let rise in a warm spot for about 45 minutes, or until doubled in bulk.

In a cup, beat egg yolk with 1 teaspoon milk and brush the top of the loaf. Dust with cracked wheat and bake in a preheated 375°F oven for 45 to 50 minutes, or until the loaf tests done when tapped on the bottom.

Remove from pan and cool on a wire rack.

It is always a delight to return to Cleveland for an appearance on "Morning Exchange." It is like coming home again, and it is one of the few shows in America where the same people seem to be there to greet me year after year. This past trip, Carol Storey brought a home-baked bread down to the studio to welcome me. And, some years ago, she gave me this recipe, originally from a Cleveland area baker named Elaine German, who had also appeared on the show. It is a cheese bread that is made either as a large, round loaf or as individual open tarts. These small tarts are so popular in the Caucasus that they're sold in the street by vendors. I make my version with whole wheat flour instead of white, and the result is marvelous!

To prepare the bread: In a large bowl, combine the honey, salt, yeast, and 1 cup flour.

In a small saucepan, heat butter and milk to about 110°F. Beat liquid ingredients into dry ingredients. Add 1 cup more flour, beat for about 2 minutes, and then add the remaining flour.

Turn dough out onto a floured surface and knead for about 10 minutes, or until smooth and elastic. Shape into a ball and let rest for 15 minutes.

To prepare the filling: Place cheese into a medium-size bowl. Add egg and egg yolk to cheese. Mix well and set aside.

Roll dough into a rectangle 6 by 24 inches. Spoon cheese mixture along the center of dough lengthwise and then roll dough and filling into a cylinder. Seal both ends and the seam firmly with your fingers and place seam-side down in a buttered 9- or 10-inch round cake pan to form a circle in the pan. Cover and let rest for 10 minutes.

To prepare the glaze: Brush loaf with egg white, sprinkle with almonds, and bake in a preheated 375°F oven for 35 to 40 minutes.

Let cool for 15 minutes before cutting.

Roll dough into a rectangle about 8 by 24 inches and then cut into 12 4 by 4-inch squares. Fill each square with some of the cheese filling and then shape into diamond shapes. Place on a buttered baking sheet, brush with egg white, and sprinkle with almonds. Let rest for 10 minutes.

Bake in a preheated 375°F oven for 15 to 20 minutes.

Cool slightly on wire racks and transfer to a serving platter.

# Khachapuri (Russian Cheese Bread)

(1 round loaf or 12 tarts)

*Bread:*
   3 tablespoons honey
   ½ teaspoon salt (optional, see page 22)
   2 tablespoons dry yeast
3½ cups whole wheat flour
   ½ cup butter
   1 cup milk

*Filling:*
1½ cups Muenster cheese, shredded
   1 egg
   1 egg yolk

*Glaze:*
   1 egg white, slightly beaten
   slivered almonds

# Individual Tarts

# Suzanne Gosar

The Breads:

**Mountain Mama
Whole Wheat *Snitzbrod*
Atomic Green Chili
Corn Bread**

*Plus:*

**The Mountain Mama
Outdoor Oven**

*Bread Winners Too*

*The outdoor oven on the back cover of* Bread Winners *created quite a stir among your readers, so I'm including the instructions for those who would like to build it themselves.*

Both Suzanne and I received letters asking about the oven, and other readers began looking for her nutritious whole wheat flour in their natural foods stores. (It's sold under the name of Rainbow as well as Mountain Mama.) The Gosar farm is in Monte Vista, Colorado:

*Mountain Mama Milling continues to flourish. We're not getting wealthy, but we have grown consistently and our wonderful stone-ground whole wheat flour is being distributed from Los Angeles to Chicago. Our son, Kris, who is now an alarming 21 years old is running the mill for us, leaving my husband, Gregg, free to attend to the farm and the production of the milling wheat.*

Recently, Suzanne and her family joined with the San Luis Valley Protein Energy Corporation, a cooperative of seven farmers and one architect, to attempt to produce 200 proof alcohol as a fuel source.

*It is one more step in our efforts toward self-sufficiency and survival on the family farm. It is not an easy struggle but we remain healthy and hopeful. I can't begin to express to you how grave the situation is. If the family farm dies, an integral part of "The American Way" will go with it and we will mourn its demise from sea to shining sea.*

Her letters have been newsy and warm. My telephone calls to Monte Vista have always left me with a feeling of awe for this woman who not only farms, but participates in the local crafts fairs, backpacks over the Continental Divide, works three days a week as a travel agent, and is so close to her family.

*I have found, sometimes painfully, that I tend to get involved in too much, work too hard, and forget to give myself some quiet time, so in recent years I've learned to pace myself a little better.*

# Mountain Mama Whole Wheat *Snitzbrod*

(3 medium-size loaves)

8 ounces pitted prunes
8 ounces dried apricots
3 cups water
½ cup butter, melted
1½ cups honey
1 teaspoon salt (optional, see page 22)
4 tablespoons dry yeast
5 to 6 cups whole wheat flour (Mountain Mama, of course)
½ cup golden raisins
1 cup chopped walnuts
4 teaspoons lemon rind
1 teaspoon ground cloves
¼ teaspoon ground ginger
¼ teaspoon ground nutmeg
3 eggs, beaten

*This aromatic bread has become another tradition with me—each Christmas I bake several loaves and give them as gifts. The original recipe came from a Mrs. Geer, whom I met on an airplane. We started talking about nutrition and health, and the conversation naturally turned to baking our own bread. She loved the story about our farm and Mountain Mama Milling, and she honored me by sending me her Snitzbrod recipe.*

Place prunes and apricots in a medium-size bowl, cover with water and soak overnight. The longer they soak, the better the final taste.

Next morning, drain fruit, reserving soaking water in a 3-cup measure. If necessary, add fresh water. Add the melted butter, honey, and salt to the soaking water and stir well.

In a large bowl, combine yeast and 5 cups flour. Add the liquid ingredients, mixing as you do so. Cover and let rise in a warm spot until bubbly, about 45 minutes.

Stir in raisins. Then add chopped walnuts. Chop prunes and apricots and add them next, followed by the lemon rind, cloves, ginger, and nutmeg. Stir well. Blend in beaten eggs and mix thoroughly. Add enough flour to make a dough that can be kneaded well. It will be quite stiff because of the amount of fruit in the bread. Though the recipe specifies 5 cups flour, you may find it is too much if you live in a dry climate. Those who live in a damp climate may have to add another cup or more of flour. Judge it by "feel."

Turn dough out onto a lightly floured surface and knead for 8 to 10 minutes. Place into a well-oiled bowl, cover, and let rise in a warm spot for 1 to 1½ hours, or until nearly doubled in bulk.

Punch dough down, turn out onto a floured surface, shape into 3 loaves, and place into 3 well-buttered and floured 8½ × 4½-inch loaf pans. Cover lightly and let rise in a warm spot until dough reaches the tops of the pans.

Bake in a preheated 325°F oven for about 1 hour. If tops become too brown, cover with aluminum foil near the end of the baking time.

Cool on wire racks before slicing.

Without meaning to be immodest, Suzanne feels that this particular Green Chili Corn Bread recipe is better than any that have been published in *Bread Winners*. I'll let you be the judge. A moist, delicious bread, it goes wonderfully with hearty winter soups, and it's perfect to take along on a picnic.

> *I sometimes give away this bread and others that I bake just on an impulse, even to perfect strangers. I'm a bit like the Lone Ranger. "Who was that person?" "I don't know, but she left this loaf of bread!"*

In a large bowl, combine the cornmeal, salt, and baking soda. Mix well. Stir in milk and oil. Add beaten eggs and corn and mix. Spoon half of the cornmeal mixture into a buttered 1½-quart casserole. Then sprinkle chilies and cheese on top. Spoon the rest of the cornmeal mixture over chilies and cheese and bake, uncovered, in a preheated 350°F oven for about 45 minutes, or until a wooden pick inserted in center comes out clean.

Cool slightly. Serve warm.

# Atomic Green Chili Corn Bread

(1 loaf)

    1 cup yellow cornmeal
    ½ teaspoon salt (optional, see page 22)
    ½ teaspoon baking soda
    ¾ cup milk
    ⅓ cup vegetable oil
    2 eggs, beaten
   16 ounces cream-style corn
    1 4-ounce can chopped green chili peppers, drained
  1½ cups shredded sharp cheddar cheese, Monterey Jack, or a combination of both

# The Mountain Mama Outdoor Oven

*Our oven is somewhat like those you see throughout the Southwest; the Pueblo Indians are famous for theirs. A fire is built inside on the brick floor, heating the walls and the bottom of the oven. Then you scoop the fire out, clean the floor, and cook in the declining heat. The thickness of the walls should be adjusted according to the climate. We live at 7,600 feet with occasional very cold temperatures, so we made the top a bit thicker than called for. However, the walls should never be less than four inches thick.*

*You simply build a fire inside the oven, leaving the back vent and front doorway open. Let it burn for about three hours, feeding it constantly. The outside of the oven will feel quite hot to the touch. Before going further, get a shovel, a hoe, and a fireproof container, plus a bucket filled with water and a broom or mop.*

*When the fire has burned for at least three hours, scoop out the remaining wood and the ashes and place them in the container. Use the hoe to reach into the back and the corners. (We have a barbecue right next to our oven so the wood and ashes just get tossed right into it.) Wet the broom or mop and finish cleaning the floor of the oven. Plug the back vent with rags—and work quickly. Place a thermometer that registers up to 700°F in the middle of the oven. If your fire burned long enough, it should register about 600°F. Leave the oven doorway open to cool the interior until the thermometer reaches 325°F (30 to 40 minutes).*

*When baking bread, it's a little tricky to do the bread making and the oven preparation by yourself, so I suggest*

*that you find someone to be your partner in the project. One person can tend the fire and the oven, while the other takes care of the bread. I also suggest that you make the dough about 1½ hours before you're ready to clear the oven, so that it can rise while you clear the oven and let it cool down to baking temperature.*

*If the bread has risen and the oven has not cooled sufficiently, refrigerate the dough. If the oven is ready, and the dough has not risen enough, just set the oven door in place until you're ready to bake.*

*The loaves are traditionally baked free-form, right on the floor of the oven. To do this, you'll need a floured bread paddle on which to place the loaves. If you bake* bollilos *or rolls, you can place them on a baking sheet.*

*When the oven temperature reaches 325°F, slide the bread onto the oven floor. Work quickly, and then set the door in place. Check the temperature in 5 minutes. If it's above 400°F, remove the door until the temperature drops to 350°F and then close it again. Continue baking for 40 to 60 minutes, depending upon the size of the loaves. If you are baking rolls, 20 to 30 minutes will do it.*

*An entire meal can be baked in the oven as well. A roast and vegetables can be placed in the back of the oven and the bread toward the front. Just follow the above directions, but leave the meat in for about an hour after the bread comes out. Needless to say, all of this takes a little practice and experimentation, but that's part of the fun.*

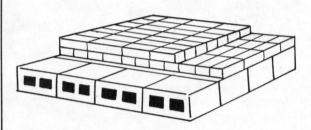

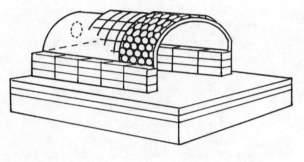

**Base**

Arrange and level 16 6×8×16 concrete blocks. Add two layers of clay bricks, placing each layer perpendicular to previous layer (150–160 bricks).

**Form**

Place one-half 28-gallon drum (paper) on side walls made from 3 rows of bricks. Make a draft hole in back of drum by cutting a hole large enough to accommodate a tin can about 3 inches in diameter. Cover the drum with piece of 4-inch concrete mesh. Cover the mesh and the back of the drum with chicken wire.

**Alternate Form for Cold Climates**

Use steel drum so that thick adobe (or bricks) can be laid over entire surface for better heat retention. If drum is not available, use a two-wire straw bale on edge and stack bricks up sides for walls. Straw can be dug or burned out later.

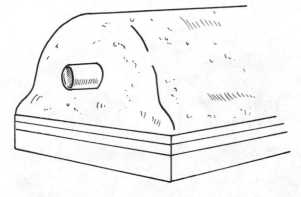

## Cover

Remove both ends from can. Fit can into draft hole, exposing 4 inches of the can. Force mud mixture (12 shovels mud, 4 shovels cement, plus water) through wire onto drum. Make walls at least 4 inches thick. If your soil is not very heavy, use some chopped straw in your mix as a binder. You'll use about 3 bags cement. Make 2-inch-thick arched-top door in place and mold mud up front of drum to fit door closely. Remove door when mud firms up a little. Smooth out surface of drum by hand with a little water. Cure under wet cloths and plastic for 4 to 5 days. Uncover and paint.

## Door

Place 2 short 2×6 boards side by side. Fasten them together by nailing 2 2×2 boards horizontally, several inches apart, on one side.

To make a handle, nail a 2×2 board on top of and perpendicular to the other 2×2's. You now have a square door. Shape the door with a hand saw to fit the opening of your oven.

# Sylvia Moore Ferguson

*The Bread:*

**Harmony Bread**

When *Bread Winners* was published, Sylvia became one of the most talked-about bakers in the book. Then a flight attendant for an international airline, she appeared with me on "Sun Up," San Diego's leading morning TV show. After our meeting on a ticket line at the airport in Billings, Montana, she had actually baked her breads aboard a 747 jet bound for Guatemala!

In September 1979, Sylvia married Bruce Ferguson, a judge in the Superior Court (Juvenile Court Division), and a master craftsman in the art of stained glass windows.

*I had been temporarily unable to work as a flight attendant due to a knee injury. Exactly one month after surgery was performed on my knee, Bruce and I got married—and me with a knee the size of a cantaloupe, using a cane to hobble down the "aisle," which was a dirt path leading to a small amphitheater at Sugarloaf Park in the Valley of the Moon, Sonoma County, California. Needless to say, when we set the wedding date, we had anticipated less drastic surgery!*

Bum knee or not, she still continued to bake bread, and two years ago she entered the Southern California Exposition in bread baking, where her Harmony Bread took third place in the quick bread competition.

Best of all, Sylvia recently informed me that the knee is now healed and she is flying again.

Sylvia writes that when she uses whole wheat flour, she usually works with the hard winter wheat variety, which she gets at natural foods stores. However, with quick breads such as this one, she uses whole wheat pastry flour for a finer texture and a better rise.

In a large saucepan, simmer the applesauce, oats, and raisins over medium heat until oats are thoroughly cooked. Stir frequently to prevent burning. Set aside to cool to room temperature.

In a large bowl, cream together the butter, honey, and eggs.

In a medium-size bowl, combine the flour, baking powder, baking soda, cinnamon, and cloves. Then, blend into butter/honey mixture, alternating with applesauce/oats mixture. Pour batter into 2 buttered 8½ × 4½-inch loaf pans. Run a sharp knife down the center of the loaves to permit expansion during baking. Bake in a preheated 350°F oven for 50 to 60 minutes.

Cool loaves in the pans for 10 minutes before turning out onto a wire rack.

# Harmony Bread

(2 medium-size loaves)

1½ cups applesauce
1½ cups rolled oats
2 cups raisins
1 cup butter
1 cup honey
2 eggs
2½ cups whole wheat pastry flour
1 tablespoon baking powder
½ teaspoon baking soda
1 tablespoon ground cinnamon
½ teaspoon ground cloves

# Stacie Hunt

Stacie Hunt, a West Coast friend and bread baker, is now married to advertising executive, Alan Pando. They still make their home in Los Angeles, and Stacie is still baking her very original recipes. I note with interest that all her descriptions and recipes use the word, "we," which leads me to believe that Alan has also joined our bread baking ranks!

# Savory Gorgonzola Cheese Bread

(2 large loaves)

½ cup minced onions
5 tablespoons butter
1½ cups milk
2 cups finely grated Gorgonzola cheese
2 tablespoons honey
2 tablespoons dry yeast
⅓ cup warm water
1 egg, slightly beaten
7 cups whole wheat pastry flour
1 egg yolk, beaten, for brushing loaves

*My husband, Alan, and I tend to prepare spicy or savory breads, usually with an Italian note. This bread is particularly good when heated or toasted. A crisp green salad would make it a complete light meal—or it can accompany a plate of warm pasta with a fresh tomato or basil sauce. On a hot summer day, try it with cold chicken.*

In a small skillet, sauté onions in 2 tablespoons butter until translucent but not browned. Set aside.

Heat the milk, cheese, 1 tablespoon butter, and honey in a medium-size saucepan over medium heat and stir until cheese is melted. Cool to lukewarm.

In a large bowl, dissolve yeast in warm water. Add the cheese mixture, onions, beaten egg, and approximately one half of the flour, 1 cup at a time. Mix thoroughly and beat until smooth. (The dough may become difficult to stir by hand.) Add enough of the remaining flour to make a firm dough, continuing to mix thoroughly.

Turn out onto a lightly floured surface to rest while you clean and butter the bowl with 2 tablespoons butter. Knead dough 6 to 9 minutes, adding flour as necessary, until smooth and elastic. Shape into a ball, turn into the buttered bowl, moving ball around until all areas are coated. Cover with a cloth and let rise in a warm place until doubled in bulk, about 1 hour.

Punch dough down and knead briefly on a floured surface for 1 to 2 minutes. Divide dough in half and shape into 2 loaves. Place into 2 buttered 9 × 5-inch loaf pans. Brush lightly with beaten egg yolk and bake in a preheated 400°F oven for 20 minutes. Then reduce the oven temperature to 375°F and bake for another 10 to 20 minutes, or until the loaves are well browned and sound hollow when tapped on the bottoms.

Cool on wire racks.

# Tangerine Ginger Quick Bread

*This recipe resulted from our discovery of some almost over-ripe tangerines in the refrigerator on the day after Alan and I had made some Indian food for dinner. We had plenty of ginger left over, so we decided to experiment. If you like, you may substitute apple juice or orange juice for the apple cider. This bread makes a wonderfully pungent morning snack with tea or coffee—and in the evening it can be served as a dessert bread topped with fresh cream (whipped or not).*

(1 large loaf)

2¾ cups whole wheat pastry
    flour
1½ teaspoons baking powder
 1 teaspoon baking soda
 ¾ teaspoon ground
    cinnamon
 ½ teaspoon ground ginger
 ¾ cup chopped walnuts or
    almonds
 2 eggs
⅔ cup apple cider, room
    temperature
⅓ cup honey
    grated rind of 1 tangerine
 3 ripe tangerines, seeded,
    membrane removed,
    and coarsely chopped
⅓ cup butter, melted

In a medium-size bowl, combine the flour, baking powder, baking soda, cinnamon, and ginger. Mix thoroughly. Then add the chopped nuts, again mixing thoroughly.

In a large bowl, beat eggs until quite light, yellow, and slightly thickened. Add cider and honey and combine well. Fold in the dry ingredients, rind, and chopped tangerines. Add melted butter and stir ingredients just enough to mix them together. The dough will be on the coarse side. Spoon mixture into a buttered 9 × 3-inch loaf pan and bake in a preheated 375°F oven for 50 to 60 minutes. When the bread begins to part from the sides of the pan, it's done.

Cool *in pan*. Do not slice until the bread has had plenty of time to settle, about 24 hours, if possible.

# Girard Franklin

*The Bread:*

**Fire Island Onion Rye**

Gerry is another of my Fire Island neighbors who qualifies as a human dynamo. A psychiatrist and psychologist in "real" life, he also plays a mean game of tennis, gardens with the best of us, backpacks and camps in the western United States and in Alaska, and bakes sensational and original breads. Each year, he and his wife, Gloria, also a psychiatrist, give a large party for their neighbors, with each guest bringing one homemade item for the menu. I would not dare bring bread at a time like this—not with Gerry around. This year, he baked the Fire Island Onion Rye; and I asked for the recipe before I left the party.

To prepare the starter: In a 2-quart glass or ceramic container, dissolve yeast in warm water. Add flour and onions and stir well. Cover loosely and keep mixture at room temperature for 2 days. Stir before using.

To keep starter for future use, add equal parts of rye flour and warm water to replace what has already been used. After it stops foaming, store in the refrigerator in a tightly covered container. At least once a week, add some additional flour and water if the starter has not been used.

To prepare the sponge: In a large bowl, stir together the starter, warm water, flour, and onions. Cover loosely and keep at room temperature overnight.

To prepare the dough: In a cup, dissolve yeast in warm water and then add to the sponge prepared the previous day. Stir in the remaining ingredients until you have a workable dough.

Turn out onto a lightly floured surface and knead until smooth and elastic, adding additional flour if necessary. This should take 8 to 10 minutes. Place dough into a lightly oiled bowl, turn to coat, cover, and let rise in a warm spot until doubled in bulk, 1½ to 2 hours.

Punch dough down, turn out onto a lightly floured surface, and divide into 2 large or 4 small free-form loaves. Place the loaves on a buttered baking sheet dusted with cornmeal. Cover and let rise in a warm spot until doubled in bulk, about 1 hour.

To prepare the glaze: In a cup, beat together egg and water. Brush the loaves with glaze. Then liberally sprinkle the tops with caraway seeds or onion flakes. Bake in a preheated 425°F oven for 40 to 45 minutes, or until loaves test done.

Cool on wire racks.

# Fire Island Onion Rye

(2 large or 4 small free-form loaves)

*Starter:*
    1 tablespoon dry yeast
    2 cups warm water
    2 cups rye flour
    1 medium-size onion,
        finely chopped

*Sponge:*
    1 cup sourdough starter
1½ cups warm water
    3 cups rye flour
    1 medium-size onion,
        finely chopped

*Dough:*
    1 tablespoon dry yeast
    ¼ cup warm water
    1 teaspoon salt (optional,
        see page 22)
    1 tablespoon caraway seeds
    1 tablespoon poppy seeds
3½ cups whole wheat flour
        cornmeal for dusting pan

*Glaze:*
    1 egg
    1 teaspoon water
        black caraway seeds or
        onion flakes

# Suzanne Corbett

*The Bread:*

**Poppy Seed Batter Bread**

*I'm finally writing that cookbook of my own. I've tested over 200 recipes for it. Now all I have to do is the typing. In the meantime, I've been teaching my cooking classes 4 to 5 days a week at the local schools and colleges—everything from gourmet and international to Americana, and of course, bread!*

In *Bread Winners*, Suzanne was a veritable gold mine of recipes, including the most superb holiday breads from Italy, Sweden, Germany, Greece, and Czechoslovakia. Here is another from her kitchen, where she bakes in flowerpots, buckets, pie pans, oatmeal boxes, and in cast-iron pots over an open fire.

Pour warm water into a large bowl. Sprinkle yeast over water. Then stir in melted butter, poppy seeds, honey, and salt. Mix in 2 cups of the flour. Then blend in enough of the remaining flour to make a soft dough. Cover and let rise in a warm spot for about 1 hour.

Stir dough down and spoon batter into a buttered 9 × 5-inch loaf pan. Cover and let rise in a warm spot until doubled in bulk, 45 to 60 minutes.

Brush top with egg white and sprinkle with poppy seeds. Bake in a preheated 375°F oven for 40 minutes, or until bread sounds hollow when tapped on the bottom.

Cool on a wire rack.

# Poppy Seed Batter Bread

(1 large loaf)

1¼ cups warm water (125°F)
1 tablespoon dry yeast
2 tablespoons butter, melted
2 tablespoons poppy seeds
1 tablespoon honey
½ teaspoon salt (optional, see page 22)
3 to 3½ cups whole wheat flour
1 egg white, slightly beaten, for brushing loaf
poppy seeds for topping

Keep in mind that homemade breads tend to dry out more quickly than the store-bought variety because they contain no preservatives. To moisten a loaf that has dried out, sprinkle it with water and bake for 10 minutes at 300°F.

Margaret Peabody

# The Farm

*The Bread:*

**Tofu Yeasted Bread**

If the Rodale Booth at the American Booksellers Association convention had the largest crowds the year we baked bread (page 205), the champions in 1982 were surely my friends from The Farm in Summertown, Tennessee. Surrounded by surging crowds, they were cooking sam-

ples from their new book, *Tofu Cookery* (Summertown, Tenn.: The Book Publishing Company, 1982). It was a chance for me to renew old friendships with Bruce Moore and Margaret Nofziger, as well as to sample the dishes made with cholesterol-free, low-calorie, low-fat tofu.

The Farm is a spiritual community, not far from Nashville, which I visited while writing *Bread Winners*. The members grow their own grains, can their own vegetables, and run their own publishing enterprise. As in the past, their recipes utilize an unbleached white flour that contains the germ of the wheat, since they mill it right on the premises and use it at once. Also, they feel that white flour does not destroy the delicacy of the tofu. This recipe is from their new book.

Tofu, high in protein and low in cost, has been a staple in the Orient for thousands of years. If you don't have a nearby Chinese market, you can generally find tofu in your regular supermarket or in natural foods stores.

# Tofu Yeasted Bread

(2 medium-size loaves or 36 rolls)

3 medium potatoes
2 tablespoons dry yeast
1 tablespoon honey
½ pound tofu
1 cup warm water
7 to 8 cups unbleached white flour
1 teaspoon salt (optional, see page 22)
½ cup vegetable oil

Boil potatoes in enough water to cover until soft. Drain, reserving 1 cup water. Let reserved water cool until just warm enough to mix with the yeast. Mash potatoes in a medium-size bowl and tranfer to a 1½-cup measure.

In a large bowl, combine the warm potato water, yeast, and honey. Stir and set aside for 10 minutes to proof.

Place the tofu, mashed potatoes, and warm water into a blender and process until smooth and creamy. Stir the contents of the blender into the foaming yeast mixture. Then stir in 4 cups of the flour, salt, and oil. Beat well. Cover and let rise in a warm place for 20 minutes.

Stir dough down. Add enough of the remaining flour to make a dough that is the right consistency for kneading. Turn out onto a floured surface and knead until smooth and elastic, 8 to 10 minutes. Form into 2 loaves or about 36 rolls. Place loaves into 2 oiled 8½ × 4½-inch loaf pans or place rolls on oiled baking sheets. Cover lightly and let rise in a warm spot for 30 to 45 minutes, or until almost doubled in bulk.

Bake in a preheated 375°F oven for 40 to 50 minutes if you are making loaves and for about 20 minutes if you are making rolls.

Cool on wire racks.

# Margaret Peabody

*The Bread:*

**Russian-Style Black Bread**

Margaret is the next-door Fire Island neighbor who first taught me to pound the dough down violently before the second rise, to throw it on the counter and take out my aggressions on the helpless, shimmering mass of bread-to-be. Recently, she has been leaving large bags of home-grown tomatoes and zucchini at our doorstep, in addition to samples of an original raspberry liqueur that she concocts from the vast array of cultivated bushes on her mainland property. With a generous neighbor like Margaret, one need never starve.

Margaret is the source of a most unusual baking tip:

*The best advice I can give a baker is—don't bake bread and watch TV at the same time. I did, and I fell asleep, and not only missed the crucial ending of "Masterpiece Theatre," but also found four charred bricks waiting for me in the oven!*

Here is a new bread recipe that Margaret has perfected, in between her teaching and her trips to Canada, Scotland, England—and Fire Island.

This is a tangy, tasty, unusual dark rye bread that uses both minced onions and caraway seeds. It will satisfy the longings of friends and neighbors who constantly ask, "Can you bake a really dark, dark rye bread like the one I ate in Germany?" Even though this originated a few countries to the left(!), everyone will love it, Margaret guarantees.

In a small bowl or measuring cup, combine the yeast, ½ cup warm water, and honey. Stir and set aside to proof.

In a large bowl, mix rye flour with 3 cups whole wheat flour, reserving the balance of the whole wheat flour for use as needed to bring dough to the correct texture. Add the salt, bran, caraway seeds, fennel seeds, and carob powder and mix well with a wooden spoon.

In a small saucepan, combine the remaining warm water, onions, vinegar, molasses, and melted butter, and blend over low heat until all ingredients are well mixed. Do not boil, but heat to just about the temperature that you would use when mixing with yeast for proofing.

Pour proofed yeast mixture into dry ingredients, and then gradually add warm mixture from the saucepan, mixing with a wooden spoon as you do so. Add more whole wheat flour and stir, until dough pulls away from the bowl and can be kneaded by hand.

Turn dough out onto a lightly floured surface, and knead for about 10 minutes, adding more whole wheat flour if it seems too sticky. (Note that all breads that use a large amount of rye flour will have a sticky texture.) Place dough into a well-oiled bowl, turn to coat, cover, and let rise in a warm spot until doubled in bulk, 1½ to 2 hours.

Punch dough down, turn out onto a floured surface, and divide in half. Shape into 2 free-form loaves and place on buttered baking sheets; or, to keep them from spreading, place them into 2 well-buttered 8- or 9-inch round cake pans. Cover and let rise in a warm spot until almost doubled in bulk, about 1 hour.

Bake in a preheated 350°F oven for 50 to 60 minutes.

In a saucepan, combine cornstarch and cold water, bring to a boil over medium heat, and cook for 1 to 2 minutes, stirring constantly. The mixture will turn clear. Brush cornstarch glaze over the tops of the baked loaves, return to the oven, and bake another 2 to 3 minutes.

Remove from pans or baking sheets and cool on wire racks.

# Russian-Style Black Bread

(2 loaves)

2 tablespoons dry yeast
2½ cups warm water
1 teaspoon honey
3 cups dark rye flour
4 to 5 cups whole wheat flour
1 teaspoon salt (optional, see page 22)
2 cups bran
2 tablespoons caraway seeds
½ teaspoon fennel seeds, crushed
1½ tablespoons carob powder
2 tablespoons minced onions
¼ cup vinegar
¼ cup dark molasses
¼ cup butter, melted
1 teaspoon cornstarch
¼ cup cold water

# Elizabeth Ebbott

*The Bread:*

**Whole Wheat Sesame Sticks**

"Since your last book, some new interests have developed, some have faded. . . ." The letter went on to tell about the busy life of one of our Minnesota State Fair prizewinners, and I wondered where she gets the time to bake bread! A member of the Minnesota Ethical Practices Board, a member of the organizing committee to research programs and problems affecting the American Indians in her state, an active member of the League of Women Voters, a student of genealogy searching for family records dating back to the 1600s, an avid gardener who has found the time to take a training program at the University of Minnesota Agricultural School, she still manages to travel.

*Last summer we backpacked in the Wind River Mountains in Wyoming (on horseback), and for the first time in my life, I caught Rainbow Lake Trout. My creative cooking runs in spurts. This past year we entertained a good deal, with one stretch of dinners for 39, 48, and 42, all in a two-week period!*

# Whole Wheat Sesame Sticks

*This is an adaptation of a recipe that I originally developed when I came back from living in Italy 16 years ago and discovered that I could no longer buy the very thin, crisp* grissini *we had grown to love. The recipe makes a dry, crisp product that keeps well in storage for months, and it has been acclaimed by all, even Italian friends, to be better than those made in Torino.*

(about 5 dozen sticks)

1 tablespoon dry yeast
¼ cup lukewarm water
1 cup milk
¼ cup plus 1 teaspoon butter
1½ tablespoons honey
1 tablespoon sesame seeds
1 egg white
½ cup rye or pumpernickel rye flour
3 cups whole wheat flour (approximate)
melted butter for brushing sticks
garlic powder or onion powder (optional)

The recipe can be made using an ordinary vegetable cutter or a pizza cutter, but Elizabeth uses a "pizzalike" five-roller cutter that makes uniform sticks exactly ⅜ inch wide. The cutters are not generally available, but you can get them by mail order at the Bridge Company (for address, see Mail-Order Sources).

In a cup, dissolve yeast in warm water and let stand for 5 minutes.

Scald milk in a small saucepan. Add ¼ cup butter and honey. When milk mixture is lukewarm, pour into a large bowl and add yeast mixture. Stir.

In a small skillet, toast sesame seeds in 1 teaspoon butter until light brown. Cool and then add to milk/yeast mixture.

Beat egg white in a small bowl until frothy and set aside. Add rye flour and half of the whole wheat flour to the milk/yeast mixture and stir. Then stir in beaten egg white. Add the remaining flour gradually until dough is the right texture for kneading.

Turn out onto a lightly floured surface and knead until smooth and elastic, 8 to 10 minutes. Place into an oiled bowl, turn to coat, cover, and let rise in a warm spot until doubled in bulk, 45 to 60 minutes.

Turn dough out onto a lightly floured surface and divide in half. Work with one half of the dough at a time. Roll out to form a rectangle about 9 by 12 inches and ⅜-inch thick. Using the vegetable cutter or pizza cutter, cut strips 9 by ⅜ inches. Place strips on a lightly oiled baking sheet ½-inch apart, but don't leave for a second rising. Bake in a preheated 350°F oven until lightly browned, about 10 minutes.

Remove from oven and immediately brush with melted butter. Then sprinkle with garlic powder or onion powder. Place on wire racks to cool. Repeat process with the remaining dough.

# Ron Kershen

When I wrote *Bread Winners,* the grain called triticale (trit-i-*kay*-lee) was not too well known. Through my long research and experimentation with this high-protein, low-gluten grain, Ron Kershen, a grower down in Canyon, Texas, was my major source of help and encouragement. Since that time, the grain has become better known, and it can now be found in almost every natural foods store across the country. Ron, currently with the ARCO Seed Company, tells me that triticale sales are increasing each year.

*We now export seed to England, while around the world triticale is planted on over 1 million acres. We still expect it to become a major crop both for food and forage during the next 20 years.*

The new varieties of triticale have some improved bread baking qualities, and Ron expects to have a series available soon with a higher gluten content, so that recipes can then be modified to contain more triticale and less high-gluten flour of other types.

*Bread Winners Too*

This is a recipe that can be used to make biscuits, dinner rolls, or doughnuts. It can be baked or you can deep fry the dough. Best of all, the dough will keep for a week if you chill it right after you make it.

In a small bowl, dissolve yeast in lukewarm water. Add 1 teaspoon honey and 1 tablespoon of the whole wheat flour. Set aside to proof.

Pour warmed milk into a large bowl.

In a medium-size bowl, cream together 1 cup honey and butter and stir mixture into milk. Add egg and then yeast mixture. Add 4 cups whole wheat flour, 1 cup at a time, stirring after each addition. At this point, dough will look like a cake batter. Cover and let rise in a warm spot for 1 hour.

Add the baking soda, baking powder, salt, and triticale flour. Then, add the remaining whole wheat flour, 1 cup at a time, until you have the proper consistency for kneading. Turn out onto a floured surface and knead for about 10 minutes. Wrap in wax paper and place into refrigerator to chill overnight.

The next morning, let dough return to room temperature. Divide dough according to your preference for biscuits, dinner rolls, or doughnuts.

To make biscuits, place dough into buttered 12-cup muffin tins, filling each cup about two-thirds full.

To make dinner rolls, shape dough into small or large rolls, and place them on buttered baking sheets.

To make doughnuts, form dough into circles and place on buttered baking sheets.

Cover and let rise in a warm spot for 25 to 30 minutes.

Bake the biscuits or dinner rolls in a 400°F oven for 30 minutes, or until brown. Start with a cold oven. It is not necessary to preheat.

For doughnuts, heat oil in a deep fryer to 450°F and drop doughnuts in one by one, using a long-handled spatula. Deep fry for a few minutes, or until doughnuts are golden brown. Remove with a slotted spoon and drain on paper toweling.

# Triticale Yeast Biscuits (or Dinner Rolls or Doughnuts)

(about 4 to 6 dozen biscuits)

1 tablespoon dry yeast
¼ cup lukewarm water
1 cup plus 1 teaspoon honey
7 to 7½ cups plus 1 tablespoon whole wheat flour
1 quart milk, warmed
1 cup butter
1 egg
2 tablespoons baking soda
2 tablespoons baking powder
1 teaspoon salt (optional, see page 22)
3 cups triticale flour
vegetable oil for deep frying doughnuts

# Isabella Groblewski

**The Bread:**

**Oat Scones**

In *Bread Winners,* Isabella was one of our more unusual bakers, with a range of achievements that included Slurry Bread, Swiss Lemon Twist, and Polish Beaten *Babka*. A potter and artist who lives in Topsfield, Massachusetts, she wrote a letter to me that included one of the most delightful stories to result from the first book:

> Our chef son-in-law, Jitendar Kumar, was sent to Europe as head of a team of cooks from the Colonnade Hotel in Boston. His assignment was to produce New England dinners of memorable distinction at the Savoy in London, the George V in Paris, the Gravenbruck in Frankfurt, and the Hassler in Rome. On the menu was a very fancy New England clam chowder with a cracker "boat" floating on top of each serving. The only crackers that floated well enough for these grand affairs were made from Beatrice Seal's recipe for "Homegrown Crackers" in Bread Winners!

The traditional Scottish scones are made on a griddle, and they generally contain unbleached white flour. These scones can be made in the traditional way, or you can use whole wheat flour as I have. They're marvelous when served piping hot, with butter and your favorite homemade jam.

Mix dry ingredients in a medium-size bowl and then work in butter with the back of a spoon. Add honey and buttermilk and stir to make a soft dough. Pat into a round shape ½-inch thick. Place on a buttered baking sheet or into a 9-inch pie plate, score into 6 or 8 triangular portions, and bake in a preheated 400°F oven for 15 minutes. Split and serve hot.

# Oat Scones

(6 to 8 scones)

1 cup whole wheat flour
1 cup oat flour
¼ teaspoon salt (optional, see page 22)
1 teaspoon baking soda
1 teaspoon butter
1 tablespoon honey
¾ cup buttermilk

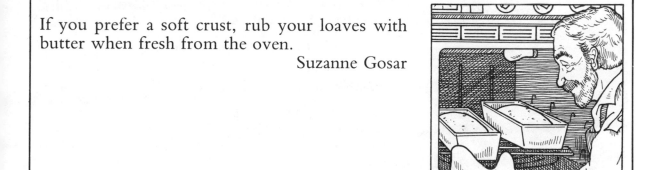

If you prefer a soft crust, rub your loaves with butter when fresh from the oven.
Suzanne Gosar

# Marjorie Johnson

*The Breads:*

**Honey Coconut Tea Ring
Oatmeal Whole Wheat
Raisin Muffins**

Marjorie is another one of our Minnesota State Fair bakers (from Robbinsdale), and she is also our all-time Blue Ribbon winner. At the time that *Bread Winners* was published, she had counted a total of 102 ribbons. In a recent letter she brought me up to date:

> Yesterday, I counted them again and I see that I now have 184 *Blue Ribbons! And each year, I have won one of the coveted Sweepstakes Ribbons (The Best of the Best Blue Ribbons), including the most recent one for the Honey Coconut Tea Ring (page 301).*

With all the baking she does, she manages to create a huge stack of large bowls, pans, and baking sheets that need washing, and even with an electric dishwasher, much of it has to be done by hand.

> So, my husband, LeRoy, is not only a Blue Ribbon dentist, but also a Blue Ribbon helper around the house. It's great to have a helping hand with the clean-up chores.

The only year that Marjorie did not enter the Minnesota State Fair, by the way, was 1980, when her daughter got married.

> I was too busy baking, baking, baking for the wedding. I made four kinds of rye bread, four kinds of nut bread, butter horn rolls, twelve kinds of fancy cookies, and a three-tiered wedding cake!

The recipes that Marjorie submitted for this new volume were Blue Ribbon winners at the State Fair, and thus we have not altered the ingredients. However, we tested the recipes with all whole wheat flour and to our taste the results were just as good as the wonderful breads that won the coveted prizes! I urge you to try them this way.

This is the bread that won the Sweepstakes at the Minnesota State Fair last year.

In a large bowl, dissolve yeast in warm water. Add nonfat dry milk, ¼ cup honey, butter, salt, and egg. Add 1 cup flour and beat at medium speed for 3 minutes. Add the rest of the flour to make a soft dough.

Turn out onto a floured surface and knead until smooth and elastic, 8 to 10 minutes. Place into an oiled bowl, turn to coat, cover, and let rise in a warm spot until doubled in bulk, 45 to 60 minutes.

Punch dough down, turn out onto a floured surface, and roll out to an 8 by 12-inch rectangle. Spread with softened butter and 1 tablespoon honey and then sprinkle coconut and nuts over dough evenly. Roll up like a jelly roll, starting with the longer side. Place seam-side down on a buttered baking sheet, forming a large ring. Join ends of the ring and seal. With scissors, make cuts two-thirds of the way through the ring at 1-inch intervals. Then turn each section on its side. Cover and let rise in a warm spot until nearly doubled in bulk, 45 to 60 minutes.

Bake in a preheated 325°F oven for 25 to 30 minutes, or until the ring is golden brown.

Cool on a wire rack.

# Honey Coconut Tea Ring

(1 loaf)

1 tablespoon dry yeast
½ cup warm water
¼ cup nonfat dry milk
¼ cup plus 1 tablespoon honey
¼ cup butter
½ teaspoon salt (optional, see page 22)
1 egg, well beaten
2½ to 3 cups unbleached white flour
2 tablespoons butter, softened
½ cup coconut flakes
½ cup chopped pecans or walnuts

# Oatmeal Whole Wheat Raisin Muffins

In a large bowl, cream butter and honey together. Add egg and beat well. Stir in buttermilk and raisins.

Combine dry ingredients in a medium-size bowl and add all at once to liquid ingredients, mixing only until flour is incorporated. Fill a buttered 12-cup muffin tin two-thirds full and bake in a preheated 400°F oven for 20 to 25 minutes.

Cool in tin for a few minutes before turning out onto wire racks.

(12 muffins)

¼ cup butter
½ cup honey
1 egg
1 cup buttermilk
⅓ cup raisins
½ cup unbleached white flour
1 teaspoon baking powder
½ teaspoon baking soda
½ teaspoon salt (optional, see page 22)
1 cup rolled oats
1 cup whole wheat flour

When I make quick breads, I mix the wet ingredients, shortening, and any nuts and fruits in a blender, then I add them to the dry ingredients. This procedure produces a lighter batter and shortens preparation time.

Beti Horvath

# Patricia Nodo

*The Bread:*

**Bumpy Barley Muffins**

Pat is another of my original Minnesota State Fair Blue Ribbon winners. She raises honeybees, gardens organically, bakes whole grain breads, raises a family and

*. . . Guess what! This old dog is learning some new tricks. I went back to school full time—will be a junior at St. Cloud Hospital School of Nursing this fall—and though the work load is just plain staggering, the sense of accomplishment, the stimulation, and the hope for the future are more than adequate rewards!*

She also reports "straight A's," as well as the fact that her daughter, Cookie, who was a tiny girl in the photograph that appeared in *Bread Winners,* is growing up.

*How can they do it without your seeing every minute of it? She is a tall, gorgeous, green-eyed, red-headed, and freckled darling! Fourth grade this fall, and boy, can that girl cook!*

Here is a new recipe from Pat—simple, delicious, and very nutritious.

# Bumpy Barley Muffins

(about 18 muffins)

2½ cups whole wheat flour
1 tablespoon dry yeast
1¼ cups water
⅓ cup mild molasses
¼ cup butter
1 egg
¾ cup fine barley flour (or you can grind about a cup of whole barley in a blender and use it in place of the flour)
milk for brushing muffins
toasted sesame seeds for topping

These tasty muffins are quite different from anything I've tasted before.

In a large bowl, stir together 1½ cups of the whole wheat flour and yeast and blend with a wooden spoon.

Meanwhile, heat the water, molasses, and butter in a small saucepan until mixture is lukewarm, stirring constantly.

Pour liquid ingredients into flour/yeast mixture, add egg, and beat with an electric mixer at low speed for about 30 seconds. Then turn the mixer speed to "high" and beat for 3 minutes. Stir in barley flour and remaining whole wheat flour, cover, and let dough rise in a warm place for about 1 hour. It won't double in size, but it will get puffy. (As with all mixer breads, you can do the process by hand. Just knead dough gently on a floured surface for 5 to 8 minutes.)

Spoon a scant ¼ cup of the dough into well-buttered 2½-inch muffin tins (use the shiny pans so that the muffins won't get too brown). Cover with lightly oiled plastic wrap and let rise in a warm place for 45 minutes.

Brush tops lightly with milk, sprinkle with sesame seeds, and bake in a preheated 375°F oven for 18 to 25 minutes.

Cool in muffin tins before turning out onto wire racks.

# Yvonne Rodahl

*The Breads:*

**Golden Carrot Muffins**
**Pumpkin Muffins**
**Pocket Bread (Pita)**

As a city-bred Northeasterner, one of the things that makes me envious is the fact that many of my baker friends across the country actually raise their own bees for the honey they use in their breads. This is particularly true of the Blue Ribbon winners out in Minnesota, among them Yvonne Rodahl.

*These past two summers, the bees have not produced as much honey as we would have liked. But, they're still one of our favorite hobbies.*

Another of the Rodahl activities that impresses this New Yorker, is a part of the vacation they took recently

*. . . in the Boundary Waters Canoe Area. Total wilderness. No cans or bottles can be taken in. This was an experience that will be remembered for a lifetime.*

One of Yvonne's bread baking tips raises a question that comes up time and time again. Most books strongly recommend that breads *not* be put out into the sun to rise. Yet, Yvonne and many of my friends do just that—and with great success. I have found that many of our old-time bakers, including our grandmothers, put the dough outside on a favorite rock to rise slowly in the warmth of the sun. That, of course, was before bread bakers read books that told them not to do it!

# Golden Carrot Muffins

(about 12 muffins)

⅓ cup butter
⅓ cup honey
3 eggs
3 tablespoons water
1½ cups shredded carrots
1½ cups whole wheat flour
1 tablespoon baking powder
¼ teaspoon ground ginger
¾ cup chopped almonds,
walnuts, or pecans

In a large bowl, cream the butter and honey. Add the eggs and water and blend until light and fluffy. Stir in the shredded carrots.

In a medium-size bowl, sift the whole wheat flour, baking powder, and ginger together and then stir into the carrot mixture. Stir in nuts only until moistened. Spoon batter into a buttered 12-cup muffin tin or a muffin tin lined with paper cups and bake in a preheated 375°F oven for 20 minutes.

In a large bowl, beat together the pumpkin, honey, and eggs. Add milk and melted butter.

In a medium-size bowl, sift whole wheat flour. Stir in the baking powder, cinnamon, and nutmeg. Add mixture, 1 cup at a time, to pumpkin mixture. Then blend in chopped nuts. The batter will be lumpy. Don't over-mix. Spoon batter into 2 buttered 12-cup muffin tins or muffin tins lined with paper cups and bake in a preheated 375°F oven for 20 minutes.

# Pumpkin Muffins

(24 muffins)

1 15-ounce can pumpkin
½ cup honey
2 eggs
1 cup milk
½ cup butter, melted
3 cups whole wheat flour
2 tablespoons baking powder
1 teaspoon ground cinnamon
½ teaspoon ground nutmeg
1 cup chopped walnuts or pecans

This is a whole grain version of the famous Middle Eastern Pita. It can be served as a "container" for salads, meats, or whole grain fillings. The secret in making the pocket is the high heat of the oven. Even if you're curious, don't open the oven door to peek as they puff up.

In a large bowl, dissolve yeast in warm water. Add honey and oil. Stir in rye flour and whole wheat flour, adding just enough flour to make dough easy to handle.

Turn out onto a floured surface and knead until smooth and elastic, about 8 minutes. Place into an oiled bowl, turn to coat, cover, and let rise in a warm spot until doubled in bulk, about 1 hour.

Turn dough out onto a floured surface, divide into 6 parts, and shape into flattened balls. Cover and let rise on the floured surface for about 30 minutes more.

Dust ungreased baking sheets with cornmeal. Roll each flattened ball to about a ⅛-inch thickness and place on the baking sheets. Cover lightly and let rise for about 30 minutes.

Bake in a preheated 500°F oven for 8 to 10 minutes, or until lightly browned and puffed up.

Cool on wire racks. The puffiness will go down, but the pockets will have been formed in the loaves.

# Pocket Bread (Pita)

(6 pocket loaves)

1 tablespoon dry yeast
1⅓ cups warm water
1 tablespoon honey
2 tablespoons vegetable oil
1 cup rye flour
2 cups whole wheat flour
cornmeal for dusting baking sheets

# George Meluso

*The Breads:*

**Four Breads for
Advanced Bakers
Ricotta Bread
Pizza Bread
Provolone Bread
Pesto Bread**

George is, above all things, a free spirit. The readers of *Bread Winners* know that he was my teacher, and that first book is, indeed, partially dedicated to him. Accompanied by his ubiquitous glass of wine, George is the easiest, the most serendipitous of bakers, measuring very little, judging water temperature by feel, putting in a "little of this" and a "little of that," and turning out the most marvelous of creations after a day in the kitchen.

One lazy summer afternoon, soon after I requested some recipes for this new volume, George called and asked me to ride over on my bicycle. The recipes were ready and tested. The loaves were warm and just right for tasting. And, they were wonderful!

Along with the slices of bread, George also gave me what was to pass as his "recipes"—two yellow legal-size pieces of paper with notes scrawled in pencil. No order of ingredients. No instructions. Size of pan? Not there. Oven temperature? Obviously not important. Procedure? He answered, "Anyone who bakes bread will know what to do!" Possibly he was right. Anyone who bakes *would* know. Most simple recipes followed the same rules. And so, I decided to present these four excellent breads in exactly the way that George gave them to me. At the beginning of the section, however, I have included some instructions that were wrung from my teacher.

RICOTTA BREAD
PESTO BREAD
PIZZA BREAD
PROVALONE BREAD

RICOTTA BREAD

1 LB. RICOTTA
1 BUNCH PARSLEY (FLAT. CHOPPED)
1 EGG
1/4 LB. ROMANO OR · PARMESAN
1 CUP
3 CUPS. WHOLE WHEAT FLOUR
1 PK. YEAST
HONEY
1/4 CUP SHORTNING
MILK · ONION

*LIQUID FIRST THEN FLOUR*

1 loaf pan

# Four Breads for Advanced Bakers

1. George uses a food processor fitted with the plastic blade for all mixing. These breads can be made, however, with the hand-mix, hand-knead, old-fashioned method.
2. All recipes make one loaf. Use a medium-size loaf pan, 8½ × 4½ inches.
3. In all recipes, combine liquids first and then add dry ingredients.
4. The oven temperature for these breads ranges from 350° to 375°F.
5. Bake the breads until they test done, about 45 to 60 minutes.

## Ricotta Bread

1 pound ricotta cheese
1 bunch flat parsley, chopped
1 egg
1 cup grated Romano or Parmesan cheese (about ¼ pound)
3 cups whole wheat flour
1 tablespoon dry yeast
honey to taste
¼ cup butter
milk (enough to make a workable dough)
onion, chopped

## Pizza Bread

3 cups whole wheat flour
1 tablespoon dry yeast
1 tablespoon dried basil
1 tablespoon dried oregano
¾ to 1 cup tomato sauce
1 cup grated Parmesan or Romano cheese (about ¼ pound)
1 egg
¼ cup butter
1 teaspoon honey
mozzarella cheese (a bit)

# Provolone Bread

3 cups whole wheat flour
1 tablespoon dry yeast
1 teaspoon honey
1 egg
butter
1 cup grated provolone
    cheese
milk (enough to make a
    workable dough)
pepperoni (some)

First prepare dough. Then chop pepperoni
into tiny pieces. Roll out dough, sprinkle
pepperoni on it, and roll up like a jelly roll
before placing in pan.

# Pesto Bread

3 cups whole wheat flour
1 tablespoon dry yeast
1 cup chopped fresh basil
    leaves
½ cup chopped fresh parsley
1 cup grated Romano cheese
    (about ¼ pound)
1 cup chopped walnuts
1 tablespoon honey
1 egg
¼ cup butter
½ cup milk (enough to make
    a workable dough)
garlic (a bit, very finely
    chopped)

# Mail-Order Sources

Even as more and more local outlets have begun to carry grains and flours such as triticale, millet, and stone-ground whole wheat, other grains have become known to us, and some are more difficult to find. If you live in an area where the local supermarket or natural foods store does not carry a specific utensil or the grains needed for a special recipe, this list may help. Indeed, I know many bakers who claim that they are too lazy to shop—and they prefer to order by mail from the convenience of their homes.

# Flours and Grains

Arrowhead Mills
Box 866
Hereford, TX  79045
806–364–0730
They carry most grains and flours (many of them organically grown) in addition to a large assortment of beans, nuts, cereals, and flakes. A catalog is available.

Birkett Mills
P.O. Box 440-A
Penn Yan, NY  14527
They carry stone-ground flour, buck-wheat groats and flour, light rye flour, and four grades of roasted buckwheat groats (kasha) from whole to fine grind. A price list is available.

Casa Moneo Spanish Imports
210 West 14th Street
New York, NY  10011
212–929–1644
This is a good source for blue cornmeal, as well as for a range of other marvelous items including tortilla making equipment. A mail-order catalog is available for $2.00.

Edwards Mill
The School of the Ozarks
Point Lookout, MO  65726
This source was originally recommended to me by Suzanne Corbett (see Index) of St. Louis. They carry stone-ground flour, cornmeal, wheat germ, rye, and cracked wheat. Send for an order blank to get a complete list. They accept small orders.

Erewhon Trading Company
236 Washington Street
Brookline, MA 02146
617-738-4516

They carry a large variety of grains, beans, seeds, and nuts. A catalog is available.

Flory Brothers
841 Flory Mill Road
Lancaster, PA 17601

This is the mill from which many of our bakers in the Pennsylvania Dutch area get their whole grains and stone-ground flour. They carry whole wheat flours, rye flours (including pumpernickel), buckwheat flour, and potato flour, and many other items, including molasses, honey, seeds, and dried nonfat milk. Send for their list.

Great Valley Mills
Quakertown, Bucks County, PA 18951

They carry a choice of whole grain flours, pumpernickel, rye meal, brown rice flour, and graham flour. Send for their free catalog.

Grover Company
330 West University Drive
Tempe, AZ 85281
1-800-528-1406 (toll free)

They are suppliers of whole grains that include triticale, rye, hard red wheat, buckwheat, millet—as well as sprouting seeds, honey, and yeast. They do not supply flour, since "flour begins to oxidize immediately after grinding, losing as much as 60 percent of its nutritional value within 24 hours." A catalog is available.

Shiloh Farms
Box 97, Highway 59
Sulphur Springs, AR 72768
501-298-3297

Many of their products are distributed in natural foods stores, but unlike other major distributors, they accept mail orders on items that cover a variety of whole grains, meals, and flours. A catalog is available for $1 (refundable).

Walnut Acres
Penns Creek, PA 17862
717-837-3874

This is a special source for me for several reasons. The owner, Paul Keene, has become a friend over the years and has been most supportive of our cookbooks. More important, perhaps, is the fact that Walnut Acres is the only source I know of for sorghum (milo) and amaranth grain and flour. In addition, they also have a large selection of other whole grains, cereals, and flours. A complete catalog is available.

Wilson Milling Company
P.O. Box 481
La Cross, KS 67548

They grow their wheat organically, and it's a high-protein, high-gluten winter variety. They also sell whole wheat berries, stone-ground whole wheat flour, and cracked wheat. They'll send a price list on request.

# Equipment, Utensils, and Kitchen Supplies

Although most of the standard baking supplies—such as medium- and large-size loaf pans—are readily available, the long French bread pans, black metal pans, and *brioche* pans may not be as easy to find. This list may help, since all of these suppliers offer catalogs.

Bazaar de la Cuisine
1003 Second Avenue
New York, NY 10022

This store provided evidence that giving the sources for mail-order items is much appreciated in many parts of the country. I walked in one day to find that they were just sorting a batch of mail that had come as a result of my publishing their name in *Bread Winners*. It is one of my favorite stores for every conceivable kind of baking accessory. A catalog is available.

Bridge Company
212 East 52nd Street
New York, NY 10022

Many professional cooks and bakers shop here to fill their special needs. The utensils are finely crafted. A catalog is available.

Dean and De Luca
121 Prince Street
New York, NY 10012
212–254–7774

This is a good source for specialty equipment, including flour mills. Retail sales, plus some mail-order service. Call or write for mail-order information.

Hoffritz
515 West 24th Street
New York, NY 10011

A great source for cutlery and special bread knives for the baker. Their retail stores are found all across the country, but they also handle mail-order sales. A catalog is available for a nominal fee. Write for information.

H. Roth & Son
1577 First Avenue
New York, NY 10028

They feature not only kitchen equipment, but a large assortment of grains and spices. It is my best source for the long, black French loaf pans. Retail sales and mail-order service. Write for a catalog.

Stone Hearth Inc.
40 Park Street
Brooklyn, NY 11206

You've probably seen their exquisitely handcrafted black steel baking equipment—bread pans, French loaf pans, baking sheets, muffin pans, and popover pans, since they are now distributed all over the country. Their items are moderately expensive, however. Write for information on the local outlet that carries their products or ask for their catalog.

Williams-Sonoma
Mail-Order Department
P.O. Box 3792
San Francisco, CA 94119
415–652–9007

They carry a large assortment of specialty baking equipment, including some loaf pans. They have several retail stores around the country, with five in California, plus shops in Dallas, Minneapolis, and Washington, D.C. Mail-order service is also available. Send for their catalog.

# Grain Mills

This is a difficult area in which to make a decision, not only because of the variety of mills on the market today, but also because of your own personal needs. There is no doubt that the flour that you grind yourself will taste better, and actually be more nutritious. However, considering the cost of a good electric mill today, the question will arise: "Do I use enough flour to make the investment worthwhile?"

For some bakers, however, there is nothing to take the place of this most basic of joys. In one of the letters that I received from Bob Adjemian (see Index), he wrote:

*Anyone who likes to make bread should seriously consider buying a flour mill. There is a special taste in flour that goes away after 24 hours. The flour sold in stores is at least one week old, probably several months old. The difference is obvious by comparison. Also, with a flour mill, you can control the grind. We have a flour mill that is 36 years old, yet runs perfectly. I won't even make bread if I can't grind the flour.*

If you *are* considering this investment, you might give some thought to the following information before you invest. And then, using the list that I have compiled, you might do well to write to each of the companies to get their literature and to find out where you might see and test the mill. I have also added a list of questions to consider, based upon the research that Sheryl and I did before we wrote our book on whole grains. Then, you can select the mill that fits your particular need.

*Hand Mills:* There are two basic types—those with steel grinding burrs or those with stone grinding burrs. With either type, the hand mill requires a great deal of effort. If the average recipe calls for two and a half pounds of flour, it will take up to 20 minutes to grind that amount. Hand mills range in price from about $50 to over $300.

*Electric Mills:* Again, you have the choice between steel grinding blades or stone grinding blades. If you choose the stone grinders, make sure you *do not* wash them after use. Cleaning them is a problem and any residue left on the stones will turn rancid. The steel-blade variety is much easier to clean. You also must keep in mind that wheat, for example, grinds better with stone blades, oats with steel blades. Electric mills can run from $200 to well over $400.

## Some Questions to Ask

The investment in a mill should be treated just as you would any other expensive piece of machinery or household appliance. I strongly suggest that you check with your friends, investigate thoroughly, take your time before you decide, and then ask yourself these questions:

• How much time does it take to grind a reasonable amount of grain? How much time for one loaf, or for six loaves?

• Grinding grains is a noisy process. How noisy is the mill? It is almost impossible to determine noise level from advertising copy.

• Is it easy to clean—are all the parts accessible and easy to remove?

• Is the mill already assembled or does it have to be put together by you or a member of your family who is adept with tools and can follow instructions? It might be more expensive if already assembled, but it might be worth the additional cost.

• What is specified in the warranty, and are any other guarantees offered by the manufacturer?

• What are the shipping charges?

• Do you expect to save money by grinding your own grain? Probably, you will not, in spite of what the manufacturer may claim. You have to grind an awful lot of grain to make the economics work for you. It's not the reason that bakers buy the mills.

• If you should need repairs, are there central service shops available in your area? Or, can you repair it yourself with some help from the company?

• If it's an electric mill, does it have heavy-duty wiring and is it grounded through a three-prong plug?

With the field becoming so very crowded due to the interest of bakers who want to grind their own grains, the problems of choosing the right mill have become incredibly complex. Whole chapters might be written on the types of mills, the special features, and the prices. I have listed below the names and addresses of the manufacturers, plus some additional information about their mills. I strongly suggest writing for their catalogs and studying them carefully. They are helpful and they are quite willing to answer questions.

Aurora Industries Inc.
P.O. Box 12
Inkom, ID 83245

They are the manufacturers of Miller Boy Mills, available in two high-speed electric models and a combination hand-pedal/motor-driven model. All three models pregrind the grain with tungsten-carbide shears before the final grinding with the stones. One interesting feature of their Independent hand grinder is that it comes with an optional bicycle sprocket and a V-belt pulley for use with the pedals, the wind, or your own electric or gas motor. Photographs and information are available by mail.

C. S. Bell Company
P.O. Box 291
Tiffin, OH 44883
419–448–0791

They make heavy cast-iron mills, including the hand-operated #2 Grist Mill and the #60 Power Mill, which can be hand operated or attached to an electric motor (purchased separately). The #60 is adjustable for fine or coarse grinding and has interchangeable burrs. These mills can be seen at a range of retail suppliers, including Sears and Southern States Cooperative stores. Send for information.

Country Living Products
14727 56th Avenue N.W.
Stanwood, WA 98292
206–652–0671 or 206–652–8913

They manufacture the Country Living Hand Grain Mill, which their president, Jack Jenkins, tells me can grind two pounds (about seven cups) of bread flour in about 12 minutes. Country Living also offers a 20-year guarantee on the body and bearings. They're probably the only manufacturer I know of who have written their own song, "The Grinding Song." Information is available by mail; possibly Jack will even send you the lyrics of the song if you ask.

Garden Way Catalog
P.O. Box 2367
1186 Williston Road
South Burlington, VT 05401

They sell the Garden Way Kit, a high-speed electric grain mill that is made by the Grover Company, manufacturers of the Marathon Uni-Mill. Their literature claims that "you don't have to be a master craftsperson to assemble the mill" since all cabinet pieces are precut, numbered, and predrilled. You can assemble the kit in about three hours. It has an auxiliary hand-crank handle in case the power goes out.

Grover Company
330 West University Drive
Tempe, AZ 85281
1–800–528–1406 (toll free)

They manufacture the Marathon Uni-Mill, as well as the Garden Way Kit (now called the Olympic, according to my last correspondence). The Uni-Mill is a high-speed electric mill that can grind one pound of flour in about a minute. The major feature of the mill is that it cracks and slices the grain before it reaches the grinding stones so that the mill grinds cooler and there is less power use. Complete information is available by mail.

In-Tec Equipment Company
Box 123
D.V. Station
Dayton, OH 45406
513–277–7102

They offer three unusual grain mills: The first is the top-of-the-line Danish Diamant that can be hand operated or attached to an electric motor. Made of cast iron, it has self-oiling bearings and must be bolted down during use. The second mill is the English-made Atlas #1, a hand-operated mill also made of cast iron, with very few moving parts. And, the third mill is the French-manufactured Gaubert, a reasonably priced mill that grinds flour, but requires sifting after the process is complete. Full information is available from In-Tec.

Kitchen Aid Division
Hobart Corporation
Troy, OH 45374
513–335–7171

They offer a cast-aluminum grain mill attachment for their Kitchen-Aid mixer. The burrs in the mill are made of hardened metal, and they're capable of grinding wheat, corn, rye, oats, buckwheat, and barley. However, the mill is limited to about ten cups at one time, and a 45-minute waiting period is required between grinds. There is a distinct advantage in another area, in that their mill can be serviced at any one of a number of authorized Kitchen-Aid service centers across the country.

Kitchenetics Corporation
1450 Del Avenue
Campbell, CA 95008
408–378–3011

Their Kitchen Mill uses a new technology, employing a "micronizer," surgical-quality stainless steel blades, rather than the conventional grinding stones of the other mills. The advantages, according to the manufacturer—based in the heart of the space-age Silicon Valley in California—are that the mill is compact and can grind grains in high-humidity climates such as my own Fire Island, without jamming or gumming up. It can also make cracked grains and it's easy to clean, though it's quite loud when in operation. Write for information.

Kuest Enterprises
Box 110
Filer, ID 83328
208–326–4084

They manufacture and distribute the Golden Grain Grinders, both the Standard model and the De-Luxe Grinder. Both will grind up to 60 pounds of flour an hour, both are electrically operated, and the De-Luxe model has self-cleaning stones with stainless steel edges. Information is available by mail.

Lee Engineering Company
2023 West Wisconsin Avenue
P.O. Box 652
Milwaukee, WI 53201

Lee manufactures four models, all of them utilizing a chamber in which centrifugal force grinds the grain against a stationery stone ring. All are fully automatic, and the feeding mechanism allows only the proper amount of grain into the grinding chamber at any given time. Flour falls into a special bag, and can be ground at a rate of 8 to 15 minutes per pound, depending upon the model. Send for information and price list.

Magic Mill III
235 West 200 South
Salt Lake City, UT 84101

The Magic Mill III and the Bosch Kitchen Mixer are available retail (see the Yellow Pages) and through local distributors. Our own Bread Winners, Howard and Agnes Arns, are still distributing the Magic Mill and the Bosch Kitchen Mixer (104 South 200 East, Cedar City, Utah 84720). The Magic Mill operates on the same principle as the Kitchen Mill—the micronizer—and, for all I know, may even be manufactured by the same company. They look exactly alike, but my latest price list indicates that the Magic Mill may be slightly less expensive. Write for information.

Platt Mill & Mix
3068 Highland Drive
Salt Lake City, UT 84106
801–487–6763

Dick Platt wrote to me saying, "I was surprised to see you mixing dough by hand on the cover of your book *Bread Winners*," and he promptly sent me information on his mills. Platt Mill and Mix handles the sales and distribution for ten different mills and mixers and they are distributors for the Braun Kitchen Machine. In addition, they manufacture their own mills under their name. Information is available by mail or phone.

Retsel Corporation
Box 47
McCammon, ID 83250
1–800–635–0970 (toll free)

When Trish Avery answered my letter asking for information, she also answered a question that I had asked: "Is Retsel really Lester spelled backwards?" Yes it is. The founder used his name spelled backwards to name the company. Retsel offers a whole range of grain mills, from small hand-crank models at very low prices all the way up to deluxe models that are electrically operated, exquisitely machined, and priced at the higher end of the range. Their catalog and literature give complete details and prices and they also offer a catalog of grain mill replacement parts and accessories.

R & R Mill Company Inc.
45 West First North
Smithfield, UT 84335

R & R offers a wide range of grain mills, including the Corona King in several models. To make a fine flour, however, it is necessary to run the grain through the mills several times. They are all easy to operate. Send for their small catalog, since they also handle other mills and it's a good way to compare prices.

Sunset Marketing
8549 Sunset Avenue
Fair Oaks, CA 95268
916–961–2896

They distribute grain mills, mill kits, hand mills, and related equipment. Write or call for mail-order information.

# Index

Diastatic malt, 138, 139
Dill
  Sourdough Dill Crackers,
    143
Double Millet Skillet Bread,
  61

## E

Earhart, Kenneth, 198–99
  recipes of, 200–201
Ebbott, Elizabeth, 294
  recipe of, 295
Eckert, Nancy Cross, 65–66,
  172
  recipes of, 66–70
Edwards Mill, 312
Eggs, added to bread dough,
  19
Electric mixer, kneading
  with an, 46
Endosperm of grain, 8, 9
Erewhon Trading Company,
  313
Esberg, Andreas, 167–68,
  258, 267
  recipes of, 169–72, 258–59

## F

Familia
  Muesli Bread, 195
  recipe for, 196

The Farm, 290–91
Fats, as ingredients in breads,
  19
Feiner, Ed, 4, 237–38,
  242–44, 271
  recipes of, 238–39, 245–51
Ferguson, Sylvia Moore,
  282–83
  recipe of, 283
Finnish Coffee Bread, 120–21
Finnish Sweet Bread, 120–21
Fire Island Onion Rye, 287
Flemish Peasant Bread,
  258–59
Flory Brothers, 313
Flour. *See also* specific types,
  e.g., Whole wheat flour
  grinding of, 14
  mail-order sources for,
    312–13
  measuring of, 37, 155
  types of, 8–13
Food processor, kneading
  with, 46
Fox, Cynthia, 182
  recipes of, 183–85
Franklin, Girard, 286
  recipe of, 287
Freezing, of bread, 54
Fruits, dried
  in dough, 172
  filling of, 162

Whole Wheat Sesame Sticks,
295
Williams-Sonoma, 314
Wilson Milling Company,
313
Winter Park Mountain Rolls,
119

## Y

Yeast, 25–28
  freezing of, 25–26
  proofing of, 26–27, 207,
    227
  Traditional Wild Yeast
    Starter, 235
  types of, 25–26
Yeast bread, 42–53, 111
  decorating of, 52
  kneading of, 44–46
  rising of, 46–47, 50
  shaping of, 48–49
  test for doneness, 53
Yogurt
  in breads, 4
  as sourdough starter, 31,
    236–37
Yogurt Casserole Bread, 193
Yogurt Sourdough Bran/Rye
  Bread, 254–55
Yogurt Sourdough Starter,
  236–37

## Z

Zeimann, Carol, 130–31
  recipes of, 132–37
*Zopf*, 170
Zucchini
  Spicy Zucchini Whole
    Wheat Bread, 200